THE AMERICAN CODIFICATION MOVEMENT

Contributions in Legal Studies
Series Editor: *Paul L. Murphy*

Philosophical Law: Authority, Equality, Adjudication, Privacy
Richard Bronaugh, editor

Law, Soldiers, and Combat
Peter Karsten

Appellate Courts and Lawyers: Information Gathering in the Adversary System
Thomas B. Marvell

Charting the Future: The Supreme Court Responds to a Changing Society, 1890-1920
John E. Semonche

The Promise of Power: The Emergence of the Profession in Massachusetts, 1760-1840
Gerald W. Gawalt

Inferior Courts, Superior Justice: A History of the Justices of the Peace on the Northwest Frontier, 1853-1889
John R. Wunder

Antitrust and the Oil Monopoly: The Standard Oil Cases, 1890-1911
Bruce Bringhurst

They Have No Rights: Dred Scott's Struggle for Freedom
Walter Ehrlich

Popular Influence Upon Public Policy: Petitioning in Eighteenth-Century Virginia
Raymond C. Bailey

Fathers to Daughters: The Legal Foundations of Female Emancipation
Peggy A. Rabkin

In Honor of Justice Douglas: A Symposium on Individual Freedom and Government
Edited by *Robert H. Keller, Jr.*

A Constitutional History of Habeas Corpus
William F. Duker

THE AMERICAN CODIFICATION MOVEMENT

A STUDY OF ANTEBELLUM LEGAL REFORM

Charles M. Cook

CONTRIBUTIONS IN LEGAL STUDIES, NUMBER 14

GREENWOOD PRESS
Westport, Connecticut • London, England

Library of Congress Cataloging in Publication Data

Cook, Charles M. 1944-
The American codification movement.

(Contributions in legal studies; no. 14 ISSN 0147-1074)
Bibliogrpahy:
Includes index.
1. Law—United States—Codification—History.
2. Law reform—United States—History. I. Title. II. Series.
KF434.C66 348.73'04 80-662
ISBN 0-313-21314-3 (lib. bdg.)

Library of Congress Catalog Card Number: 80-662
ISBN: 0-313-21314-3
ISSN: 0147-1074

First published in 1981

Greenwood Press
A division of Congressional Information Service, Inc.
88 Post Road West, Westport, Connecticut 06881

Printed in the United States of America

10 9 8 7 6 5 4 3 2 1

For my three best friends
Maureen, Emily, and Jeremy

CONTENTS

PREFACE

This book was begun a number of years ago while exploring antebellum law journals in search of a doctoral dissertation. In my reading, I was struck by the tremendous energy the legal profession was expending in a debate over the efficacy of codified law. It was my initial assumption that the argument focused on the issue of the relative merits of adopting a common or a civil law system. Being convinced by Roscoe Pound, and the results of more recent research, that this was "the formative era of American law," it seemed logical that the law guild, recognizing the need to develop an appropriate legal system, would debate the applicability of the two dominant Western legal traditions in the United States. However, more analytical and comprehensive research forced me to modify my assumptions substantially and to conceptualize the reform movement as something other than a study of competing legal systems.

The American codification movement, which existed as a significant force in the legal environment from roughly 1820 to midcentury, was a powerful effort motivated by a desire to make codified law an essential element in American legal development. The debate was real. At no other time in our legal history have the merits of codification been so thoroughly argued about by lawyers and laymen alike. But contrary to my first assumptions, the antebellum effort on behalf of codes was not a confrontation between civilians and common lawyers in an environment where a choice had to be made between genuine and distinct alternatives, though some of the radical codifiers acted as if this were the case. Rather, the American codification movement is best understood as an attempt to deal with the problems of antebellum legal development that occurred within an already well-established legal tradition. This study was ultimately conceptualized and completed on that premise.

Pound was correct in suggesting that the American legal system experienced its formative era during the first half dozen decades of the republic. But an entirely new legal system was not being fashioned. Instead, the English common law, both as a set of rules and as a means to organize and operate a legal system, was being adapted to the American circumstance.This occurred during a period of extraordinary socio-economic change that intensified the process of legal development. Contemporaries were well aware that their legal system was in an acutely developmental state. Some were troubled by the dominant methodology adopted to produce the American legal system and by the resultant content of the law. They and others also voiced concern over a variety of problems attendant on legal growth and change. Regardless of the defects perceived in the process of legal development, nearly every concerned individual saw codification as an appropriate remedy. By focusing on the resulting reform effort, I hope I have added a significant increment of knowledge to our understanding of the development of the American legal system in its most vigorous period of growth.

My approach, then, has been a limited one. I have not attempted to write a history of codification in America. I shall leave that to some later, more ambitious scholar than I, though I hope my efforts are useful in its completion. The period surveyed in depth here stretches from about 1820 to 1850—the reform movement had no clear starting point or end. A discussion of legal reform the postrevolutionary years is included to set the stage and to suggest some of the historical constraints that were placed upon the codification effort.

An explanation of Louisiana's codification experience, which occurred at about the same time as the effort to codify in the common law states, may appear conspicuous by its absence. A chapter on Louisiana was included in earlier drafts. However, while it contained many of the same themes developed in the larger study, Louisiana's essentially successful effort to codify its laws seemed, upon deeper reflection, to be apart from, or possibly ancillary to, the codification movement in the common law states. It occurred in its own very special milieu, quite independent of law-reform efforts elsewhere. Some will be disappointed that I have not attempted to shed new light on colonial codification efforts, limited though they were. Others may wish that such things as the American Law Institute and the various uniform codes developed in this century would have received more than brief mention. To them, I offer no apology, as these matters were well outside the scope of my concern. Of course, I hope that those interested in the colonial codes find something relevant here. Similarly, I trust that others who seek to understand better the more recent American efforts to codify the law see the importance of the antebellum experience to their concerns. For these individuals, I have attempted to point the way.

Many people assisted me in my efforts here. I should like to acknowledge those who were most important. Mary F. Berry convinced me that the study of history was a worthwhile endeavor. As my doctoral advisor and friend, she encouraged me to undertake an examination of antebellum legal reform. I benefited from her acute perception and wise advice along the way. I hope this book does not disappoint her.

Maxwell Bloomfield was kind enough to read the initial draft and to offer numerous suggestions for its improvement. Always generous with his time and unselfish with his knowledge, he helped to improve the manuscript in innumerable ways. R. Kent Newmeyer, Donald Roper, and Morton J. Horwitz also read an early draft and recommended useful changes. In addition, several faculty members of the history department at the University of Maryland, at College Park, provided helpful critiques. Among them were James Cockburn, David Grimsted, and Herman Belz. The university provided much needed support by way of a fellowship during the initial research and writing.

Martha Norkunas was the last in a series of typists. Her good-natured enthusiasm made the final stage of manuscript preparation easier than it would otherwise have been. Ted Manning of the North Central Association's Commission on Institutions of Higher Education provided greatly appreciated encouragement and support.

A good friend, Nancy Arnson, offered thoughtful suggestions in matters of form and content and a special sort of encouragement at every step. To her, I am especially indebted.

My children, Emily and Jeremy, helped me not at all in my research and writing. In fact, with their constant entreaties to play with them, they were a positive hindrance to progress. But they, more than anyone else, helped me maintain a sense of perspective and a grasp on what is real and what is important.

To my wife, Maureen, I owe the greatest debt of all. Without her, I would never have attempted the task, nor would I ever have completed it.

Of course, any failings or shortcomings are my responsibility alone.

Charles M. Cook
Evanston, Illinois

THE AMERICAN CODIFICATION MOVEMENT

1

AMERICAN ATTITUDES TOWARD THE LEGAL ENVIRONMENT, 1776-1815

Certain historical circumstances frequently contain the potential, even the demand, for legal reform. Revolutions, with their implicit stress on change over continuity, at least in modern times, have brought about drastic transformations in the law. Both the Russian and French revolutions, for example, resulted in the reform of their respective legal systems. In Russia, the new Soviet dictatorship undertook to refashion existing law into a code that would fit the acute economic and social innovations of the new regime. For the French, the creation of the Code Napoléon eliminated the myriad of unjust legal systems that were a source of revolutionary discontent in *l'ancien régime.*

The American Revolution, atypical of the revolutionary experiences of other nations in so many respects, did not occasion reforms in the form and content of existing law. Rather, the immediate impact of independence on the colonial legal legacy was not innovation but conservation. All but two of the thirteen new states specifically provided that pre-existing law would remain in force.[1] New York's first constitution, adopted in 1777, dealt with the matter in a representative fashion. It declared that "such parts of the common law of England and the statute law of England, and Great Britain, and the acts of the legislature of the Colony of New York as did form the law of the said colony...shall be and continue the law of the State."[2] While New York and other states added the limitation that none of the colonial law or received English law that was repugnant to their constitutions should be considered binding, and while each quite naturally provided for possible future changes in the law through legislative alteration, there were no significant departures from the legal past except for those obviously necessitated by independence—for example, the abrogation of all provisions relating to colonial status and allegiance to the British Crown. Beyond this and the largely symbolic abolition of primogeniture and entail in some states, and other modifications in the law that may have merely institutionalized existing practice, American patriots felt little need to work a revolution in private law as profound as they had completed in public law.[3]

There are several reasons why legal continuity was considered preferable to change. First, an inequitable legal system had not been a source of revolutionary discontent as it had been in France. If any grievance arose from the legal system, it was that the English government was attempting to subvert what was believed to be the well-established law that the colonist enjoyed. Among the "repeated injuries and usurpations" of George III that Thomas Jefferson and the Second Continental Congress submitted to "a candid world" to justify independence was that the English king had "made judges dependent on his will alone" and that he had "obstructed the administration of justice." The English monarch was also accused of acting with others for the purpose of "abolishing our most valuable laws" and for "abolishing the free System of English laws in a neighboring province."[4] Second, changes in the legal system were not ideologically mandated as they were in the newly created Soviet Union. The American revolutionaries claimed their purpose was not to create but rather to preserve and guarantee rights, liberties, and immunities already propounded in existing law and now threatened by English usurpation. The First Continental Congress declared in 1774 that as subjects of the English Crown, Americans had "all the rights, liberties and immunities of free and natural born subjects of the realm of England." Among these were the "Common Law of England" and "the benefit of such English statutes...found to be applicable to the local and other circumstances" as well as "all the immunities and privileges...secured by the several codes of provincial law."[5] The existing law, then, was a repository of liberty. To reject it or even to reform it significantly was contrary to the goals of the patriots.[6]

There were other, more pragmatic reasons for sustaining the inherited legal system. On the one hand, there were the practical difficulties of creating a wholly new system of law. Declaring that the existing law would remain in force, the newly independent Vermont legislature asserted that this was necessary as "it is impossible at once to provide particular Statutes applicable to all causes wherein Law may be necessary for the happy Government of the People." On the other hand, breaking legal continuity would bring uncertainty and instability to the law, thus jeopardizing existing property rights. The American Revolution was not fought to upset established property relationships. The same Vermont statute declared that the established law should remain binding as "the inhabitants of the State have been habituated to conform their manners to English laws, and hold their real Estates by English tenures."[7] Likewise, the commission appointed in Virginia in 1776 to revise the laws of the new state rejected the suggestion of one of its members that they "abolish the whole existing system of laws, and prepare a new and complete Institute." Thomas Jefferson, one of the commissioners, later recalled that he and his colleagues George Wythe and George Mason, not beguiled by visions of a new law, rejected the idea because "the imperfections of human language, and its incompetence to express distinctly every shade of idea," would render each word of any new text "a subject of question and chicanery... and thus would involve us in ages of litigation and render property uncertain."[8]

The three Virginians were undoubtedly right in their appraisal. Yet, maintaining legal continuity did not prove to be a satisfactory solution. Disillusionment with the existing legal system soon followed the Revolution. Independence had a greater impact on the law than had been foreseen. It unleashed uncontrollable forces that, coupled with the nature of legal growth and the socio-economic changes of the postwar years, led to demands for law reform.

The felt abuses were in three broad areas. First, the law was said to be inaccessible and uncertain, a lament made most often by the law guild. Second, the law, it was claimed, was unnecessarily mysterious, complex, and overly technical, a charge usually leveled by laymen. Third, complaints were made about the English, or foreign, form and content of the law. These were not separate and unconnected grievances. For example, the uncertain and/or the mysterious nature of the law was often seen as a function of its alien identity. Of the three general areas of dissatisfaction, the first, that the law was inaccessible and uncertain, was the most important and evoked the greatest remedial response.

The establishment of republican government was quite naturally accompanied by sentiments stressing the need for citizens to be familiar with the laws by which they governed themselves. As Robert and George Watkins, two Georgia lawyers, remarked in 1800, "In a representative government, it is of the utmost consequence to the body of the nation to be rightly informed of those laws and regulations by which their duties are defined and their rights secured."[9] Zephaniah Swift, a contemporary Connecticut jurist, voiced agreement: "Every citizen ought to acquire a knowledge of those laws that govern his daily life and secure the invaluable blessings of life, liberty, and property." But, Swift pointed out, while "no country is favored with a more perspicuous code... yet in no country is it more arduous and difficult to obtain a systematic understanding of the law."[10] Swift was referring to Connecticut, but the "singular inconvenience" he was addressing was not unique to that state. John F. Grimke declared in 1790 that, because the laws of South Carolina were "wrapped up in... profound confusion and Sibylline obscurity," the citizens of that state were "degraded to the condition of a slave," a strong statement for a South Carolinian.[11] A Pennsylvanian spoke uneasily of the "involuntary disobedience in the subject to the laws of his country when he might be disposed cheerfully to conform to them, if he understood them."[12] The compilers of Georgia's statutes related in 1800 that they were prompted to undertake the compilation by "the great uncertainty in municipal regulations of the State, and the embarrassments thereby introduced into every department of government."[13] William Cranch, reporter of the United States Supreme Court, in his first volume of case law lamented the *"uncertainty of the law* which is so frequently and perhaps so justly the subject of complaint in this country."[14]

Grievances about the unknown and therefore uncertain nature of the law were not unique to the early republic. The history of many legal systems, and certainly that of the common law, are replete with such complaints. In the seventeenth century, for example, Sir Francis Bacon bewailed the "great uncertainties" of the law in England and proposed its reform. A strikingly similar charge was made by the prestigious American Law Institute some three hundred years later. Its program for improvement was not unlike that recommended by Bacon.[15] In the young American nation, however, this persistent problem of uncertainty was greatly exaggerated. It was a result of numerous and interrelated difficulties encountered in giving practical meaning to legal continuity.

In declaring that the law theretofore in force would continue, the newly independent states settled the question of the source of the law but not its content. Unfortunately for contemporaries, knowledge of the pre-existing law was not easily obtained. A chief difficulty was the almost complete lack of usable objective legal materials—statutes, reports, or texts—from the colonial period that could be consulted to discover the content of the law. Furthermore, the problem was compounded, as the first postrevolutionary generation was little better at preserving the law they had created than were their predecessors.

It might be assumed that statute law, being promulgated in a written form, would have been readily available. Such was not the case. In all the colonies, the statutes passed during the generally annual sessions of their legislatures were published in pamphlet form. But, according to Samuel Allinson, who finished a compilation of New Jersey's provincial statutes in 1776, these pamphlets or session laws came "into the hands of only a few" and were "easily lost." As a result, "a complete set was rarely to be found: Hence it became difficult to know what the law was."[16] A similar situation existed in Virginia, where St. George Tucker claimed in 1803 that session law pamphlets were "extremely difficult" to obtain. "Few gentlemen, even of the profession," he declared, "have ever been able to boast of possessing a *complete* collection of its laws." His own efforts to gather an entire set, he lamented, were "ineffectual." Simple compilations, usually the work of private individuals, were only sporadically printed. A few colonies did undertake to revise their statutes, but nowhere was it an ongoing process, and never was it done at regular intervals.[17]

Even if an individual had a complete set of session law pamphlets or some other collection of colonial statutes, they were difficult to use. Indexes were unknown. Private acts outnumbered public laws, and they were often interspersed chronologically on the same page. Furthermore, according to

Tucker, "inexperience, inattention, or other accidental circumstances" resulted in "a variety of modifications, provisions, suspensions, and repeals" throughout the statutes of "almost all the colonies."[18] Allinson estimated that at least one-third of the colonial public statutes of New Jersey were no longer in force because they were either obsolete, expired, or repealed. Given the inaccessibility of the statute law, in many cases it was impossible to determine with any certainty which statutes were in fact law and which were not. It was little wonder that Allinson, trying to make sense out of this morass of New Jersey statutes, declared that "[a] few good laws, well understood and executed, must be a Happiness to a people, and are much preferred before a large Code, which by their very Number, became intricate, are sooner forgotten, and of consequence, are oftener violated."[19]

Unfortunately, for a generation or more following the Revolution, few states attempted to effect an official revision or even a compilation of colonial laws. Indeed, in most, the methodology of disseminating and managing the growing corpus of statute law was little improved. In 1803, Tucker bewailed

> That obscurity into which the laws of the state [Virginia] have been thrown, by *partial editions,* and by the *loose* and *slovenly* manner in which the acts of the legislature are *stitched* together, and dispersed throughout the country in *unbound,* and even *uncovered* sheets, more like ephemerous than perpetual rules of property, and of civil conduct in a state.[20]

Some states did attempt compilations of their laws. Faced with the problem of the inaccessibility of its statutes, South Carolina ordered its laws compiled in 1785. However, the effort was hampered by the "impossibility of obtaining" a collection of the state's session laws.[21] Similarly, Massachusetts authorized the compilation and publication of its public laws, but not until 1789, fourteen years after the legislature had been meeting without sanction of the Crown. In that time, nearly one thousand pages of laws were published in forty-three separate pamphlets.[22] It is no wonder that a "great complaint had been made for the want" of a complete statement of the state's statute law.[23] The compilation proved to be less than adequate. It took as its starting date 1780, the year the commonwealth constitution was promulgated, and thus ignored the five years following independence as well as the entire colonial period. Another compilation of the public law of Massachusetts was not completed until 1793, but, because it was done privately, it did not carry the weight of official authorization.

This persistence of technique in dealing with objective legal materials was in keeping with the spirit of legal continuity. The old law was maintained, as were the methods of making it accessible. But just as the old laws would prove inapplicable to new circumstances, so, too, did the methodology of making the law accessible. The colonial way of doing things, which was no doubt an inconvenience sometimes strongly felt, as the periodic revisions of provincial statutes in some colonies demonstrate, was generally adequate for the legal needs of pre-revolutionary America. In the years following the Revolution, however, the conditions of lawmaking changed severely. No longer feeling the weight of imperial restriction, and being forced by independence to take cognizance of matters previously handled by parliamentary regulation, state legislatures greatly expanded their field of action. This meant, of course, an increasing corpus of statute law. Maryland's case was typical. In the eleven years preceding independence, each session of the provincial legislature added an average of slightly more than 20 pages, or a total of 649 pages to the statute book. During the decade following independence, the legislative output was 1,233 pages, containing approximately the same lineage or an average of 58 pages per session.[24] This growth of the statute book was seen by some contemporaries as setting off what might be seen as a legislative chain reaction that only made things worse. As James Sullivan, a Massachusetts lawyer, observed unhappily in 1801 about the growth of the statute law, "[t]here is no truth more manifest than this, that the multiplication of statutes increases the demand for more, and that the multitude of laws calls for a multitude of expositions, increases the uncertainty of disquisition, and involves the national jurisprudence in mystery and perplexity."[25]

The problems of uncertainty that resulted from an inaccessible statute law were compounded by the fact that state statutes were unstable creations. This problem persisted until well into the nineteenth century. James Madison spoke of laws being "daily...repealed or superceded, before a trial can be made of their merits." The superabundance of repealed statutes found in any early American statute book confirms this observation. Madison asserted that this "vicious legislation" was "a nuisance of the most pestilent kind."[26]

Mutability was but one side of the coin. Faulty draftsmanship was the other, and it, too, would prove to be a persistent problem in the nineteenth century. Jefferson asserted that it led to a scandalous "instability of the Law."[27] Another found the laws of his state "blemished" by overly lengthy sentences in which "are crowded... multifarious sometimes heterogeneous and disjointed circumstances and materials." The consequence was "obscure and confused" laws.[28] Still another pressed his desire for "a few good laws" passed after mature consideration rather than the confused array that annually received legislative assent.[29]

Common law was no more certain than was statutory law. Again, this uncertainty was due in good measure to its inaccessibility. The legacy of colonial decisional law bequeathed to the postrevolutionary generation was nonexistent. Decisions were made orally, and opinions were not published. As one individual lamented in 1789, the colonial courts left no "proper histories of their adjudications."[30] Such an arrangement probably worked reasonably well in provincial America. Society was simpler then, and no heavy burdens were placed on the legal system. The bar that practiced before the appellate courts was everywhere a small guild. Attendance at court, keeping a commonplace book, and personal associations with other lawyers apparently met the needs of the legal profession.

The postwar years soon proved different. "The uncertainty and contradiction of oral reports of cases," one jurist claimed in 1795, "has been the subject of much complaint."[31] Another commentator in 1804, recognizing the necessity of looking "to our own courts" for the resolution of numerous legal controversies, expressed his concern that unpublished oral opinions led to legal uncertainty. "Must they float in the memories of those by whom they are pronounced," he asked, "and the law instead of being a fixed and uniform rule of action, be thus subject to perpetual friction and change?"[32] This absence of reported decisions led to the situation faced by James Kent when he was elevated to the New York Supreme Court in 1789. Before he was appointed, Kent noted that he had "never dreamed of volumes of reports and written opinions. Such things were never heard of." As a result, he declared, "[w]e had no law of our own and nobody knew what it was."[33] Until decisional law was preserved and made readily available through regular publication, there would be no American common law.

The legal uncertainty in postrevolutionary America probably would not have been so great had not the best of the colonial bar and many of the superior court judges become self-exiled Tories, taking with them not only their knowledge of the law but also their law books.[34] In 1775, there were seventy-one lawyers in Massachusetts, but less than half remained five years later. Their numbers increased to ninety-one by 1790 and continued to rise rapidly.[35] But these new additions were largely young men attracted to the profession by the exceptional opportunities available to lawyers in the early years of the republic, and they were not overburdened with training or knowledge of the law.[36]

Possibly because these were years of enlarged opportunity for the profession, few lawyers wrote texts or treatises on the law before 1815. More importantly, because there was no easy access to the authoritative sources of the law—statutes and decisions—text writing was made most difficult. While their numbers would eventually increase to avalanche proportions, almost no American legal texts or treatises existed before 1800 beyond practice manuals for justices of the peace. Between 1800 and 1815, there were probably less than thirty books written about American jurisprudence, and few of these dealt with substantive law.[37] This lack of native law books forced the practitioner into a dependence on English legal works as increasing demands were made on the legal system. The availability of these texts proved, at best, a mixed blessing. While the English law books provided a potentially helpful resource in the absence of American legal texts, they of course expounded English law. Consequently, they did not give definitive answers to the questions of American attorneys relative to the law of their jurisdictions. As one familiar with the situation said, English texts, "though consulted through necessity, are not only imperfect but often erroneous." While English law was adopted in American jurisdictions, "the various architects have not always adhered to the model; in many respects there is a material difference" which "naturally bewilders."[38] Joseph Story, in his *Selection of Pleadings,* came to a similar conclusion:

> A variety of English books on this subject [pleadings] are at once elaborate and learned, yet such is the difference of our customs, statutes and common law, that they will be formed, in many respects, inadequate to supply the necessities of our own judicial practice.[39]

The dearth of native legal materials compounded another source of legal uncertainty that was quite specific to the newly confederated American states—the impact of the federal structure on the law. Lawyers, old and new, had learned from Coke and Blackstone that the common law consisted of transcendent, enduring legal principles, but the reality of the federal system, with its numerous, largely autonomous jurisdictions, stood in contradiction to such notions. The law affecting those things that mattered the most in interstate affairs—commerce, contracts, real property, and descent—often varied from state to state. While the difficulties arising from this situation would increase as the society became more mobile and economically interdependent, in these early years, the situation was just beginning to be felt strongly. As one individual observed in 1808, when a citizen "leaves the state or vicinity to whose laws and jurisprudence he is accustomed, he is lost." Consequently, "[a]n American becomes a stranger in his own country... subjected to involuntary prejudice and error."[40]

The scantiness of authoritative native legal materials and associated difficulties were only partially responsible for the legal uncertainty experienced in the early republic. No less important was the difficult process of adapting the English legal heritage to American circumstances. In declaring that the existing law would remain in force, the revolutionary state governments, either expressly or by implication, declared that English law, both statute and common, frequently as of a certain date, was considered the law of the new government. Of course, those portions of English law considered incompatible with the new government were excluded through some general provision. The Massachusetts constitution of 1780, for example, excepted "such parts only as are repugnant to the rights and liberties contained in the Constitution."[41]

These so-called reception provisions recognized the realities of the American legal environment and gave sanction to use of English law as the primary source of American law. Of course, this was not a new departure. While there was some legal experimentation with new law during the colonial period, especially during the early years, the English colonists consciously brought their law with them. They found that not all their native law was applicable or appropriate in the American circumstance. Some were received, some modified, and some rejected. The adaptation of English law was, however, barely under way by the time of the Revolution. Lacking an indigenous system of law, the newly independent governments had no real recourse but to continue the process of reception.

Reception was not easily accomplished. The states provided no clear and easy way to determine which portions of English law were binding and which were not. Taking the Massachusetts example cited above, what did "repugnant to the rights and liberties contained in the Constitution" mean? Such generalities were of little use, except in the most obvious situations to attorneys faced with the very real problems of advising a client or pleading a case. Zephaniah Swift complained that such provisions offered "no general rule" that could be easily applied. Consequently, the extent of the adoption of English law was "bounded by no known line." Therefore, he declared, "[t]he operation of English laws can be learned only from the decisions of our courts."[42] Determining the applicability of English law became "an inescapable incident of litigation," which created a far from stable legal situation.[43] And, as one unhappy contemporary pointed out, "certain information" about the reception of English law could be obtained in the courts after "much argument, delay, expense and embarrassment."[44] Still another said that the sole method of discovering whether a given English statute or common law rule was actually in force was "by turning over a multitude of books, and by spending a great deal of time in our courts of justice."[45] Of course, the process of reception, being given practical meaning through adjudication, worked only on a piecemeal basis, never offering a complete solution. This situation, according to Governor Tiffin of Ohio, led to "the embarrassment of the courts and to the extreme oppression of the people."[46]

The absence of any reporter system in most of the states until after 1800 greatly magnified the problem of reception. Without written opinions published regularly, it was impossible for lawyers and citizens to have practical access to the courts' determinations, however fragmentary. Unless other measures were taken, the meaning of reception would only move out of the realm of speculation with the development of a system of accessible American common law in the states, and then slowly. Most, but not all, states eventually adopted this method to receive English law; but even that was no guarantee of certainty. Richard Coxe, New Jersey's first reporter, presented the problem. "[Q]uestions have frequently arisen, and probably will continue to arise, how far" English law had "obligatory force among us." Unfortunately, "[d]ifferent opinions have been entertained and expressed upon this subject by judges of equal ability and worth."[47]

The immensity of the task of determining what English law was binding after independence can be comprehended by examining the list of British statutes declared in force in the various states between 1776 and 1836, as compiled by a careful student of the problem, Elizabeth Gaspar Brown. Beginning with an act for abjurations and sanctuaries and ending with an act for the public registry of deeds within West Riding of the County York, she listed in over one hundred and fifty double-columned pages of fine print the hundreds of acts declared binding in thousands of court cases and state statutes.[48] Presumably, a comparable list could be created of those statutes rejected or somehow modified. Regrettably, no one has attempted to compile a list of received common law rules. Perhaps such an inventory would be impossible to compose. Nonetheless, a rapid perusal of almost any of the early state reports soon brings an awareness of the frequency with which the problems of reception came before the courts.

The difficulties associated with reception were only exacerbated by the other sources of legal uncertainty in the early republic. The absence of suitable authoritative legal materials made knowledge about what English law had been received and what had not illusive, indeed. Together, these problems created, according to St. George Tucker, "a labyrinth of uncertainty" for the postrevolutionary generation.[49] It was, to summarize, a time when statute law was, at best, inaccessible and the common law was often little better than slippery darkness. Judges, lawyers, and laymen alike rested uneasily. They felt the constant fear that lurking somewhere in the murky legal unknown was a law they were unapprised of that would appear, as out of Pandora's box, and would wreak legal havoc in matters they believed or hoped were settled. As one contemporary put it,

> We are looking forward to the happiness of prosperity; and, unless we have a certain known system of maxims and principles of jurisprudence, and a certain known and definite construction of settling statutes, we can have no security for our lives and property.[50]

Complaints about the inaccessibility and uncertainty of the law came largely from lawyers; but laymen, the consumers of the law, also found much to condemn in the legal environment of the early national period. The content and thrust of their criticism, however, differed markedly. Laymen perceived the law as having a utilitarian function: it was a tool to achieve desired goals. The end of law, simply put, was justice, cheaply and speedily effected.[51] In other words, laymen wanted the law to fulfill the functions they might daily assign to it—whether making a deed secure, insuring heirs their proper legacy, bringing a horse thief to justice, or enforcing a contract—without undue cost or delay.[52] Anything that thwarted this utilitarian purpose was considered a proper object for law reform.

Laymen, by definition, had little understanding or appreciation of the complex legal subleties that were the basis of the black-letter art. Doing justice was a simple matter of choosing between right and wrong. There were no shades of gray. "[A]ny man of common abilities," Benjamin Austin, a vituperative lay critic from Boston, asserted in 1786, "can easily distinguish between right and wrong." Unfortunately, the workings of the legal system did not appear to reflect this simple truism, and the form and content of the law was seen as the chief cause of this discrepancy. Instead of having, as Austin observed, a "plan [sic] concise system, calculated on the plainest principles"[53] that would produce quick just results, the law, according to "Caution's" anonymous letter printed in a Boston newspaper in 1798, was "cloy'd with... numberless difficulties, perplexities, and embarrassments."[54] The common law was singled out for special censure. What Lord Coke called "nothing more than reason," the *Aurora,* a Philadelphia newspaper that led the fight for law reform in Pennsylvania, labeled an "unbounded trackless ocean" of "dark, arbitrary, unwritten, incoherent, cruel, inconsistent maxims."[55]

As one might expect, procedural law was also considered especially odious. Jesse Higgins, a law critic from Delaware, spoke of "those absurd rules of evidence [and] pleadings" as little better than "gamblings" or "hazards" that "changed simple justice into a *professional mystery*" and "contributed to oppression and plunder rather than happiness and security of the people."[56] In short, according to a defender of the legal status quo, the lay critics claimed that law, especially the common law, was "a mass of magical mysteries, full of hidden dangers to life, liberty and property; a dark cloud, pregnant with mischief, and... dripping poison and death."[57]

As far as the interested layman was concerned, cheap and speedy justice was often subverted by artificial technicality. Intricate law, the *Aurora* claimed, led to enormously expensive litigation, where a law suit became not an effort to achieve a just result but a "contest of wealth."[58] Sometimes, it was claimed, the results of going to the law were economically disastrous. "Many inhabitants," asserted Hector St. John Crevecoeur about his fellow countrymen in his famous *Letters from an American Farmer,* "while contending perhaps for the right to a few hundred acres, have lost by the mazes of the law their whole patrimony."[59] While it is difficult to determine the frequency of the type of situation Crevecoeur described, justice was clearly not cheap. The typical cost of litigation in the mid-1780s before a court of common pleas in Massachusetts, which had jurisdiction over all cases involving sums above four pounds, was between five and seven pounds if the case was speedily settled and not appealed, a circumstance that did not often occur.[60]

If litigation was expensive, it was also slow. The *Aurora* complained to the Pennsylvania legislature that "[t]he evasions [in the law] are so numerous, and by technical forms so established, that the plainest and most incontestable questions stand for years on the records of our courts."[61] Such situations were not uncommon. Possibly one of the worst contemporary examples of slow justice was the final settlement of a case in North Carolina in 1802, thirty-three years after it had first been brought into chancery.[62] If we are to believe Benjamin Austin, legal complexity embarrassed and perplexed every judicial proceeding to the extent that litigation often was lost because of some punctilio in the law. In such situations, "every principle of *equity* and *justice* is destroyed."[63]

The lay critics concluded that this predicament arose not from any inherent and necessary characteristic of law, as the legal fraternity claimed, but rather that lawyers were to blame. Their "principal study," it was claimed in 1797, "was to render the law as intricate as possible and as far out of reach of common sense as professional interest would render them."[64] Purposefully, then, the law waxed complicated under the guiding hand of self-interest, as practitioners created a situation where "a man of the soundest sense, and best judgement, is disqualified from defending his own rights, except through the medium of a hired pleader."[65] This analysis is not unique to the period or peculiar to the United States. In fact, wherever a legal system has spawned professional craftsmen, similiar assertions have been made. Jesus of Nazareth, nearly two thousand years before Austin published his diatribe, came to the same conclusion: "Woe unto you lawyers ...for ye have taken away the key to knowledge; ye entered not yourselves, and them that were entering ye hindered."[66]

According to American lay critics, it profited the attorney to keep the law as technical and mysterious as possible. Thus the uninitiated would-be intruders, who might deny him his unjust exactions, were kept out. A complex law created infinite possibilities for scheming chicanery to subvert the principles of justice. Their willingness to perpetrate this subversion was demonstrated by the fact that lawyers were not adverse to defending either side of a dispute right or wrong for a fee. Their mastery of the mysterious science also allowed them to take advantage of the public's misfortunes and vices. As one caustic critic put it, lawyers grew out of other people's adversity and error, "as mushrooms out of dunghills in a rain shower."[67]

The charge that lawyers intentionally made law as complex as possible was only part of the public's case against the profession, but it was possibly the most convincing evidence that they were an unholy lot who oppressed society. It was artificially technical law that made it a profession and gave it its unique powers. By definition, a profession is a monopoly of talent and learning; and monopoly, of whatever sort, has usually been disagreeable to Americans. Benjamin Austin asserted that it was "a duty of the *government*" to examine the principles and practices of any group claiming to be a profession to determine if it tended "to the ruin and danger of the community."[68] The mastery of the clerical calling was subverted by what was considered a healthy competitive religious freedom from which numerous sects derived their existence.[69] Similarly, if we are to believe contemporary accounts, there were as many cures for a given physical malady as there were physicians.[70]

The fact that the legal profession seemed to have control of the public's earthly goods made the situation seem especially pregnant with danger. According to Crevecoeur, "no plantation is secured, no title is good, no will is valid, but what they [lawyers] dictate and approve. The whole mass of provincial property is become tributary to this society." He asked, "[W]ho can tell where this may lead in a future day?" The *Farmer* answered his own question: "In another century, the law will possess in the north, what the church possessed in Peru and Mexico."[71] This situation, an angry Jesse Higgins claimed, required "the most strenuous interference of the legislature and the jealousy of the people."[72]

The lay law reformers were not ideologues isolated from the mainstream of society. By and large, they were men of affairs who often went to the law and found the legal system wanting.[73] Benjamin Austin, besides being an abrasive critic of the law craft, was also a Boston merchant who must have had first-hand knowledge of its workings. Duane, who edited the *Aurora,* also had personal experiences with the legal system.[74] While rhetorical excess marks the work of both men, there was a degree of truth in their criticism. It is doubtful whether lawyers alone were responsible. A good deal of the problem lay in the inherent characteristics of the common law system. Sir Frederic William Eggleston has pointed out that the inherent uncertainty and want of system in the unwritten common law has made it "a costly burden on the community." Because of its difficulties, a trained and highly paid professional class is required to operate it. This, and the fact that in any litigation of importance "a score of legal points could be argued," made going to the law very time-consuming and expensive.[75] Further, as Maxwell Bloomfield has correctly observed, "the very structure of common law justice... places a premium upon aggressive individualism, pitting the self-interest of the client against that of his legal representative in matters of cost and efficiency." The lay remonstrance against the law craft was not the radical rhetoric of legal anarchists. It was an "overwhelmingly middle-class protest," reflecting a need that "centered on demands for cheaper and speedier justice."[76] It is not surprising that the new state of Kentucky, where land disputes were complicated by the difficult question of the applicablity of Virginia law, was the scene of a major law-reform movement directed toward that end. Similarly, Pennsylvania, at the turn of the nineteenth century, experienced a strenuous effort to simplify her legal system largely because it was not meeting its legal needs. In these two states and elsewhere, the demands for cheap and speedy justice was evidenced by calls for modifications of the states' judicial machinery as well as for a simplified law. Each aspect of reform had the purpose of removing the lawyer as much as possible from the legal system.[77]

Recent studies had adequately demonstrated the widespread desire to reform the machinery of justice in the early republic.[78] The demand for a simplified law was another element in the movement to reform the legal system. One of Austin's fundamental demands was to abolish the "mystery of *law craft*" by adopting "a plan [sic] system, calculated on the *plainest principles* and agreeable to our Republican Government."[79] Eleven years later, pleas were still heard in Boston for simplified law. The Boston *Independent Chronical* in 1797 sympathetically reported the wish of a state senator, expressed in debate, for "a plain system of laws calculated to the understanding and information of the citizens."[80] "A Real Democrat," writing in a Pennsylvania newspaper some years later, expressed a similar desire.[81] A Kentuckian felt his new state should promulgate "a simple and concise code of laws...adopted to the weakest capacity."[82]

Given the popular simplistic notion of justice and the belief that legal complexity was a function of lawyers' greed and chicanery, it is not surprising that laymen thought it possible to reduce the law to a series of fundamental and unadorned principles, a point most lawyers vehemently opposed. Laymen contemplating the results of such a reduction waxed ecstatic. Once the simplified ordinances were adopted, the "forced *magic* or *inspiration*" of lawyers "would dissolve like morning fog." Men "would see the purpose of all law is real justice, and instead of purchasing protection from *lawyers,* they would rely on righteous actions and a good cause." Then "virtue would abound, and a crime would be seldom heard of."[83] Or, as another put it, "reduced as *to bulk*... our laws would be adopted to every man's information, and most persons could spare some leisure moments to be acquainted with their general principles."[84]

Practitioners were familiar with lay complaints, and popular pressure frequently stimulated the legal fraternity to support moderate reform. Motivated by prevalent fears of lawlessness and anarchy, professionals desired to create respect for the law by making it efficient and fair.[85] Furthermore, widely held notions of republicanism stressed the need of the citizenry at large to know the law. Zephaniah Swift, for example, complained that "the jurisprudence of the country was surrounded by such thick clouds of technical jargon and abstruse learning, that it is inaccessible to the mass of the people." The law, he continued, should be reformed and made popularly available. This would be an "experiment" that the "republican form of government will have the fairest chance to put to the test." If this were done, Swift suggested, it could be determined "what portion of political happiness, a people are capable of attaining when they are informed, and the quantity of civil liberty which is compatible with the energy of government, which is necessary to preserve the peace and good order of the community."[86]

The sort of reform suggested by both practitioners and laymen, as well as its limits, however, were quite different. The desire for justice—unambiguous and inexpensive—and popular accessibility to the law were ideals among lawyers, but they stressed the fact that human complexity inevitably made those ideals incapable of perfect realization. Consequently, while the legal fraternity thought it, in the words of one lawyer, "desirable" that laymen have accessibility to the law, they also were convinced that there was "no great danger that everyman" would become "his own lawyer."[87]

A formula often suggested by laymen as a likely first step to redeem the law from its complexity was the development of an American law freed from English influences.It was a common lay assertion that the legal profession introduced the British legal science into American practice "to render the laws as intricate as possible."[88] But the dissatisfaction with English law, and its corollary—a desire for an indigenous legal growth—were built on something broader than a belief that English jurisprudence was a source of legal complexity. That notion was only one facet of a widely held conviction that independence must be declared from English law because it was believed inapplicable to the genius of American government and institutions. Austin, a foremost critic of English jurisprudence, stated the case to his readers:

> Why should these states be governed by British laws? Can we suppose them applicable to the circumstances of this country? Can the monarchical and aristocratical institutions of England, be consistent with the republican principles of our constitution? Why should a young Republic be ruled by laws which are applicable to Kings, Lords and Commons of England?... We may as well adopt the laws of the Medes and Persians.[89]

Lay critics like Austin were not the only ones to observe the inefficacy of the British legal science in America. Nearly everyone paid at least some lip service to the notion and the attendant desire for a native law, including well-respected and established lawyers and jurists. Some, indeed, were intensely critical. Nathaniel Chipman, the first professional lawyer to sit on the bench of the Supreme Court of Vermont, expressed a strong wish for "a system of laws applicable to our own governments," because the English legal inheritance was the "jurisprudence of a foreign nation" that contained a mixture of "heterogeneous principles" unsuited to American conditions.[90] If the practical results of reception taught anything, they taught that at least some occasional changes had to be made in the fabric of common law to insure its utility in America. Even those who found much that was praiseworthy in the common law shared this opinion.

While Austin and Chipman might sound essentially alike, there was a profound disparity in their views. The Boston layman found all English borrowings positively dangerous. He would destroy every vestige of Westminster Hall's influence in America. The entire system, he believed, should be abolished as irredeemable. Chipman felt otherwise. While he found much of the common law inappropriate, he discovered in it "many things which accord with the principles of American governments." The Vermont jurist claimed it was necessary to borrow selectively from the English as the time was probably not ripe for the creation of a totally new system of laws congenial to American principles.[91] Jesse Root, a Connecticut jurist, made a similar, but more inclusive, observation. He urged Americans "to rear a system of jurisprudence purely American, without any marks of servility to foreign powers or states." Like Chipman, he believed careful borrowing was appropriate to effect this end. But, unlike the Vermont judge, Root suggested "all countries and nations" possibly had something to offer. He observed that the American states should be like a "republic of bees," extracting "their honey from innumerable flowers."[92] While the two New England jurists expressed their attachment to the idea of American law, they were not willing to go as far as Austin was to achieve it. For them, the creation of a native jurisprudence would be a slow process, using established institutions and methodology for which Austin had little liking. Root and Chipman wanted an American law, not only because they found English law in part inappropriate to American conditions, but also because its very creation would establish a certainty in the law so greatly desired by their craft.

Isaac Parker, Chief Justice of Massachusetts and Royall Professor of Law at Harvard University, represents a very different position. He eulogized the English common law in 1816 as "common sense and sound reason...the result of the researches and profound meditations of the wisest sages." But he pointed out that the legislature must repeal "such parts, as changes of circumstances may render inconvenient, or simplify those which may be obscure.[93] While Austin, Chipman, and Root were essentially legal nationalists critical of English law, Parker was laudatory and believed it should be the basis of American law. The common law, he asserted, should be "cherished as *our own.*" This was his answer to the felt need for a corpus of law appropriate to American conditions. Simply stated, the common law of England, as corrected by local legal institutions, was "the *Common Law of Massachusetts.*" Unlike Austin, Parker found English jurisprudence redeemable; indeed, he found it redeeming as it could "correct defective legislation." Any serious innovation would be a positive danger calculated to destroy "the general safety and certainty of the laws as we now enjoy them."[94] Of course, Parker's position was the same as that espoused by the American revolutionaries who did not look beyond the need for an authoritative reception of English legal principles. By 1816, efforts had been undertaken to make that reception workable. Parker's viewpoint, was, in part, dictated both by his apparent satisfaction with the results of those reception efforts as well as by his love of the common law.

NOTES

1. The exceptions were the two corporate colonies, Connecticut and Rhode Island. Both elected to live under their colonial charters following independence, making any declaration of what law was in force unnecessary.

2. N.Y. Const. art. XXXV (1777).

3. A typical example of a relatively minor change in the law occasioned by the Revolution is an article in New Jersey's constitution of 1776, which declared that the estates of suicides would not be forfeited. N.J. Const. art. XVII (1776).

4. Henry Steele Commager, ed., *Documents in American History,* 2 vols., 7th ed. (New York: Appleton-Century-Crofts, 1963), I:101.

5. Ibid., p. 83.

6. Bernard Bailyn, *The Ideological Origins of the American Revolution* (Cambridge: The Belknap Press of Harvard University Press, 1967), pp. 30, 78. See also Gordon Wood, *The Creation of the American Republic, 1776-1789* (Chapel Hill: University of North Carolina Press, 1969), pp. 7, 8-10, 292-93.

7. John A Williams, ed., *Laws of Vermont,* vol. 14 of *State Papers of Vermont* (Montpelier, Vt.: State of Vermont, 1966), p. 238.

8. Thomas Jefferson, *The Writings of Thomas Jefferson,* H.A. Washington, ed., 12 vols. (Philadelphia: J. B. Lippincott and Co., 1864), I:42-43.

9. Robert Watkins and George Watkins, eds., *A Digest of the Laws of the State of Georgia*... (Philadelphia: R. Aitken, 1800), p. iv.

10. Zephaniah Swift, *A System of Laws of the State of Connecticut,* 2 vols. (Windham, Conn.: John Byrne, 1795-96), I:1.

11. John Faucheroud Grimke, ed., *The Public Laws of the State of South Carolina*... (Philadelphia: R. Aitken and Son, 1790), p. iii.

12. [Hugh Henry Brackenridge], *Consideration on the Jurisprudence of the State of Pennsylvania, No. 1* (Philadelphia: [W. Duane?], 1808), p. 6.

13. Watkins and Watkins, *Georgia,* p. iii.

14. 1 Cranch (U.S.) i (1804).

15. Benjamin N. Cardozo, *The Growth of the Law* (New Haven: Yale University Press, 1924), pp. 3-4.

16. Samuel Allinson, ed., *Acts of the General Assembly of the Province of New Jersey*... (Burlington, N.J.: Isaac Collins, 1776), pp. iii, iv.

17. Sir William Blackstone, *Blackstone's Commentaries: With Notes of References to the Constitution and Laws, of the Federal Government of the United States, and of the Commonwealth of Virginia,* St. George Tucker, ed., 5 vols. (Philadelphia: William Young and Abraham Small, 1803), I:iv. On statutory revision in colonial America, see, generally, Erwin C. Surrency, "Revision of Colonial Laws," *The American Journal of Legal History* 9 (1965): pp. 189-202.

18. Ibid.

19. Allinson, *Province of New Jersey.*

20. Tucker, *Blackstone's Commentaries, p. 21.*

21. Grimke, *South Carolina.*

22. Grace E. MacDonald, comp., *Check-List of Session Laws* (New York: H.W. Wilson Co., 1936), pp. 97-98.

23. Isaiah Thomas, ed., *The Perpetual Laws of the Commonwealth of Massachusetts* ... (Worcester, Mass.: Isaiah Thomas, 1788), p. 1.

24. MacDonald, *Check-List,* pp. 81-82.

25. James Sullivan, *History of Land Titles in Massachusetts* (Boston: I. Thomas and E. T. Andrews, 1801), p. 342.

26. James Madison, *The Writings of James Madison,* Gaillard Hunt, ed., 9 vols. (New York: G.P. Putnam's Sons, 1901), II:365.

27. Jefferson, *Writings,* II:355.

28. James Wilson, *The Works of James Wilson,* Robert Green McCloskey, ed., 2 vols. (Cambridge: The Belknap Press of Harvard University Press, 1967), I:62.

29. Allinson, *New Jersey,* p. 60.

30. Richard Hening, ed., *The Statutes at Large*... 13 vols. (New York: R. & W. & G. Bartlow, 1819), IX:175.

31. Swift, *System,* p. 45.

32. 1 Johnson (N.Y.) iv (1804).

33. Association of American Law Schools, ed., *Select Essays in Anglo-American Legal History,* 3 vols. (Boston: Little, Brown and Co., 1907), I:842-43.

34. Lorenzo Sabine, *Biographical Sketches of Loyalists of the American Revolution*

with an Historical Essay. 2 vols. (Boston: Little, Brown and Co., 1864) I:59-60. See also Charles Warren, *A History of the American Bar* (Boston: Little, Brown and Co., 1911), p. 213.

35. Gerard W. Gawalt, "Sources of Anti-Lawyer Sentiment in Massachusetts, 1740-1840," *The American Journal of Legal History* 14 (1970): 285.

36. Anton-Herman Chroust, *The Rise of the Legal Profession in America,* 2 vols. (Norman: University of Oklahoma Press, 1965), II:34 ff.

37. Kate Wallach, "The Publication of Legal Treatises in America from 1800 to 1830," *Law Library Journal* 45 (1942): 143-45. She places the number at twenty-three, but her list is incomplete.

38. William Wyche, *A Treatise on the Practice of the Supreme Court of Judicature of the State of New York in Civil Actions* (New York: T. and J.Swords, 1794), pp. vii-viii.

39. Joseph Story, *A Selection of Pleadings in Civil Actions, Subsequent to the Declaration* (Salem, Mass.: Barnard B. MacNulty, 1805), p. iii.

40. [Brackenridge], *Considerations,* p. 6.

41. Mass. Const. art. 6, sec. 6 (1780).

42. Swift, *System.*

43. Julius Goebel, *Antecedents and Beginnings to 1801,* vol. 1 of *The Oliver Wendell Holmes Devise History of the Supreme Court of the United States,* Paul A. Freund, ed. (New York: Macmillan Co. 1971), p.111. On the problem of reception, see pp. 109-18. The treatment given English law was, as might be expected, far from uniform. Some judges felt bound to follow British authority, while others did not. See William E.Nelson, "Emerging Notions of Modern Criminal Law in the Revolutionary Era: An Historical Perspective," *New York University Law Review* 42 (1967): 475.

44. [Brackenridge], *Considerations,* p. 7.

45. James Sullivan, *Land Titles,* p. 13.

46. Quoted in William T. Utter, "Ohio and the English Common Law," *Mississippi Valley Historical Review* 16 (1929-1930): 325.

47. *State v. Mairs,* 1 N.J. 335, 338 (1795).

48. Elizabeth Gaspar Brown, *British Statutes in American Law, 1776-1836* (Ann Arbor: University of Michigan Law School, 1964), pp. 203-355.

49. Tucker, *Blackstone's Commentaries,* p. ix.

50. Sullivan, *Land Titles,* p. 345.

51. Maxwell Bloomfield, "Lawyers and Public Criticism: Challenge and Response in Nineteenth Century America," *The American Journal of Legal History* 15 (1971): 270.

52. On the utilitarian function assigned to the law by nineteenth-century America, see, generally, J. Willard Hurst, *Law and the Conditions of Freedom in Nineteenth Century America* (Madison: University of Wisconsin Press, 1956), esp. pp. 4-9.

53. [Benjamin Austin], *Observations on the Pernicious Practice of the Law* (Boston: Adams and Nourse, 1786), pp. 1, 19.

54. *Independent Chronical and the Universal Advertiser* (Boston), March 2, 1797, quoted in David Mellinkoff, *The Language of the Law* (Boston: Little, Brown and Co., 1963), p. 230.

55. *Aurora* (Philadelphia), Jan. 30, 1805.

56. Jesse Higgins, *Sampson Against the Philistines...* (Philadelphia: William Todd, 1807), pp. 15-16.

57. [Joseph Hopkinson], *Considerations on the Abolition of the Common Law in the*

United States (Philadelphia: W.P. Farrand and Co. 1809), p. 10.

58. *Aurora* (Philadelphia), Nov. 9, 1804.

59. J. Hector St. John Crevecoeur, *Letters from an American Farmer* (Gloucester, Mass.: Peter Smith, 1965), p. 165.

60. Jonathan Smith, "The Depression of 1785 and the Daniel Shays' Rebellion," *William and Mary Quarterly*, 3rd ser. 5 (1948): 81. Theophilus Parsons, Jr., *Memoir of Theophilus Parsons* (Boston: Ticknor and Fields, 1859), pp. 200-11.

61. *Aurora*, Nov. 9, 1804.

62. Frederick C. Hicks, *Materials and Methods of Legal Research* 2d ed., (Rochester, N.Y.: Lawyers Co-Operative Publishing Co., 1933), p. 93.

63. [Austin], *Observations*, p. 6.

64. *Independent Chronical*, March 2, 1797.

65. *Aurora*, Nov. 9, 1804.

66. Luke 11:52.

67. "An Industrious Man," "On Redress of Grievances," *American Museum* 1 (1787): 115.

68. [Austin], *Observations*, p. 14.

69. Perry Miller, *The Life of the Mind in America from the Revolution to the Civil War* (New York: Harcourt, Brace and World, 1965), pp. 40-43.

70. On the medical profession in the early republic, see J.C. Furnas, *The Americans: A Social History of the United States, 1587-1914* (New York: G.P. Putnam's Sons, 1969), pp. 332-39.

71. Crevecoeur, *Farmer*, pp. 164-65.

72. Higgins, *Sampson*, p. 12.

73. Bloomfield, "Public Criticism."

74. Raymond Walters, Jr., *Alexander James Dallas* (Philadelphia: University of Pennsylvania Press, 1943), pp. 77-79. Interestingly, Duane chose as his attorney, Alexander James Dallas, an archetypical Philadelphia lawyer and staunch defender of the common law.

75. Sir Frederic William Eggleston, "Legal Development in a Modern Community," in *Interpretations of Modern Legal Philosophies*, Paul Sayre, ed. (New York: Oxford University Press, 1947), p. 174.

76. Bloomfield, "Public Criticism."

77. See, generally, Richard E.Ellis, *The Jeffersonian Crisis: Courts and Politics in the Young Republic* (New York: Oxford University Press, 1971).

78. Ibid.

79. [Austin], *Observations*, pp. 11, 12.

80. *Independent Chronical*, March 2, 1797.

81. Quoted in Elizabeth K. Henderson, "The Attack on the Judiciary in Pennsylvania, 1800-1810," *The Pennsylvania Magazine of History and Biography* 61 (1937): 116.

82. Ellis, *Jeffersonian Crisis*, p. 124.

83. Higgins, *Sampson*, pp. 66, 69.

84. [Austin], *Observations*, p. 37.

85. Parsons, *Memoir*.

86. Swift, *System*, pp. 4-5.

87. Hugh Henry Brackenridge, *Law Miscellanies*, (Philadelphia: P. Byrne, 1814), p. 300.

88. *Independent Chronical,* March 2, 1797.

89. [Austin], *Observations,* p. 12.

90. Nathaniel Chipman, *Sketches of the Principles of Government,* (Rutland,Vt.: J. Lyon, 1793), pp. 235-38.

91. Chipman, *Sketches,* p. 238.

92. 1 Root (Conn.) xiv, xliii (1798). In expressing the idea that American jurisprudence could benefit from gleaning its content from a variety of foreign sources, Root was possibly twenty years ahead of his time. He told his readers that in creating "a system of jurisprudence purely American," while they should not be "humble imitators," the lawmakers could "derive instruction and improvement from the observations, discoveries, and experience of the literati, in all countries and nations, respecting jurisprudence." pp. xiii, xiv.

93. Isaac Parker, "Inaugural Address Delivered in the Chapel of Harvard University, by the Hon. Isaac Parker, Chief Justice of Massachusetts, and Royall Professor of Law," *North American Review,* 3 (1816): 23.

94. Ibid.

2

ATTITUDES INTO ACTION: AMERICAN LAW REFORM, 1776-1815

The strong dissatisfaction with the form and content of the law in the early republic and the concomitant demands for reform induced a variety of amelia-tory responses in nearly all the states by 1815. The actual business of erecting the specific reforms was undertaken by lawyers. Believing the law was a delicate commodity that could easily be bruised by the rough popular hand, they carefully maintained this monopoly, and not a few laymen, usually those with a conservative orientation, agreed. When the legal profession takes up the business of perfecting the law, its efforts are usually limited to careful, technical improvements designed to meet its own particular needs.[1] Most attempts to improve the legal order in the young republic proved no exception. Consequently, of the three areas of complaint, the first, largely a professional grievance that the law was inaccessible and uncertain, received the most attention. The second, that the law was overly complex and mysterious, was satisfied only as much as the needs of the law guild required. The third, the demand for an indigenous system of law, was, by comparison, only infrequently a specific object of reform. Yet, the very process of facilitating access to the law fostered the growth of American legal materials and thus a distinguishable native law.

Since elected assemblies were often considered pre-eminent among the three branches of government in these early years, it was quite natural that lawyers and laymen looked to them to effect the desired reforms. In dealing with the problems of inacessible law, the legislatures were encouraged to act by the fact that if they did not fix the law's content, the courts would take the responsibility by default. This prospect was not appealing to those imbued with the prevailing notions of separation of powers. John F. Grimke cautioned the legislature of South Carolina to "give as little opportunity as possible to the Magistrates of the Courts" to work reform in the law, "as it invests them with legislative power."[2] However, some individuals saw courts as decidedly reluctant agents of reform. Hugh Henry Brackenridge, a justice of the Pennsylvania Supreme Court, citing attachment to precedent and "[t]imidity of mind," claimed that it was "extremely difficult, if not altogether impossible, to get a court to budge in a matter of reform."[3]

Certainly the action of the several state courts relating to reception almost uniformly indicated a disinclination to deal effectively with the problem beyond cases being adjudicated. Consequently, no holding or dicta offered a general and easily applicable rule that could be applied to English law with any certainty. For example, the highest court of Massachusetts declared in *Commonwealth v. Hutchinson,* an early case on the matter, that it would not adhere to English law if "necessity, convenience or public policy required" a departure.[4] As this principle gave little indication of the future direction the court would take, it was little better as a guide for action than the reception provision itself. Reports of the Massachusetts court would soon stand as testimony to the fact that one man's "necessity" was another's frivolity, and what one man considered convenient, another would find dangerous. Hence the claim of a respected contemporary law writer and judge that "only...the interpositions of the legislature" could remedy the "serious evils" that existed in the legal system. Once the lawmakers had completed their work, he asserted, the law would be "just in principle, clear, concise, and equal in expression, uniform and permanent," and "it would enable the courts to do justice in all cases."[5]

One reform adopted to solve the problem of inaccessible law in these early years was statutory revision, which one of its advocates claimed, "would exempt our laws from...obscurity and confusion, and would lessen our statute volume."[6] Since revisions had been periodically taken up by several of the colonial governments, the reform carried a redeeming element of tradition.[7] The term "revision" had a well-defined meaning, at least until the mid-1820s. Specifically, it meant a consolidation of statutes reprinted in a uniform style and usually in chronological order, from which were eliminated dead laws (repealed or expired legislation), private acts, and sleeping statutes (obsolete laws).[8] The result was a complete and authoritative statement of the statute law of a jurisdiction in a manageable size.

Considering the disorderly and confused condition of state ordinances, revision was potentially a tremendous boon to the research needs of the legal profession. Not only would the chaos of session laws be dealt with, but revision also offered the real possibility of dealing with British statutes once and for all by including them as part of the revision. For example, William Patterson, New Jersey's revisor, was empowered by the state legislature in 1792 to "collect and reduce to proper form...all Statutes of England or Great Britain...which by the

Constitution extend to the State," in addition to revising state ordinances.[9] Once Patterson completed his efforts and the review was given legislative sanction, the general assembly made the revision definitive. It declared that except for the British statutes therein reenacted, "no statute or act of Parliament of England or Great Britain shall have force or authority in this State."[10] Local statutes were dealt with similarly. The revised laws of New Jersey were collected in one volume of 455 pages and published in 1800, eight years after the project was begun. By 1815, ten of the original thirteen states and Vermont had provided for the revision and digesting of their ordinances.[11] Three of those states, for reasons unique to each, failed to complete the project.[12] Four of the states that successfully executed a revision attempted to tackle the problem of British statutes by reenacting those determined to be in force and abrogating all others.[13]

The most significant impulse behind the revisions did not derive from a desire for substantive reform, even if received English law was included as an object of improvement. The premise most often argued within the profession was not that English law was unhealthy for the republic, but that it was uncertain. The Virginia repeal statute of 1803 declared that it was necessary to repeal unrevised English law because "the good people of this Commonwealth may be ensnared by an ignorance of acts of Parliament which have never been published in any collection of laws."[14] "To have the law certainly known," asserted a contemporary Massachusetts law writer, "is as much consequence, as to have it certainly right."[15]

While the impetus behind statutory revision in the early republic was quite similar to that which encouraged the codification of statutes in subsequent decades, and while these early revisions did result in a single authoritative statement of the law where they were undertaken, they could hardly be considered codifications.[16] Instead, those statutes found to be in force were merely reproduced in the revision as they were originally enacted; this was true of both American and British statutes. While the latter was generally well drafted, American laws were notorious for their lack of precision and lack of careful formulation.[17] Instead of a systematic arrangement, the tried and true chronological organization was used. Nothing beyond the circumstances of random legislative action established the arrangement of the revision. In the New Jersey revision, "An act for the Preservation of Deer and Game and to Prevent Trespassing with Guns" was followed by "An act for Establishing the Boundary of Partition Line Between New York, Nova Caeseria or New Jersey, and for the Conformation of the Title and Possession," which was, in turn, followed by "An act to Enable All Persons...to Inherit Real Estates."[18] Tradition dictated this arrangement in regard to local laws, but certainly the reenactment of English law offered an opportunity for more systematic classification. Instead, English laws were also included chronologically, being placed in the revision in their order of reenactment by the New Jersey legislature. Thus, "An act Respecting Amendments and Jeofails" was preceded by "An act for Supporting Idiots and Lunatics and Preserving Their Estates" and was succeeded by "An act Concerning Justices of the Peace, and Courts of General Quarter Sessions."[19] The system adopted by Samuel Jones and Richard Varick, New York's revisors, was a slight variation on this style. Whereas Patterson simply included one act after another, each being considered a separate piece of legislation, the two New York revisors followed the British practice of making each law, for purposes of citation, a chapter in the statutes of each regnal year. However, Jones and Varick replaced the regnal years with legislative sessions.[20]

The revisors should not be judged unfavorably for completing their work as they did. They simply followed a customary methodology that seemed most likely to produce the desired effect without sending shock waves throughout the legal system by creating an entirely new statement of the law. Their efforts were in keeping with the principle of legal continuity embraced in revolutionary America.

The completed revisions, on the whole, were thoughtfully undertaken. Usually, the best legal talent in the states was pressed into service for the task. While the format adopted would be found wanting in later years, no matter how carefully done, at the time, these inventories of statutes seemed to meet the needs of the law craft and the government for an accessible law. However, they did not satisfy the demands of lay consumers for a law simplified enough for universal common understanding. Given the increasing complexity of American society, it is possible that that wish could never be satisfied. But it is certain that neither the revision formula nor any of the other reforms directed toward improving the law were aimed in that direction. Occasionally, though, revisions were seen as opportunities for a degree of simplification aimed at meeting the lawyers' demands. For example, New Jersey called on its revisor, Patterson, to translate into English any Latin or French terms found in the law and to place the translation in the margin.[21]

Perhaps there was more than a kernel of truth in the lay critics' claim that the profession purposely maintained the law's complexity and mystery. However, a more persuasive explanation can be found in the inherent conservatism of the legal profession, which tended to view any modification of the status quo as a serious threat to legal stability. Indeed, strange as it may seem, considering the chaotic condition of statute law, the enthusiasm of the profession for revision actually did not wax very strong. It would appear that those states with a tradition of revision undertook and completed the process with the greatest zeal.[22] Statutory revision was defeated in Pennsylvania and South Carolina. In the latter state, a draft revision was completed and lacked only legislative sanction. Virginia went through three separate commissions of revisions before the legislature voted approval of a completed compilation. Even a privately executed digest of Georgia's law, while in great demand, met opposition in the legal profession during the process of compilation.[23] Nine of the eighteen states in existence in 1815 did not undertake, or failed to complete, the revision of their laws, preferring some less adventuresome formula, or they did nothing at all.[24] Perhaps some of their reluctance resulted from what was thought to be the less successful experience of other states with statutory revisions. St. George Tucker, the respected Virginia lawyer and judge, claimed in his widely read edition of Blackstone that Virginia's revision was "the parent of new complexities, by the introduction of new law; and the reenaction, omission, or suspension of former acts, whose operation is thus rendered *doubtful* even in the most important cases."[25]

Such concerns had little meaning for, and carried little weight with, laymen who wanted a functional knowledge of the law. The layman faced insurmountable problems in gaining more than a superficial understanding of the law that applied to his situation without professional aid, even if he had a copy of his state's latest revision, which was unlikely. First, there was the problem of finding the law or laws that might be applicable. Only indexes, which were required of all the revisors, made the statute books readily usable, but usable for whom? The were filled with professional argot, not terms that were commonly understood. How was a man to know that his house and the ground it stood on was a messuage? or what coverture or abatement meant? If he desired a general knowledge of the laws of his state and sat down to read the statute book from cover to cover, he found it filled with words like "whereas," "wherein," "aforesaid," and "notwithstanding," all repeated with confusing frequency, to say nothing of technical distinctions quite foreign to his thinking. Until a lawyer or a court informed the layman, he would never know that his well was realty whereas his cow was a chattel, and the legal significance of the difference.

Unfortunately, even for the legal profession, revision did not always result in the desired effect. Even though New York's revision of 1788 included a provision, substantially reproduced in the revision of 1830, that repealed all English statutes not therein reenacted, the courts in 1833 expressed a view that seemingly ran contrary to legislative intent. Chancellor Wolworth, in *Bogardus v. Trinity Church,* held the English statutes to be a part of the common law, which, of course, was not affected by the revision-repeal process. In effect, his ruling abrogated the repeal statute and put the question of reception of British statutes back to where it had been before 1788.[26]

The states adopted other lawyer-like remedies to deal with the problems of legal uncertainty and inaccessibility, sometimes in combination with revision and other renovations. One such effort taken by four states was the compilation of lists of British statutes considered in force in the state.[27] Of those completed, the inventory compiled for Maryland by William Kilty, a physician turned lawyer, was probably the best.[28] Usually, judges of the highest state courts made the lists at the mandate of the legislature. These inventories were neither authoritative nor definitive. While Pennsylvania Supreme Court Judge Hugh Henry Brackenridge considered Pennsylvania's formulation of a list "a wise and necessary policy," he pointed out that even though the justices of the supreme court compiled it, "[i]t cannot be understood that this report had the force of decision by the Court; much less that it could be considered, as to any statute so reported, to be conclusive."[29] The statutes themselves were not reenacted, nor were others not in the list declared inoperative. The fact that several states made subsequent calendars and that one state abandoned the process for the revision-repeal scheme points up the inadequacy of the results.[30] Nonetheless, the profession no doubt believed such compilations were helpful, especially when coupled with the printing of the actual text of the statutes themselves, as was done in Pennsylvania. The lists offered a degree of knowledge, however incomplete, of which British laws the judges of the states' highest courts considered in force. These efforts were in keeping with the general reluctance to deal boldly with the law and with the problems of the legal system. Obviously, the inventories could hardly be said to meet the demands of lay critics for a more simplified law.

Other methods were adopted in the early republic to deal with the problems of uncertainty. Revisions were occasionally brought up to date with the publication of supplements or appendices of laws enacted since their completion.[31] Some states periodically published simple compilations of their statutes in one or two volumes. Before attempting revision, New York published a collection of her statutes from 1777.[32] In 1792, Pennsylvania provided for the publication of a compilation of her statutes in force, while almost simultaneously rejecting a bold scheme by James Wilson to renovate completely the whole of her law. Instead, Alexander James Dallas was authorized to make the collection, which came out in individual volumes more or less regularly over the next decade. While the several volumes in the series bear the marks of revision by deleting repealed, expired, and private acts, Pennsylvania and the other states adopting this method stopped short of that formula by declining to adopt a repeal statute that covered all statutes not included in the compilation.[33]

In providing for a new compilation in 1810, Pennsylvania added an interesting supplement. The construction of each statute made by federal or state courts in Pennsylvania was included. Hugh Henry Brackenridge considered this "[a] very useful step... towards giving the people some idea of our law."[34] It seems likely that the legal profession, not "the people," were the real beneficiaries. Another avenue was taken by Maryland to facilitate access to her statutes. In 1814, the legislature directed an index to be made of the state statutes passed since 1800.[35] This, again, was helpful to the legal profession, but proved of little aid to the confused layman.

Occasionally, partial revisions were taken up to improve access to the law as well as to reform its content. Maryland in 1797 enacted a statute "amending and reducing into a system" all laws relating to testaments, executors, and guardians because the laws concerning these subjects were "complicated and difficult to be understood."[36] Included in the legislation were sections repealing local as well as British statutes that were not therein reenacted. While this bore the characteristics of a partial codification, subsequent legislation dealing with the same subject found elsewhere in the statute book nullified the progress. Pennsylvania in 1812 similarly dealt with her penal laws when the state legislature required the attorney general "to draught and prepare a bill, consolidating the whole of the penal laws of this commonwealth."[37]

Efforts to achieve a reasonably certain statute law did not stop with measures designed to improve access to the statutes themselves, nor could they. Statutes, as Jesse Root observed, were "like the most perfect system of human composition, however well intended and wisely devised, [they] would often if lightly pursued, fail the good ends proposed, through some ambiguity in the expression, or some defect in the remedy provided." The solution to these inherent difficulties was found in the courts that construed the law. But their work was not limited to statutory construction. As Root pointed out, "it is the province of the courts to explain and declare what both the written and unwritten laws are, and from their decisions we learn the law and determine its meaning."[38] Root was possibly thinking especially of received English common law. Because the state legislatures failed or refused to resolve this problem of reception of English law by statute, the courts alone had this responsibility. All attempts to achieve legal certainty would fail if knowledge of the results of the adjudications of the courts, the common law, was not functionally available. Nor could there be said to be a complete system of American law without the development of some means by which case law was readily accessible.

The response of the states to an inaccessible and uncertain statute law was generally quicker and more direct than the attempts to deal with the same problems in the common law. Perhaps the strongest reason for this tardiness was a certain squeamishness within the legal profession about any attempt to make the common law more certain. Unlike the statute law, which was periodically added to or subtracted from, the common law was viewed by most as a complete system of jurisprudence, or, as Judge Isaac Parker of Massachusetts put it, the common law was "a vast amalgamation of principles, axioms, and precedents applicable to every relation of life." It contained all the necessary "remedies to reach continually and changing mischiefs." Any attempt to change its format by reducing it to a written system would result in rendering it incomplete. Parker cautioned the citizens of his state to "beware of hasty innovation" in dealing with the common law. He contended that "[t]he most comprehensive list of statutes, which political ingenuity could devise, would leave innumerable cases unprovided for."[39] Joseph Hopkinson, a Federalist and a Philadelphia lawyer, asserted that any attempt to modify the traditional modes of treating the common law would be "most fatally abortive, and produce confusion that would destroy the very rights and distinctions of property; rob us of our certain remedies against wrong, and take away... our most simple and obvious rights."[40] The common law had been accorded a potent mystique that precluded the possibility of its innovative reform and insured the courts total power to determine the applicability of the English common law in America.[41]

That mystique also required the states to develop some form of making the common law more accessible within the traditional framework of the jurist's opinion, even though there were no recognized models for state action.

Connecticut made an exceptionally early attempt to deal with the problem of making the common law more accessible. In 1785, four years before any American reports were published, that state required the judges of its highest court to render written opinions in cases where the pleadings closed on an issue at law. These were then made available for professional examination. The results, according to one familiar with the situation, were less than satisfactory because the opinions, "written on loose paper, were exposed to be mislaid, and soon sunk into oblivion."[42] Nonetheless, the existence of written opinions, even if some were not carefully preserved, offered a tremendous stimulus for their publication. The fact that the opinions were not adequately maintained prompted further action. It should come as no surprise that it was these opinions that were brought together in the first volume of American reports. The task of compiling the written opinions was taken up privately by Ephraim Kirby, who hoped, not only to aid lawyers in their quest for knowledge of the law, but also to make a small profit.[43] The effort was unique to Connecticut for only a short time. Soon thereafter, Francis Hopkinson and Alexander James Dallas privately compiled and published reports of Pennsylvania decisional law, and others soon followed.

While the existence of privately reported judicial opinions may have delayed the commitment of the states to work out an acceptable official reporting system, they did point the way for subsequent state action to meet the problems of an inaccessible common law. By 1803, when Massachusetts appointed the first official American reporter, sixteen individuals had already published twenty-two volumes of American reports. Private reporting was a well-established British practice, but, in the long run, it would not do for the new American nation. The unofficial American reports were too irregular. Kirby's volume covered the years 1785-1788. No other Connecticut reports were published for a decade. Then, in 1798, Jesse Root issued two volumes covering the intervening years in addition to some colonial cases. It was several more years before Chancellor Day took it upon himself to continue the work, but his reports commenced in 1802, thus leaving four years of case law unreported. In a country searching for its own legal system and for a means of making the law more accessible, this was not acceptable.

At first, it was suggested that these private reporters be subsidized. Addison, in his volume of Pennsylvania reports published in 1800, proposed that the state promote his work. He claimed, with good reason, that the reports, being evidence of the law, should be purchased and distributed just as were copies of the statute law.[44] But the states were slow to adopt the route taken by Massachusetts—the appointment of an official paid reporter. The Bay State legislature, on a trial basis, authorized the governor to appoint "some suitable person, learned in the law, to be a reporter of the decisions of the Supreme Judicial Court... to obtain true and authentic reports of the decisions... by the said court, and publish the same."[45] For this, the first appointee received the then rather large sum of $1,000 per year plus any profits from sales after a certain number of copies were provided to the state government. By 1820, nearly all the states had followed Massachusetts' lead, though usually finding a smaller stipend appropriate.

The establishment of official regular reports was well received by the legal profession as a positive remedy for their complaints, but professional needs alone were not wholly responsible for these developments. There were also the needs created by the principles of republican government, which were not only a stimulus to action, but which gave to American reports their distinctive comprehensive and official characteristics. Whereas in most colonial governments only the lower house of the legislature was directly responsible and responsive to the citizenry, the establishment of a republic made the people sovereign and the whole government a function of their authority. In the words of the North Carolina constitution of 1776, "all political power is vested in and derived from the people only."[46] A natural consequence was a felt need for all government to be made responsible to the people. The election of the executive and the upper house of the legislature, which had previously been appointed by the Crown, made them accountable to the electorate. The judiciary was a special case not so easily dealt with. From England and from the American revolutionary experience came a strong tradition of judicial independence that stood at loggerheads with the newer notions of republicanism. How were republican theory and judicial autonomy to be reconciled? The answer came in the publication of reports. Nathaniel Chipman claimed they gave citizens "an opportunity for reviewing as well what is wrong and what is right" in the decisions of their courts.[47] If they were wrong, they could be corrected, though Chipman failed to point out how the public's wishes could be effected. William Cranch claimed that public knowledge of court opinions put a proper check on the discretion of the judges and thus checked any abuses of judicial power. When reports were published, he stated, "[e]very case decided is a check on the judge. He cannot decide a similar case differently, without strong reasons, which for his own justifications, he will wish to make public. The avenues of corruption are thus obstructed."[48]

The appointment of official reporters and the regular public circulation of their reports broke away from British practice. Also contrary to the British tradition of including only important cases was the requirement that every decided case be included, no matter how redundant, trivial, or unique. How else could reports effectively check the judiciary? Following British custom in this matter probably would have, if well developed, satisfied the requirements of the American legal profession, but such imitation would not have met the needs of republican theory. Unfortunately, the path followed in the United States did not effectively meet the theoretical requirements, and, in the long run, it created serious problems for the legal profession. In both cases, codification of the common law would eventually be prompted as a remedy. Of course, the layman who complained of the complexity of the law found little solace or assistance in published opinions. He, too, would ultimately see codification as a proper solution to the problem he perceived.

Some of the legal reforms undertaken in the early republic addressed, at times indirectly, another source of complaint—the foreign, or English, content of American law. In 1806, the then western state of Ohio adopted a forthright, if rather peculiar and distinctly frontier-like, solution to the problem caused by reception of the common law.[49] Governor Edward Tiffin in 1805 pointed out to the legislature the oppressive problems of uncertainty with regard to English law. He claimed, probably appealing to an anti-English prejudice always near the surface of any debate about the law, that "an almost boundless field of research" was open to the person who desired to discover what English law was applicable to Ohio.[50] No doubt having first-hand knowledge of the situation themselves, and certainly feeling no love for things English, the legislature needed little prompting to action. They went to the source of the complaint and simply repealed the reception statute and thus abolished all English law in the state.

Unfortunately, the immediate impact of the action has never been studied, nor would it be easy, as there are no reports of Ohio cases decided before 1816. But a glimpse of the results can be gained by examining Judge Tappan's opinion in *Ohio v. Lafferty,* decided in 1817. Lafferty was charged with the common law offense of selling unwholesome provisions. His indictment alone suggests that the legislative action was less than fully effective. The defense claimed that because of the 1806 repeal legislation, there was no common law of crimes in Ohio. Judge Tappan, admitting that there was much dispute within the courts over this point, concluded that, as far as he was concerned, "[n]ot only is the common law necessarily in force here, but... its authority is superior to the written laws."[51] Citing the Ordinance of 1787, which confirmed the validity of the common law in Ohio, he paid little attention to the act of 1806. The matter did not end here.

The state's highest court subsequently took up the question the same year in *Landerback v. Moore.* While the court, speaking through Judge McLean, refused to uphold the common law in the case as valid in Ohio, it did not clarify the situation. The court declared that only "the shadow of the common law would disappear" if it were expressly repealed by statute, but "the life and spirit would remain."[52]. In fact, the courts of Ohio, traditionally common law jurisdictions, found it impossible to do completely without the common law, despite legislative enactments. While they upheld the abolition of common law crimes in the state, they could not go so far as to abolish it in civil matters. Indeed, given the fact that the common law was the basis of legal relationships in the state and that court procedure was built on it, resort to it was absolutely necessary.[53] Like other state courts, the Ohio courts faced the problem of determining what portions of the common law were applicable in their jurisdiction.

The action taken by Ohio was prompted by more than a desire for legal certainty. Anti-British prejudice and a deep dislike of English law also constituted part of the motivation.[54] The abhorrence of British jurisprudence was a widespread American phenomenon, fed by the worsening relations between the two countries in the years preceding the War of 1812. But the plea to abandon the English legal inheritance largely fell on deaf ears. The effective and significant factors in American legal development were not the demands that the states free themselves from English law, but were the complaints that the law was uncertain. To be sure, several states did act on the matter of English law in a manner that seemingly lessened its pervasiveness, but these were, in effect, limitations on the degree of its direct influence, not declarations of independence from the common law tradition.

In 1799, New Jersey passed a law that forbade any English adjudications, decisions, or opinions from being "received or read in any court of law or equity in this State, as law or evidence of the law, or elucidation or explanation thereof."[55] Significantly, the prohibition applied only to English decisions handed down since independence, thus leaving the great bulk of British jurisprudence available to draw upon to form the law of the state. The following year the law was repealed, and a new date of exclusion was declared—June 13, 1799, the date the first act was passed.[56] But this did not end the matter. The next year, 1801, in a fine example of the mutability of American legislation, the New Jersey General Assembly acted once again, readopting the date of independence as the date of exclusion, and in a display of American chauvinism, the legislators also broadened the act to prohibit the reading of any authorities "without the present boundaries of the United States of North America."[57] Finally, in 1819, this act was repealed and apparently there was no more action taken on the matter.[58] Kentucky passed similar prohibitory legislation, as did Delaware and Pennsylvania. These acts seem to have made no difference in the legal development of these states. In each, the opportunity to build on the English legal tradition was not severely limited, and the essentially English character of the legal system was not changed. The opportunity to borrow from English law, if circumscribed, was retained. Given the relatively weak state of American legal literature, the ability to adopt doctrines from foreign jurisprudence was a necessity.[59] It was only with the development of an accessible native law that the direct continuing ties with English law began to snap.

Not all the motivation for this sort of legislation came from a distaste for English law in general. Thomas Jefferson, for example, favored measures excluding recent developments in the English common law so that the innovations of Mansfield would be proscribed and the pristine common law would be preserved.[60]

If there was any desire to do away with the English legal legacy, it was generally believed that the replacement should be a native creation, not another foreign system. There was no general movement whatever in these early years to adopt the general form or content of French or civil law as a substitute. To be sure, portions of the content of the civil law were occasionally received, but within the format of common-law cases and usually in matters where the English law was deficient, such as in commercial law. The individuals who occasionally saw the appropriateness of continental law in the American situation were not wild-eyed Jacobins, but were conservative common lawyers like James Kent and Joseph Story, who had a reading knowledge of the language in which the foreign law was written, access to continental legal texts, and a desire to strengthen the content of American common law through selective adaptation of foreign law.

Except for Ohio's unique experiment, and the legislative attempts to set chronological limits to the influence of English law, the law reforms adopted in the early republic were, in the main, careful, conservative responses to the felt legal problems of the times, not efforts to change the course of American legal development. Even Ohio's innovation and the attempts to circumscribe the Americanization of English jurisprudence really made very little difference, if any, in its legal experience. The law everywhere (except in newly purchased Louisiana) continued to be fundamentally English in content and in form. Reception was motivated by a desire to maintain legal continuity and thus the security and stability of the American legal order. The reforms adopted to make reception a viable response to the legal needs of the young republic were similarly prompted. Problems had to be solved, but in such a way as to prevent new ones from developing, and without disturbing the fundamental relationships and characteristics of the legal order. Revisions, compilations, indexes, even statutory lists were all reasonably safe traditional formulas. Although the use of official reports was an innovative device, their content was not. They were merely a means by which accessibility to judicial opinions was facilitiated and insured.

But not everyone was committed to traditional methodology. Several far-sighted members of the legal profession made concrete proposals that broke with past practice in varying degrees. At least two attempts were made to deal with the statutes of a state in a way that escaped from hide-bound tradition. While none of the proposals recommended that the content of American law be changed, all suggested alternatives to the time-honored methods of dealing with the extrinsic body of the law. None of these departures seems to have been very influential, and all were ultimately rejected. They are, however, significant as early evidence of codification sentiment years before codified law became the object of a general movement in the United States.

The earliest of these innovations was a privately executed compilation of Massachusetts public statutes covering the eight years before its publication in

1788. What was unique about the work was its internal arrangement. The compiler, Isaiah Thomas, Boston's foremost publisher, grouped all the "[l]aws of a *similar nature* under a general head," and each had a letter of the alphabet assigned to it. Thus, section "A" included statutes relating to towns and parishes. Succeeding it was "B," county officers, and "C," lands in common, and so on. Thomas "presumed" this arrangement would "be found more convenient for practice" than the chronological division by chapters.[61] His divisions were not as logical or as systematic as they could have been, and there was no attempt to rewrite and condense the statutes themselves, but the collection was a distinct step forward in American legal literature. It was also an improvement over the alphabetical system found in some other private compilations (where lay the logic of "divorce" following "deed," or "oath" preceding "orphans"?) and was far superior to the chronological arrangement. Interestingly, the following year witnessed the publication of a second compilation of Massachusetts statutes, encompassing the same years "By Order of the General Court." This official publication adopted a format similar to that employed by Thomas, but the arrangement was perhaps more logical and systematic, its groupings being somewhat like the divisions used by Blackstone in his widely used *Commentaries.* The first section included public and private rights, the second, real and personal estates, the third, courts and forms of process, and so forth.[62]

These innovations were apparently not well received since, in subsequent compilations, either public or private, no attempts appear to have been made to maintain the new system. While numerous other private compilations were made, the next successful official compilation of Massachusetts law was completed in 1823, along the traditional lines of chronological arrangement.[63] Thomas published a second collection in 1799, covering the statute law in the intervening eleven years since his first digest was completed. The convenience he had believed his new arrangement would offer evidently was not appreciated. In the second edition, the Boston publisher adopted the nearly universally used chronological arrangement by chapters, which he stated was suggested by "several eminent law characters."[64]

Virginia's statutory revision, ratified in 1803, came the closest to a codification of the statute law of a state. The laws in force were, not only rearranged by subject, but they were also rewritten to a limited extent. However, the modification of the text of the laws was aimed more at bringing unity to the law under each heading than at conciseness and clarity, two cardinal objectives of codification. Furthermore, the composition of the revision left much to be desired. St. George Tucker asserted that it rendered "a complete acquaintance with the laws of this country, one of the most difficult of human acquirements." As a result, the operation of the law was *"doubtful,* even in the most important cases." Significantly, it was never cited among the American codifiers as a precedent of what could be done to improve the law.[65]

These experiments only went part way toward solving the problem of inaccessibility by what came to be called "codified law" in another quarter century. They dealt with statutes, that portion of the law most easily codified. But at least one lawyer proposed, in 1792, a thorough reworking of all the law of a jurisdiction that would have, had it been completed, resulted in a codification. (The specific term "codification" was not used then, being a Benthamite creation unknown at the time.) The innovator was James Wilson, a Scotsman imbued with the rationalism of the Enlightenment, who proposed to take up the task of perfecting the law of his adopted state of Pennsylvania.

While men like the fiery newspaperman William Duane or the radical Bostonian Benjamin Austin proposed thoroughgoing reformations of the law, few competent professionals were actually willing to take up the business of law reform on a grand scale. Wilson, then Associate Justice of the Supreme Court of the United States and a law lecturer at the College of Philadelphia, had both the willingness and the ability to execute the difficult enterprise. He made his sweeping proposals in a report dated 24 August 1792 to the Pennsylvania House of Representatives, which had unanimously authorized him to revise the state's statutes and determine what British law was actually in force in the state.[66]

Justice Wilson had his work cut out for him. While a few private compilations existed, Pennsylvania's statutes had not been revised for nearly a century, and, according to Wilson, they were blemished by disgracefully poor draftsmanship. All manner of subjects were often bunched together in single sentences. Consequently, the statutes were "obscured and confused."[67]

Deploring this situation, Wilson asserted that "simplicity and plainness and precision should mark the texture of the law." His desire was to lay down a body of law that would be "compacted and well proportioned." As such, he asserted, "[i]t claims the *obedience*" of the citizen. He proposed to accomplish this end by completely rewriting the statutes to remove the extraneous materials, resolve ambiguities, and reconcile the several parts. Thus, the first criterion of what would come to be called "codified law," that the law be precisely and concisely laid down, would have been met. But Wilson did not stop there. How irrational it would have been for this creature of the Enlightenment to refine the text of the law and then neglect a logical scientific arrangement of the whole. In discussing the general format of the revision, Wilson rejected a chronological organization as "impractical" because of "the nature of the collection." Likewise, an alphabetical system was excluded as "unnatural and unsatisfactory." Instead, he proposed that "[t]he order of a legitimate system" be adopted, or a "natural series... reduced to a just form... compacted and well proportioned."[68] Unfortunately, he did not elucidate a definition of his system, but we can surmise from the systematic treatment of the law in his later law lectures that he had a logical and analytical order in mind. In the lectures, Wilson divided the law into rationally consistent and comprehensive categories. His son, Bird Wilson, suggested that the format of those lectures reflected the divisions and plan of organization that the elder Wilson would have applied to Pennsylvania law.[69]

Not satisfied with merely a rational restatement of statute law, Wilson further proposed a comprehensive legal reformation. He also suggested that the common law, which he claimed was "the most important part" of the state's law, should be "reduced into a just and regular" system of written law and become part of the final rational legal edifice. He asserted that exclusion of common law materials would leave the legal system he proposed incomplete.[70] Although Wilson did not discuss this aspect of his recommendations at any length, he was clearly one of the most farsighted jurists of his time in this matter as well as in the whole business of statutory revision. Regrettably for Pennsylvania and possibly for Wilson, while the house of representatives desired that the idea be pursued, the upper house, in a fit of constitutional pique, demurred, and a less adventuresome scheme was adopted.[71]

Another prominent Pennsylvanian and jurist, Hugh Henry Brackenridge, observed that the rejection of the Wilson project "was considered a great loss by intelligent men." Brackenridge believed that the Wilson proposal, if completed, would have determined conclusively the extent of English law in force in the state, a problem that he and the other members of the state supreme court faced. A man of no small vision himself, he saw Wilson's project as offering more than a definitive statement on reception or even a helpful digest of statutes. According to the judge, there was "perhaps a still more important object" that would be

> greatly conducing to the convenience of all officers of the commonwealth; to the legislature; and most greatly satisfactory to the people themselves. It would be desirable to have a single law on every particular subject, embracing the provisions of the several laws on that head, and contained in other acts and supplements.

He further suggested that the law in such a comprehensive system would be stated so simply and perspicuously that it could preclude much litigation.[72]

Brackenridge was a man of immense practical legal experience, and, like Wilson, he deplored the uncertainty and obscurity in the law that he was mandated to apply in his court. And, like so many of his contemporaries, he was especially distressed by the problems arising out of reception, especially those related to the common law. It was probably Brackenridge who anonymously wrote a slim pamphlet in 1808 entitled *Considerations on the Law of Jurisprudence of the State of Pennsylvania.*[73] While he had all the admiration and love of the most zealous anglophile for the content of the common law, he had none of the squeamishness of his professional colleagues in dealing with the matter of its form. The unassuming title of his tract carried no portent of its contents. In a carefully reasoned argument, tempered with a great moderation of tone, the Pennsylvanian proposed that the common law, as an unwritten body of legal rules, be abolished in the state. The temperate quality of the essay cannot be overly stressed. Proposals of this sort had been made in America before, but usually as part of fiery diatribes based on little more than angry passion against both the form and the content of the English law.[74] But Joseph Hopkinson, a common lawyer to the core and a staunch defender of the legal status quo, considered the argument so potentially, if falsely, persuasive that he wrote a carefully reasoned and temperate rejoinder. The anonymous author of the *Considerations,* Hopkinson remarked, "from the skill of his pen, and the candor of his demeanor," was not a "vulgar reviler" of the common law, and he should not be "classed with those who assault the Common Law merely to indulge a passionate prejudice."[75]

Brackenridge did not propose to abolish the content of the common law, which he saw as the source of American liberty. "Certain it is," he stated.

> that if liberty shall be permanent in the United States of America... it is to the common law of England that the original impulse is to be attributed, and the primary goal assigned. THE COMMON LAW OF ENGLAND, may be justly stiled, THE FOUNTAIN OF AMERICAN RIGHTS, and the CRADLE OF HUMAN LIBERTY.

He recommended, instead, that form be separated from content. Specifically, he proposed that the common law of England, as applicable to Pennsylvania, should be "reduced to writing and enacted by *Statute.*" Once this had been done, and the portion not abridged declared not in force, Brackenridge correctly pointed out that the written result "ceased to be the common law."[76]

The measure was advocated to deal with the problems of legal uncertainty that attended the reception of the common law. At the time it was published, when the common law was under a general attack in the state, this essay was an isolated and thoughtfully reasoned, but apparently ineffectual, argument that favored what most lawyers believed was unthinkable. But it carried with it a great significance. What the Pennsylvanian was suggesting became, in a somewhat broader form two decades later, one of the core issues of the codification movement—the reduction of the common law (both English and American) to a written systematic form. Wilson did not elaborate on his proposals to the same effect; he simply stated that it should be done. The desire to reduce the common law to writing was not new when Wilson proposed it; moreover, occasional demands of this sort among practitioners may be found as early as the seventeenth century in England.[77] What makes the Brackenridge statement so special is that for the first time, this desire was seriously and responsibly adapted at length to American conditions and circumstances, and designed to meet America's particular legal needs. While very few responsible spokesmen at the time saw such legislative enactments as an alternative to the uncertainty of the common law, within twenty-five years, the suggestion had become a basic demand within the legal profession, and one of the most seriously debated issues in law. It was in the Brackenridge pamphlet that the issues were first outlined. In addition, like the later codificationists, Brackenridge suggested that the system resulting from the abolition of the common law should have "simplicity and purity" as well as a "perfect congruity of all... its parts."[78]

The basic point of Brackenridge's case against the common law was that while it was the source of liberty, for its own good, America had to declare independence from the form of the common law if knowledge of the law was to be certain. He listed six cogent reasons for taking such action. First, the fundamental identity of the common law was impossible to maintain. Changes in its content were being made both in England and in the several states of the American union. "When the common law becomes different in the two countries, and in different parts of the same country," he declared, "its identity as a system is subverted, and must be gradually lost." Second, in many particulars, the common law was not applicable to American conditions. What was and what was not applicable was not known. Thus, through ignorance, citizens easily ran afoul of the law. Third, even in England the common law was not uniform. Consequently, only "professional characters" could explain the law. But "[e]very person cannot affort the time and expense" of being professionally informed. Again, the citizen might involuntarily disobey the laws that he might happily conform to "if he understood them." The fourth reason Brackenridge gave was a variation on the second and third. In the United States, a native common law had grown into existence, that often varied from its parent. Indeed, subvarieties existed in each of the several states. Therefore, "[m]ore and more difficult it must become, with the course of time, to ascertain with precision, what is the common law and what is not." Expressing anxiety over the impact of federalism on the common law, Brackenridge asserted that "[a]n American becomes a stranger in his own country" when he goes to a different state or vicinity. There he finds "[a] different rule of conduct is prescribed for him, and for the want of an acquaintance of it, he is subjected to involuntary prejudice and error." Fifth, the common law in England had been modified by acts of Parliament and by her courts. These changes were recognized in some states but not in others, while still others accepted only a part of these changes. "It is therefore an impossibility, even for a professional character, to ascertain to what extent, and what manner, a particular construction of the common law will prevail in a particular American court." The sixth reason was an argument that it was possible to reduce the common law to a written form. Brackenridge pointed out that much of the common law—indeed its best parts—had been reduced to writing and could be found in the federal and state constitutions, while much had been superceded by legislation.[79]

Brackenridge elaborated little beyond this simple but meaningful catalog, except to stress that if the proposal reached fruition, the law would be "comprehended in a small compass." He further suggested that the result would be a first step "[i]n laying the foundation of an original and national system."[80]

Possibly more significant was the response that the ten-page pamphlet evoked. Joseph Hopkinson's reply of some seventy pages outlined the basic position of conservative lawyers in regard to codification. While the issue would dominate much of the interest of the American bar for several decades, no one significantly expanded or improved on the initial defense by this Federalist of the American legal status quo against codification.

Hopkinson's reply represented the view of conservative lawyers, who felt either little need for change in the legal system or, probably more to the point, a positive fear of it. The scope of the essay, entitled *Considerations on the Abolition of the Common Law in the United States,* written two years after Brackenridge published his *Considerations,* is somewhat wider than the ostensible object of its argument. No doubt it was aimed at a broader set of demands for legal change that were then being experienced in Pennsylvania. Hopkinson addressed his essay to lay citizens, asserting that the facts he outlined had so frequently occurred in the lawyer's experience and the conclusions were so obvious that the professional "will observe nothing but what he has been long familiar with."[81] He was probably right in believing that most of his fellow legal craftsmen would agree.

Compatibly with Brackenridge, Hopkinson stated his belief that the common law was the "best friend of rational liberty, and the boldest protector of the just rights of the people." Simply stated, his argument was that the common law could not be effectively reduced to a written form. Such a change in form, he asserted, would destroy the salutary results that accrued from the legal system as it presently existed. Unlike his opponent, he refused to separate form from content. To him, form was function and was essential to preserving content.[82]

If there were some truth to the arguments of Brackenridge, Hopkinson believed, it was not unique to the common law. In fact, such problems of uncertainty arose "necessarily out of the very nature of an extensive system of jurisprudence, whether *written* or *unwritten.*" If the law was complex and uncertain, he argued, "these difficulties and embarrassments are not created by the law or by lawyers; they arise out of the very nature and intricacy of human affairs; from the variety of transactions between man and man." Citing English authorities, no doubt with little effect on his intended audience, Hopkinson attempted to refute the argument that unwritten law is by its nature uncertain and that statute law was naturally more certain. Citing the multitudinous opinions about the meaning of the federal and state constitutions to demonstrate the chimerical certainty that written law offers, he claimed, "the contrary was more easy to be demonstrated." "If descending from our constitutions," he continued, "we look at some of the laws that have been enacted by the legislature, we shall fall upon volumes of proof of the intrinsic uncertainty of statutes, in instances where more than ordinary care has been taken to avoid it." After listing several examples, especially the Pennsylvania law concerning intestate estates, Hopkinson declared, "while [the] Common Law proceeds on fixed, determined, and uniform principles, the statute law, opening a wide range of constructions, leaves so much to the opinion of the judge, as, in fact, to cease to have certainty of a rule." Without common law rules, "every case committed ... will be without a rule of decision; unless referred to the *discretion* of the *judge,* which heaven forbid!" He continued:

For heaven's sake, do not let us, in a search after certainty throw down the permanent rules of the Common Law, to erect in their place, the opinions, caprices, and prejudices of judges and juries, who will deal out one measure of justice to-day and another tomorrow, as humour, favour or affect may induce them.[83]

Attacking the issue from another angle, Hopkinson claimed that if the common law were reduced to writing, the result would be a work of enormous bulk and vast toil, and then, when finished, "the experience of a day will discover something to have been omitted that ought to have been provided for; and something ambiguous and obscure that needs explanation." Like so many common lawyers, this Pennsylvanian believed the common law to be a complete system of jurisprudence that could be applied to and remedy all controversies. The common law was a vast accumulation of discrete rules, each fitting a particular situation. Therefore, if any code were to have any pretense of being complete, it "must be a mere transcript of the numerous volumes of judicial opinions upon these subjects or it must fail in providing for very many cases." The law was the result of gradual experience and growth that could not be duplicated by a mere legislator. It was a great compendium, the limits of which were not comprehensible. No legislator had the foresight to form a system of statutes that would take in all the matter covered by the common law.[84]

Hopkinson believed that any attempt to form a comprehensive code would doubtless create confusion that would destroy well-established and regulated aspects of the law, most significantly those involving property rights. Only the courts could bring order out of the chaos that would result, but a settled legal system would not come easily or quickly following the reduction of the common law to writing. He suggested that

after wandering a century or two in darkness and doubt... we shall be most fortunate indeed if we find ourselves just where we are now. We shall leave the fast land to be driven about by every tempestuous gust and restless current, and the utmost of our hope must be to escape ruin and wreck; and regain the shore we deserted.

The common law represented the security of the known, while a new law represented the chaotic unknown. He cautioned that if the states took up the project "[w]e shall look to it with the tears of sorrow, and in the bitterness of self reproach." This would be the result of any overzealous quest for certainty. In place of the "permanent rules of the Common Law," there would not be a single easily interpreted uniform written system. Only chaos and confusion would exist.[85]

As to the argument that the inherited common law could gradually be lost in the rise of an American common law, Hopkinson responded, "surely if it must be lost, this is the best way of losing it. It is the safest way, and of itself renders a murderous extinction unnecessary at least." In relation to this, he saw the rise of an indigenous common law as the most desirable ("if really desirable") way of freeing the United States from English jurisprudence, as it "will be gradually replaced by *time* and *experience.*" He concluded that

> it is wiser and safer to continue the Common Law AS THE BODY AND BASIS OF OUR JURISPRUDENCE...modifying and changing it, from time to time...than to prostrate the admirable structure...with one fell blow, under the vain expectation we may gather up as many of the fragments as will be useful to us.

His message clearly was to leave well enough alone.[86]

He probably had to convince few lawyers of his case against legal change; they were inherently ill disposed to it. If the legal profession did not favor change, given their influence and authority in these matters, change would not come. For them, the conservative safe reforms directed toward making the law more accessible, without making changes in form or content, were enough. When supplemented with private works—compilations, treatises, and reports—the reforms worked well enough for most lawyers. But neither law nor society stood still. Increasingly, men looked beyond the bounds of traditional methodology in dealing with the body of the law as these older modes appeared inadequate in a changing legal environment. Increasingly, they looked to codification.

NOTES

1. On this point and the historical trends of law reform in the United States, see Lawrence M. Friedman, "Law Reform in Historical Perspective," *St. Louis University Law Journal* 13 (1969): 351-74.

2. John Faucheroud Grimke, ed., *The Public Laws of the State of South Carolina* ...(Philadelphia: R. Aitken and Son, 1790), p. iv.

3. Hugh Henry Brackenridge, *Law Miscellanies* (Philadelphia: P. Byrne, 1814), pp. 73-74.

4. *Commonwealth v. Hutchinson,* 1 Mass. 7, 8 (1804).

5. 1 Root (Conn.) xiv (1798).

6. Grimke, *South Carolina.*

7. On the colonial revisions, see, generally, Erwin C. Surrency, "Revision of Colonial Laws," *The American Journal of Legal History* 9 (1965): 189-202, esp. p. 202.

8. Frederick C. Hicks, *Materials and Methods of Legal Research,* 2d ed. (Rochester, N.Y.: The Lawyers Co-Operative Publishing Co., 1933), p. 51. Connecticut's revision of 1784 was an exception. Instead of the chronological approach, that state used an alphabetical system to catalog its laws. Also, Virginia, in its revision of 1803, placed its statutes under subject headings and partially rewrote the laws.

9. Acts of the Sixteenth General Assembly of the State of New Jersey, 794 (1792).

10. William Patterson, ed., *Laws of the State of New Jersey*...(Newark: Matthias Day, 1800), p. 436.

11. The states were Connecticut, Georgia, Massachusetts, New Jersey, New York, Pennsylvania, Rhode Island, South Carolina, Vermont, and Virginia.

12. The states were Massachusetts, Pennsylvania, and South Carolina.

13. The states were New Jersey, New York, Vermont, and Virginia. Elizabeth Gaspar

Brown, *British Statutes in American Law, 1776-1836* (Ann Arbor: University of Michigan Law School, 1964), p. 46.

14. I Collection of Acts of the General Assembly of Virginia, cxlvii, 291. (1803).

15. James Sullivan, *History of Land Titles in Massachusetts* (Boston: I. Thomas and E. T. Andrews, 1801), p. 345.

16. Some scholars have, however, refuted these statutory revisions as codifications. See, for example, Gordon Wood, *The Creation of the American Republic, 1776-1789* (Chapel Hill: University of North Carolina Press, 1969), pp. 299-305.

17. Virginia's revision of 1803 approached the idea of codification. In it, laws were placed under subject heads and were partially rewritten. However, the arrangement was far from scientific, and the draftsmanship was seriously defective. On the revision, see St. George Tucker's comments in Sir William Blackstone, *Blackstone's Commentaries: With Notes of References to the Constitution and Laws, of the Federal Government of the United States, and of the Commonwealth of Virginia,* St. George Tucker, ed., 5 vols., (Philadelphia: Wiliam Young and Abraham Small, 1803), I: xiii-xiv.

18. Patterson, *New Jersey,* pp. 19-26.

19. Ibid., pp. 125-32.

20. Samuel Jones and Richard Varick, eds., *Laws of the State of New York*... (New York: Hugh Gaine, 1789).

21. Acts of the Nineteenth General Assembly of New Jersey, 1074 (1795).

22. Surrency, "Revision," p. 202.

23. Robert Watkins and George Watkins, eds., *A Digest of the Laws of the State of Georgia*... (Philadelphia: R. Aitken, 1800), p. iii.

24. The states were Delaware, Kentucky, Maryland, Massachusetts, New Hampshire, North Carolina, Ohio, Pennsylvania, and South Carolina.

25. Blackstone, *Commentaries,* p. xiii.

26. Paige (New York) 178 (1833).

27. The states were Georgia, Maryland, North Carolina, and Pennsylvania. Brown, *British Statutes,* p. 32. See also pp. 33-34 on this method.

28. William Kilty, *A Report of All Such English Statutes*... (Annapolis: William Chandler, 1811).

29. Brackenridge, *Miscellanies,* p. 28.

30. Brown, *British Statutes,* p. 34.

31. For example, Georgia provided in 1810 for the decennial revision of her statutes.

32. Laws of the State of New York...(1782).

33. Acts of the General Assembly of the Commonwealth of Pennsylvania, 243 (1792).

34. Brackenridge, *Miscellanies,* p. 36.

35. State of Maryland, *Index to the Laws and Resolutions of the State of Maryland from 1800 to 1813, Inclusive*... (Annapolis: F. Green, 1815).

36. William Kilty, ed., *The Laws of Maryland*... (Annapolis F. Green, 1799), ch. 101, sec. 1.

37. Brackenridge, *Miscellanies,* p. 31.

38. 1 Root (Conn.) xiv-xv (1798).

39. Isaac Parker, "Inaugural Address Delivered in the Chapel of Harvard University, by the Hon. Isaac Parker, Chief Justice of Massachusetts, and Royall Professor of Law," *North American Review* 3 (1816): 22-24.

40. [Joseph Hopkinson], *Considerations on the Abolition of the Common Law in the*

United States (Philadelphia: W. P. Farrand and Co. 1809), p. 57.

41. Apparently the mystique did not apply to decisions relating to the construction of specific statutes, as the desire to include that information in a compilation of Pennsylvania statutes indicates. Brackenridge, *Miscellanies,* p. 36.

42. Kirby's Reports (Conn.) iv (1789).

43. On Kirby, see Alan V. Briceland, "Ephraim Kirby: Pioneer of American Law Reporting," *The American Journal of Legal History* 16 (1972): 297-319.

44. Addison's Reports (Pa.) iv (1800).

45. Acts and Laws Passed by the General Court of Massachusetts, (1803), chap. 133.

46. N.C. Const. art. I (1776).

47. Chipman's Reports (Vt.) preface, n.p. (1793).

48. 1 Cranch (U.S.) iii (1804).

49. On this episode, see William T. Utter, "Ohio and the English Common Law," *Mississippi Valley Historical Review* 16 (1929-1930): 321-33, from which this account is taken.

50. Quoted in ibid., p. 325.

51. Quoted in ibid., p. 328.

52. Quoted in ibid., p. 330.

53. Even the most vociferous opponent of the common law in Ohio, John Milton Goodenow, accepted the validity of the common law in civil matters. "Civil actions," he said, "are founded in the private rights and private wrongs of the individuals, in which the legislative power of the civil state has nothing to do." *Historical Sketches of the Principles and Maxims of American Jurisprudence in Contrast with the Doctrines of the English Common Law on the Subject of Crimes and Punishments* (Steubenville, Ohio: James Wilson, 1819), p. 36.

54. Utter, "Ohio," pp. 326-27.

55. Patterson, *New Jersey,* p. 436.

56. Acts of the Twenty-fifth General Assembly of New Jersey, 28 (1800).

57. Acts the Twenty-sixth General Assembly of New Jersey, 127 (1801).

58. Acts of the Forty-third General Assembly of New Jersey, 25 (1819).

59. Lawrence M. Friedman, *A History of American Law* (New York: Simon and Schuster, 1973), p. 98.

60. See Julius Waterman, "Thomas Jefferson and Blackstone's Commentaries," *Illinois Law Review* 27 (1933): 629-49.

61. Isaiah Thomas, ed., *The Perpetual Laws of the Commonwealth of Massachusetts* (Worcester, Mass.: I. Thomas, 1788), p. 3.

62. *The Perpetual Laws of the Commonwealth of Massachusetts*... (Boston: Adams and Nourse, 1789).

63. Asahel Stearns, Lemuel Shaw, and Theron Metcalf, eds., *General Laws of Massachusetts,* 2 vols. (Boston: Wells & Lily and Cummings & Hillard, 1823).

64. Isaiah Thomas, *The Perpetual Laws of the Commonwealth of Massachusetts*... 2 vols. (Boston: I. Thomas, 1799), preface, n.p.

65. Blackstone, *Commentaries,* p. xiii.

66. James Wilson, *The Works of James Wilson,* Robert Green McCloskey, ed., 2 vols. (Cambridge: The Belknap Press of Harvard University Press, 1967), I: 62.

67. Ibid., pp. 60, 62.

68. Ibid., pp. 60, 64.

69. Ibid., pp. 69-440, and II: 441-720 contains the text of the lectures.

70. Ibid., p. 61.

71. Charles Page Smith, *James Wilson: Founding Father, 1742-1798* (Chapel Hill: University of North Carolina Press, 1956), p. 352.

72. Brackenridge, *Miscellanies,* pp. 28, 31.

73. [Hugh Henry Brackenridge], *Considerations on the Law of Jurisprudence of the State of Pennsylvania, No. 1* (Philadelphia: [W. Duane?]. 1808.)

74. The vituperative lay critic, Benjamin Austin, made such a proposal. See [Benjamin Austin], *Observations on the Pernicious Practice of the Law* (Boston: Adams and Nourse, 1786), p. 1.

75. [Hopkinson], *Considerations,* p. 11.

76. [Brackenridge], *Considerations,* pp. 5, 7.

77. In the early seventeenth century, Francis Bacon, then lord chancellor, made a proposal to reduce the common law to writing. In the law-reform movement that accompanied the English Revolution, similar proposals were made.

78. [Brackenridge], *Considerations,* p. 9.

79. Ibid., pp. 5-7.

80. Ibid., pp. 7,9.

81. [Hopkinson], *Considerations,* p. iii.

82. Ibid.

83. Ibid., pp. 23, 54, 61.

84. Ibid., p. 65.

85. Ibid., p. 58.

86. Ibid., pp. 64, 71.

3

CHANGING ATTITUDES TOWARD A CHANGING LEGAL ENVIRONMENT, 1815-1830

The many improvements undertaken in the young republic to establish the content of the law and to make it accessible resulted in an unprecedented outpouring of American law. However, the growth of a sizable native legal product was not a consequence of legal reform alone. It was also the result of meeting the increased and various legal needs that constantly arose in America's rapidly developing economy and society in the nineteenth century. A restless America created hothouse conditions for legal growth. As one contemporary said in 1826,

> the unexampled prosperity of the nation... the almost incredible growth of population, and immense extension of commerce, a vast and rapid accumulation of wealth, wonderful inventions and discoveries in machines and the arts, the great public schemes of large capital in trade and manufactures have these past forty years combined to create a real demand for law adopted to the improved constitution and modern exigencies of society.[1]

Another observer gave a more succinct, but no less accurate, explanation when he declared that the abundance of American law grew "out of our liberties, and is the exuberance of excessive fertility."[2]

The development and expansion of the law was reflected in an ever increasing supply of native legal materials—reports and statutes—in which the law became manifest and was at the same time preserved. Considering the meager indigenous legal resouces available at the close of the Revolution, the growth of American law was indeed remarkable. As Nathanial Haven observed of the situation that had existed before 1800, "[t]he best library of American reports that could be summoned by money or magic, within the circumference of the Union, might have been born on [the] circuits in a portfolio."[3] Yet, by 1815, there were well over one hundred volumes of native case law alone, as well as a greatly enlarged corpus of statutory materials. The very number of law books, and their presumably erudite and useful contents, was first taken as evidence that the problems of the postrevolutionary years were being solved, and that the working legal order was moving well along on the road to perfection. Consequently, by 1815, the legal profession generally regarded the legal system with self-satisfaction and contentment.

In 1815, Richard Rush, a Jeffersonian Democrat and President Madison's Attorney General, expressed a widely held view in the legal fraternity when he asserted that "[i]n the department of jurisprudence the United States probably approach...excitements of the mind nearer to a par with the old nations than any other that could be named." Describing American law as "a science of great extent," he claimed that a native jurisprudence was being developed "to meet the exigencies of our incessant enterprises, our growing population, and the genius of all our institutions." Furthermore, Rush declared that the inherited legal tradition had been largely perfected and adapted to American circumstances by "shaking off...the shackles fixed upon it in early rude periods." Seemingly, a distinct American legal system was emerging that would more than adequately meet the needs of the young republic.[4]

Stressing the arduousness involved in pursuing a legal career in America as a result of the increasing size of the objective body of American law, Rush observed that American lawyers, unlike their English counterparts, did not specialize in one branch of the law. Being so to speak "general practitioners," they had to study the whole body of American jurisprudence. The scope of the consequent difficulties were magnified, Rush said, by the myriad of American courts in a large number of jurisdictions, each adding its own increment to the body of law. The resulting availability of an ever increasing corpus of native law, he believed, "provoked and improved" the mind of the bar.[5]

Such contentment with the state of the law was short-lived. Increasingly, after 1820, criticism of the legal order, accompanied by demands for reform multiplied as men perceived the realities of the changing American legal environment. Many thought that Rush's pronouncement that the American legal system was headed toward perfection was premature, and held that the creation of an effective legal structure would not be achieved if existing patterns of development were maintained.

Lawyers noted a variety of ills besetting the legal order. Their complaints fell into four broad areas: problems arising out of the magnitude and diversity of the emerging legal product; the institutional role of the judiciary in the common law system; the continued close affinity of American law to English jurisprudence; and the difficulties encountered in dealing with statutory materials. While none of these felt deficiencies emerged without warning, it was only after 1820 that they were considered serious enough by large numbers of the legal profession to require special efforts aimed at their correction. Laymen also perceived the legal system to be in need of reform. While their critique of the legal order was superficially similar to that of the legal profession, in essence, it was quite different.

In a few states, there was little criticism of the legal status quo because their legal systems seemed adequate to meet local needs. Virginia was a case in point. Unlike most other states, it had largely succeeded, at an early date, in solving the legal problems of the postrevolutionary years. Furthermore, in keeping with the state's legal tradition, the statute law was clarified periodically in order to insure the continued effectual functioning of the legal system. The revision-repeal remedy adopted to deal with the difficulties created by the reception of British statutes, coupled with the publication of its statutes at large beginning in 1809 and the thorough revisions of its statutes in 1803 and again in 1819, had the effect of creating an accessible and reasonably certain written law.[6] The same condition was attained in the state's common law. By 1815, there were numerous volumes of Virginia reports. While their publication, as in most states, was begun as a private endeavor, it was regularized by the appointment of an official reporter in 1820. The precision and certainty of the state's laws were also promoted by the publication of St. George Tucker's edition of Blackstone's *Commentaries* in 1803, which contained an exposition of the common law received in that state.[7] Besides this valuable work, there were many private compilations and digests that made the plentiful supply of local authoritative materials manageable.

Efforts to make the law accessible were not the only reason for the satisfactory state of affairs in the Old Dominion. The fact that Virginia's well-established economy and society created no inordinate pressures on the legal structure also encouraged satisfaction with the state's legal environment. The upshot was the creation of an adequately functioning and stabilized, but not static, working legal order by 1820, marked by the precision and clarity of its laws. While it was not flawless, the Virginia bar saw little need to go beyond techniques traditionally used to insure the good operation of the legal system.

Circumstances were not so auspicious elsewhere, however. Rush had given some indication of the serious problems that were beginning to be felt in the emerging American legal order when he spoke of the difficulties and arduousness of pursuing the vocation of the law in the United States because of the size and diversity of the American legal product. He chose to see this as a cause of self-congratulation, but others began to place a different interpretation on that situation.

Joseph Story's address to the Suffolk Bar on the "Progress of Jurisprudence" six years after Rush's ebullient encomium illustrates the changing attitude of the legal profession that reflected changing legal conditions. Like Rush, Story took pride in the march of indigenous law, which he declared to be "remarkable throughout all America." But what Rush considered beneficial, Story found distressing, if not alarming. Commenting on the magnitude of the American legal product, manifested by more than 150 volumes of American case law all published in the previous two decades, Story declared that "our law is... sufficiently extensive to occupy all the time, and employ all the talents, and exhaust all the learning, of our ablest lawyers and judges." The fact that the body of the law had grown so large and was continuing to increase "with almost incredible rapidity" was laden with danger. The accumulation, Story claimed, was "a fearful calamity, which threatens us of being buried alive, not in the catacombs, but in the labyrinths of the law."[8]

Story emphasized another troubling aspect when he spoke of the law's increasing lack of uniformity as a result of twenty-four largely autonomous state jurisdictions developing their own systems of law. While he did not consider the resultant diversity altogether bad, he believed that the fact that the jurisprudence of each of the states was "perpetually receding farther and farther from the common standard" was "a subject of very serious contemplation and interest to the profession" that "will not be less distressing to the philosophical jurist, than to the practical attorney." The lack of legal uniformity within the body of American law, he asserted, created "perplexities that strain the human mind to its utmost bearings."[9]

Three years later, a youthful Caleb Cushing made a similar evaluation when he queried,

> [w]here is this rapid increase of reports to lead us, and what is to be the consequence of it [?] If year after year is to be... prolific of its annual harvest of reports, we do not ask what fortunes will ere be capable of compassing the purchase of a complete law library, but we ask what mind will be adequate to the task of storing up the infinite variety of decided cases.

Because the number of reports was increasing so fast, a situation he declared to be "a standing subject of complaint... like the national debt of Great Britain," Cushing submitted that their "benefit is becoming a very chargeable one." Like Story, he also expressed concern over the doctrinal diversity found in the legal system. "[A]s these discrepancies multiply," he warned, speaking of the frequently antagonistic decisions found in reports from different jurisdictions, "the uncertainty of the law increased."[10] In short, according to these two commentators, American law had become so large and confused with heterogeneous principles that it was unmanageable and uncertain. Instead of the soaring legal edifice that Rush saw reaching toward perfection, it appeared that American law was becoming an incomprehensible tower of Babel. The problems with which the legal fraternity had to contend had come full circle in the span of a few decades. In the years following the Revolution, lawyers complained about uncertainties arising out of a deficiency of native legal materials, chiefly law books. By 1820, widespread grievances were again heard that the law was uncertain, but for the opposite reason: dearth was replaced by a no less troublesome deluge of legal materials.

The particulars of the situation about which Story and Cushing generalized were striking enough seemingly to discourage anyone from entering the maze of American law. Story observed in 1821 that there were over 150 volumes of native case law. Actually, a more accurate figure would be 170, and, within three years, their numbers would swell to over 200. All but eight of these volumes were printed after 1804. Excluding session law pamphlets, 157 distinct volumes of state statutes had been published since the turn of the century. The 1820s brought not respite but increasing inundation. Because American law was grounded in English jurisprudence, lawyers frequently felt it necessary to continue to consult British law books, both ancient and modern. This added to the difficulty the attorney faced in acquiring a knowledge of the law. Nathan Dane spoke for the profession when he observed in 1823 that "a common life" was "too short to be well read in the immense mass of law and equity...readily applicable to our affairs."[11]

The picture of doctrinal diversity that the reports revealed was no less distressing. While every state's legal system except Louisiana's was based on the common law, which gave a degree of similarity to the whole, the particulars of the law, both statute and common, manifested wide variation. For example, in 1821, on the important, but relatively uncomplicated, question of whether a scroll was sufficient as a seal on a deed, thirteen states, departing from the English common law, held that it was; in seven, it was not; and in four, the matter was in doubt. The same lack of uniformity was found in the issue of whether judgements could bind real property, a matter of no small moment to a society of landholding debtors. Eighteen states, in conformity with the inherited doctrine, declared by a statute or by case law that they could, and many of these placed limitations on such judgements and mandated specific requirements for their proper execution.[12] American law had never been uniform, but, as it became accessible and as practitioners had to confront the problem, increasing numbers became aware of the divergence and contradictions in the substantive body of the law and the practical difficulties thus created.

Lawyers' complaints about the enlarged size of the native legal product and its internal diversity focused on the common law in particular, although the growth of the statute book was considered part of the problem. Case law was simply more important in legal practice, as it played a more significant role in human affairs. Dane estimated that over 90 percent of the law in the states was common law.[13] Furthermore, the doctrinal growing point of American law in the early nineteenth century was to be found in the courts, not in the legislatures.[14] The fact that the common law had to be distilled laboriously from the written opinions of jurists found in the numerous volumes of cases that had no systematic arrangement beyond chronological compilations gave added impetus to the grievance.

Anxiety was frequently expressed about the consequences of the magnitude and internal inconsistency of the American legal product. George Bibb, a Kentucky lawyer, observed in 1826 that the evidences of the law were "so voluminous and multiplied and contradictory... that the lucubrations of twenty years cannot derive at certainty." He remarked that law had become so confused and ambiguous "that the responsibility and obligations of judges to decide according to the law, is mostly confined to their own consciences." Indeed, the judges of the highest court of one state, Bibb related with a sense of well-justified fear, had laid down the doctrine "that they are not responsible, for error of judicial opinion, unless it can be traced to corrupt motive." Such a situation was filled with danger, as "another Jefferies might now riot in wicked and unjust sentences forfeited by the precedents."[15]

Peter S. Du Ponceau saw another potential calamity arising out of the confused state of American law. If the tendency toward legal diversity were not corrected, he predicted, "the United States will find themselves at last in the situation of France, with her hundred provincial codes previous to the last revolution." No codifier himself, this Philadelphia lawyer feared that the remedy eventually adopted might be the same as had been embraced by France, and

> the sovereignty of the states would be sacrificed to the vast, unlimited and uncontrolled power in the general government of the Union, when some new Napoleon, perhaps by a code that will bear his name, will cut the gordian knot of uncertain litigation, and subject this extensive empire to some novel and uniform system of legislation.[16]

A writer for the conservative *United States Law Journal* found the state of American law no less troubling. He suggested that, if the "rage for reporting" continuing unabated, it would "be the work of a lifetime to learn even the names of all the reporters," and eventually "the paths of the law will completely blocked by the constant accumulations of these enormous masses of type and paper and binding." The writer suggested, with imagery characteristic of the age, that "some future generation, in the height of their vexation and despair, may be tempted to apply the Torch of Omar, and burn their way through it."[17] Even Chancellor Kent, a man not known for his advocacy of legal reform, commenting on "[t]he evils resulting from an indigestible heap of laws, and legal authorities," expressed his belief that "[t]he spirit of the present age, and the cause of truth and justice require more simplicity" in the system of American law.[18]

Of course, complaints of this sort are not unique to the period. Nearly two hundred years earlier, Matthew Hale, one of England's greatest judges, made a representative expression of discontent when he spoke of the law as

> rolling like a snow ball, it increaseth in bulk in every age, till becomes utterly unmanageable. very age did retain somewhat of what was past, and added somewhat of its

own... And this produceth mistakes... It must necessarily cause ignorance in professors and the profession itself; because the volumes of the law are not easily mastered.[19]

Similar complaints are found so frequently in the modern era of Anglo-American legal development, to say nothing of other legal systems, that it should be considered a basic theme in the history of law. Contemporaries were well aware that they were not the first to face the problem of an enlarged and contradictory body of law. "Our age is not peculiar in its complaint of the increase of law books," said one law writer of the time.[20] This, of course, was small comfort.

While the specific grievances the legal profession expressed in the 1820s about their legal environment were not new, the distinctive characteristics of that environment exacerbated the enduring difficulties of the law. This environment created serious practical problems for a law craft that seemed to require reform. When the legal fraternity wishes to change the legal system, the impulse is, with some few exceptions, derived from utilitarian needs, not from theoretical considerations. The desire for legal reform in the 1820s was typical in this regard.

The developmental state of the law amplified the basic problems of an unwieldy and uncertain jurisprudence. This was a remarkably vital period of legal growth, whether or not it was "the formative era of American law" as Roscoe Pound suggested.[21] The United States was engaged in the necessary process of developing an adequately functioning system of laws. Not only was it necessary to apply the inherited legal tradition to American conditions, but new circumstances encouraged legal development in new areas as well.Cases of first impression frequently made up an extraordinary portion of the work of the courts. Judges were not confined by a well-established body of doctrine to applying precedent; they were creating law, as legal scholar and historian Morton J. Horwitz has explained. Judges, he contends, had an instrumental conception of the law, as they "conceive[d] of themselves as legislators and leading agents of legal change." They looked upon "the common law as equally responsible with legislation for governing society and promoting socially desirable conduct." This "encouraged innovation and allowed judges to formulate legal doctrine with the self-conscious goal of bringing about social change."[22]

While not everyone is convinced that American judges held such notions, it is indisputable that they frequently acted as if they did.[23] Much of the inherited legal tradition was inapplicable to conditions in America, and the vitally developing American society demanded a vitally developing law. Consequently, the received law was undergoing dramatic changes in the process of being shaped by the courts to fit America's practical legal needs. Old doctrines were thrown over or modified, and new law, often totally at odds with English jurisprudence, was being created. English law had offered a handle of sorts by which to grasp the law, but this was being destroyed in the process of legal change.

Most lawyers were pleased that English legal science was undergoing change by being exposed to the genius of American institutions, but they discovered that change in the material details of the law was formless and inconsistent. Each state made its own determination of the viability of English law for its needs and shaped its own legal structure in a piecemeal fashion. Consequently, it was difficult to know which portions of English law were in force and which were not, to say nothing of what may have replaced the inherited doctrines. One writer in 1830 spoke of the "real difficulty in determining" what part of the common law "has been transmitted from our ancestors" and thus would "demand the obedience and protect the rights of the people."[24] Another spoke of a different aspect of the problem when he expressed his concern that "[a]ncient precedents could be roused up, like so many sleeping lions, to destroy the innocent and unwary."[25] Of course, the problem was not new, but, in this period of accelerated legal growth, the problem was enlarged and more troublesome than it had been before.

The fact that the law was undergoing doctrinal transformation made it imperative to follow the American reports closely so as not to be caught unaware by some important change or modification in what was thought to be a well-established doctrine. However, keeping abreast of the law was no easy task, given the rapidity of legal growth. Indeed, as Nathan Dane gloomily asserted in 1823, it was "almost impossible for any man to keep pace with the increase and changes in American law."[26] He knew because he had attempted the task.

To a large extent, the effluence, as well as the lack of uniformity that the American legal product exhibited, sprang from the impact of federalism, as each state produced its own corpus of law. Peter S. Du Ponceau described the situation when he said, "there is no polar star to direct our uncertain wanderings," as reflected in "the discordant judgements of so many coordinate judicial authorities."[27] In retrospect, little else but legal diversity could have been expected, given the reality of federalism and the great variety of local circumstances that the United States exhibited.

Perhaps the legal fraternity's anguish over the size and diversity of American law would not have waxed so strong in the 1820s if each segment had thought only in terms of the law of its own state rather than American law as a whole. There was, however, reason enough for dissatisfaction concerning the multiplicity, uncertainty, and instability of the law within most states, and the expressed discontent was often limited to the working legal order within individual states. In part, the concern about the condition of American law was the cumulative function of the legal circumstances faced locally. Furthermore, the inherited conception of the common law, as well as the practical realities of working with the law in a federal system that overlaid a greater interdependent socioeconomic system, strongly encouraged a concern for the aggregate body of American law and prompted a more general indictment.

Because of the received legal tradition, many lawyers and jurists persisted in thinking of the common law in terms of a body of jurisprudence with general and enduring application. While the concept had no institutional basis, the notion still persisted and was based on the assumption that the common law consisted of transcendent and enduring legal principles or truths. If these abstract assumptions encouraged the idea of a national jurisprudence, the operative realities that the law guild faced in the United States were strong inducements to hope that American law could be more than a geographical expression.

American society was mobile, increasingly interdependent, and divided by political subdivisions that were largely free to form their law as they wished. The difficulty of administering the law in such a society created serious practical problems. As the editors of the *American Jurist* wrote in their first issue in 1829,

> the frequent migrations and active commerce among the different states, and consequent intermixture of the interests and affairs of subjects of distinct jurisdictions, make it important, and indeed necessary that the members of the profession in one state should have some knowledge of the legislation and legal administration in the others...It frequently happens that instruments of writing, which are duly authenticated according to the laws of one state, when opened in the courts of another, are found to be perfectly nugatory, and the unfortunate suitor, after incurring heavy expense, is unable to assert his right or must submit to an unjust claim, because he was ignorant of the law which prevails where the controversy existed.

Such situations, they suggested, occurred so frequently that "they must be familiar to the experience of everyone."[28] James Kent claimed that "[t]housands have been lost" for want of an accurate knowledge of the law of the several states.[29]

The business of the law required a reasonably certain knowledge of the law's substantive contents, and, of course, this meant keeping pace with the changes and developments of the legal science. If it was important to have access to knowledge of the laws of the other states, it was even more important to develop and maintain a mastery of the laws of the state where the attorney practiced. William H.Gardiner, a prominent Massachusetts practitioner, stressed this theme when he stated that "many a client might have been saved the expense and vexation of a suit instituted and resisted for the purpose of ascertaining and settling some point of the glorious uncertainty of the law" if his lawyer had a sound up-to-date knowledge of the law.[30] To be sure, materials were generally available, but how could a lawyer sustain a firm grasp of the law given its abundance? And, of course, in this period of unusual legal growth and development, there was little assurance that what was thought to be settled would be free from reinterpretation.

If the practitioner needed a reasonably certain knowledge of the law to advise his clients, he also needed reliable weaponry for the legal battles he would fight in the adversary process. But the conditions of the legal order rendered the outcome of the legal jousts before the bench and jury extremely problematical.

The common law had no ultimate repository. Rather, it was to be found in the opinions of jurists in decided cases. Common lawyers, as a result, had to reason from existing case law by analogy. This created an inherently uncertain legal situation, given the variety of case law and the fact that no two law suits were exactly alike. In England, the intrinsic defects involved were modified by the existence of a unitary system of common law courts, which created a limited body of case law that could be drawn upon by a highly centralized bar. But the American federal setting exacerbated the natural uncertainty of the common law. The several common law jurisdictions in the United States were not considered self-contained. Rather, as one contemporary law writer observed, the "decisions of each" were considered "a commentary on those of the others, all of them mutually imparting light, and confirming, qualifying, and correcting the decisions of each."[31] English cases were admitted nearly everywhere by courts as evidence of the law, which added to the number of law books that had to be consulted. While the common law of the other states and of England was not considered authoritative, it was nonetheless considered "persuasive" or "respected" authority. Given the immense body of American law and the imported English cases, serious problems were created for the attorney. Certainly, as Caleb Cushing observed, it was

> not necessary nor desirable for the practitioner to study every case that may be reported. But still it is very convenient to find, that the portion you wish to establish has been decided agreeably to your views, and for sufficient reasons assigned by one respectable court of law; and if your antagonist cites an adverse case precisely in point which you have overlooked, your situation is at least a very awkward one, even though the case adduced be not of conclusive authority as a precedent where you practice.

He suggested, in effect, that no relevant case should be overlooked. But, as Cushing remarked, "the same point is not seldom differently considered in England and America, in Massachusetts and New York."[32] This doctrinal conflict within the growing body of the law, according to Henry Dwight Sedgwick, tended to "weaken the authority" of every case and "perplex the judgement." Sedgwick asserted that "[s]carcely any doctrine can be advanced, or decisions made to which an ingenious man cannot give respectable authority."[33]

The upshot, according to one unhappy commentator, was that "legal discussion" was rendered "an array of cases against cases, [rather] than a reference to well-settled principles bearing on the question before the court."[34] William Sampson, a New York practitioner and law reformer, put it somewhat differently when he asserted that "great delays are occasioned by the great multitude of books which it is now necessary to read and cite." This was "an evil that increases hourly, and is now become not only inconvenient, but too absurd to be endured."[35] Jared Ingersoll declared in 1824 that "[t]he camel load of cases which it is said to have been necessary to gain a point of law in the decline of the Roman empire is...already insufficient for the purpose in America."[36] The comparison was apt, considering that the solution adopted by Justinian and suggested with increasing frequency in the 1820s by American lawyers was codification.

The difficult professional task of searching out the germane precedents from the huge body of common law was magnified by the style of American reporting. Unlike their English counterparts, the American reporters generally included the opinions handed down in all cases, however redundant, insignificant, or unique. Some also quoted the arguments of opposing counsel at length, thus adding to the size and cost of the reports. Others used their reports as vehicles for extensive, though not always appreciated, discussions on points of law. Not a few attorneys saw an improved system of reporting, which would concentrate on succinctness and the inclusion of only important cases, as a solution for their overabundant law. Daniel Webster, no stranger to common law reports, complained of "the rage for bookmaking" among the reporters that arose "from the growing habit of reporting cases not sufficiently important to merit publicity." If the practice were not checked, Webster declared that the result would be "deeply injurious" to the profession.[37] However, while improved reporting would have lightened the lawyer's task, it would only have been a cosmetic that would have had little effect on the true source of the proliferation of the law.

The perception of legal problems exhibited by many lawyers extended no further than the areas already outlined. In effect, they desired only that the law be given precision and clarity, be stated concisely, and that all nonessentials be removed. For others, this was not enough. Such improvement would not attack what they considered to be the true source of many of the country's legal problems—the institutional role of the judiciary in the common law system.

Thomas Cooper, who had himself been a state judge in Pennsylvania, was one of the leading exponents of this position. He asked, "[h]ow can there be anything like certainty in the law, when the whole of the common law is the mere creature of judicial legislation, changing its character as the bench of judges changes its occupants?"[38] As evidence of his contention, Cooper cited Simon Greenleaf's publication in 1821 of a compilation of approximately twelve hundred American and British cases that had been doubted, limited, or overruled in subsequent decisions.[39] "Is it not a disgrace," he asked, "that the glorious uncertainty of the law should be verified by 1200 conflicting decisions?"[40] He expressed his conviction that the number would double in a dozen years.[41] The law itself, he declared, did not vary, suggesting that there were fundamental changeless legal principles. Rather, the cause of uncertainty lay in the "fluctuating character of bench legislation" and in the fact that the "natural talents, the acquired knowledge, the prejudices, the inclinations, and the interests of the judges vary. Judges make the immutable principles of justice depend on the color of the spectacles through which they read them."[42] Cooper believed that this was the real cause of legal uncertainty in America.

Such notions were contrary to Blackstone's classical description of the workings of the common law system, which stressed the idea that judges were bound to follow clear authority and had little discretion to pick and choose precedents to suit their fancy. "[I]t is an established rule," the English commentator declared, "to abide by former precedents," except "when they are flatly absurd and unjust," if they are in agreement with ancient principles.[43] Instead of the common law being a collection of hard and fast rules that insured the certainty of the law, Cooper argued, in rebuttal, that it was "at no time certain, it is a nose of wax; it may be moulded into a Greek form by one judge; and into a Roman shape by another."[44]

Cooper was not alone in condemning judge-made law as capricious. Edward Livingston of Louisiana also attacked the common law system as a source of legal uncertainty because of the discretionary power it accorded judges. Called upon by the Louisiana legislature to prepare both civil and criminal codes, he berated the system of judge-made law in the reports that accompanied the projected statutes. Louisiana went only part of the way in accomplishing the goals Livingston outlined. Nonetheless, Livingston's reports were widely read and influential in the common law states.

Livingston's basic argument about the uncertainty of judge-made law varied little from Cooper's. Laws, he said, must be known to be obeyed, "and, to be known, they must be promulgated." This could never be so with the common law, found only in the opinions of judges and announced case by case. While frequently published, these were a recondite repository for the law. They rarely stated the rule of law clearly. Furthermore, judicial opinions also existed in legions.[45]

Examining Edward Coke's seventeenth-century declaration that the common law was nothing more than reason, Livingston asked, "what more uncertain rules can be referred to than *human reason*?... What may appear reason to one, is folly to another." He observed that what passed for reason was often the "caprice, or bigotry, or the enthusiasm of the judge." He believed judicial discretion had to be bridled by definite written laws, if the law were to be made certain. The alternative was to remain subject to the "vacillating authority" of the common law and the "quackery of judicial authority."[46]

These sentiments were not new.[47] But the confused state of American law in the early nineteenth century, with all its contradictory decisions, gave added impetus to the concern over the judge's power. Indeed, even orthodox common lawyers complained of a tendency among judges to change the law capriciously. Peter S. Du Ponceau declared that a "spirit of innovation" infected the courts, and he expressed the fear that if this continued, "we shall be reduced to a state of confusion."[48] A writer for the *United States Law Journal* critically remarked about "an habitual... irreverence beginning to grow up in some of our courts" for certain well-established common law rules.[49] But these men did not believe that the variations in the common law that were occurring in the United States resulted from any defective characteristic inherent in the common law method. If anything, they believed that judges were deviating from established practices in adjudication. Nonetheless, their depreciation of judicial alteration or abandonment of theretofore well-accepted rules indicates that men like Cooper and Livingston were not chasing phantoms.

If lawyers believed the legal machinery to be in need of reform, large numbers of the same individuals believed the substantive body of the law itself required rehabilitation and fundamental reconstruction. "[T]he science of law throughout the union," one of their numbers declared, "stands in need of reformation as much as religion did in the time of Luther."[50] The content of the law was seen as filled with convoluted and arbitrary forms, practices and fictions. It seemed to be full of legal maxims and rules that ill suited American legal needs and rendered the law unnecessarily mysterious and uncertain. Consequently, it was believed, progress toward legal perfection, thought so possible in the nineteenth century, was being retarded, if not completely blocked, and America's natural advance in civilization and freedom was being hindered. The source of the abuse was detected in the English origins and content of American law.

One of the strongest, and certainly the most influential, indictments of the received law was William Sampson's discourse before the New York Historical Society on the "Origins, Progress, Antiquity, Curiosity, and Nature of the Common Law," delivered in 1823. Sampson had, for many years, preached the necessity of abandoning the inherited legal tradition; but he had never made such a provocative and all-inclusive statement of his position. Sampson treated his audience to a sketch of English legal history because, as he said, "[h]aving adopted the common law of England, so far as it is not repugnant to our constitutions, we have a mighty interest to know clearly what it is, and from what stock it comes." His purpose was to demonstrate that English law, arising out of essentially different circumstances, had no place in America.[51]

Anglo-Saxon jurisprudence received the most extended treatment, as Sampson desired to put an end to the widely held notion that the common law could be perfected by restoring the unadorned simplicity or "pristine vigor" to the law that had existed before the Norman invasion of 1066. To Sampson, the idea was "delusive cant," which hid the basic fact that English law was irredeemable for American purposes. Saxon law, he declared, manifested the barbarism of its age in such institutions as trial by ordeal and atonement for crimes by socially graduated compensation. While the Anglo-Saxon legal system may have been suitable for primitive needs, it was "utterly inconsistent with any advanced state of civilization," as the "semi-savage Saxons" had "no knowledge nor comprehension of the objects" that comprised modern law.[52]

Norman jurisprudence was not better. The French conquerors created an artificially subtle and overly complex system built around feudal institutions that still indelibly marked English law. Norman jurists, he declared, spent their time, "frittering...law...into logical distinctions and metaphysical subtleties, till what ought to be a plain rule of action, became a science of the greatest intricacy." Although subsequent statutes were enacted "to pare off the excrescences," its essentially mysterious and "metaphysical" nature remained. Courts, in attempting to apply it to modern conditions, were "frequently obliged to have recourse to unaccountable fictions and circuities" in order to establish "equitable and substantive justice." As a result, the law became even more complex and synthetic.[53]

Built on "the three great pillars... the monarchy, the hierarchy, and privileged orders," the common law was a "mazy labyrinth" filled with sophistries and dangerous principles. Attorneys, he said, were "ever baffled" in their "efforts to reconcile the irregularities, explain the anomolies, sustain the paradoxes and solve the riddles of our entangled jurisprudence." To be sure, he conceded, English law, "secures our rights and liberties," but even this portion of the law was "not untainted with pedantry, nor free from absurdity." Sampson's point was clear: America should forsake the received law and establish a system of laws "suited to our high destinies."[54]

Sampson's condemnation of English law was hardly new, although the furious impiety with which he pursued the common law made his address seem anything but redundant. Since the Revolution, nearly everyone paid at least lip service to the notion that the United States should establish some sort of legal self-identity, and it was a rare lawyer, indeed, who could find nothing in the received law that needed improvement. After 1815, the restless and changing American society and economy placed increasing pressures on the legal system. The inherited legal tradition, with its ancient and often cumbersome and intricate content, appeared less and less suitable and was increasingly thought to be the source of inefficacy in the legal system. In this atmosphere, there was a growing willingness within the profession to challenge what had previously been unquestioned, and to determine whether the law was providing the most efficient and just solutions.

Sampson's criticism of English law was a general indictment that did not delve into specific abuses. But writers in contemporary legal literature set forth numerous examples where reform was needed in the content of the law. As might be expected, the common law relating to real property was considered especially odious. It was originally designed to help sustain the feudal system, and marks of that purpose still remained. Consequently, the law of English real property was fundamentally at odds with the realities of the American land system. Thomas Cooper spoke to the issue when he asked, "[w]hat harmony is there between allodial property and feudal law?"[55] Attempts had been made in England to apply the old law to changed circumstances, the writ of ejectment with its fictitious John Doe and Richard Roe being a case in point. Yet these reforms made the law even more convoluted and artificial, to say nothing of uncertain. One American law reformer declared that the law involved in this form of action was so enveloped in "Egyptian darkness" that it would require "three of Judge Gould's law lectures" to explain it.[56] According to Henry Dwight Sedgwick, there was nothing "more simple than the ownership of real property," but the law relating to it was so filled with "subtleties, quibbles, refinements, and false analogies... that it can excite little admiration except in the eyes of a thoroughbred common lawyer."[57] In a society where land was abundant and frequently changed hands, where titles were often in dispute, and, consequently, where real property matters often made up sizable portions of an attorney's practice, it was little wonder that English law was looked upon as an abuse that required reform. Special pleading, foreign terminology, the forms of action, the law of evidence, uses and trusts, and contingent remainders were among the other aspects of English law singled out for special criticism and held up as examples of the infirmity of the British legal product and its unsuitability for the United States.

It was bad enough that the inherited legal system of the states bore the mark of English law, but the continued borrowing from the contemporary English legal product seemed especially galling. Not only did it add to the lawyer's expense and to the confusion already entailed in keeping up with the burgeoning American law, but it was also considered bad policy, as the nineteenth-century English judges were no more capable of creating law for the United States than were their sixteenth- or seventeenth-century counterparts. Sampson, citing the fact that the English judiciary was "appointed by the king" and that "[o]ur condition is essentially different from theirs," declared that "they are not fit persons to legislate for us." Continued appropriation from the English legal product, he believed, would merely strengthen the felt stranglehold of English jurisprudence on the United States. Of course, it was also insulting to American independence. "Dependence," Sampson declared, "can never cease if one nation is always to teach, and another to always learn."[58] The *American Jurist* quoted an "eminent jurist" who expressed "the universal sentiment of the profession" in asserting: "I do not like this everlasting copying of British publications, this everlasting waiting for the ford of the fugleman beyond the seas."[59]

Such sentiments reflected the long felt desire for true legal independence; they also reflected the reality of the American legal environment. American jurists and lawyers continued to drink at the fountain of the common law, hoping for pure waters. Not only was it a matter of long established habit, but the confused and frequently incomplete picture of the law presented in the United States made the flow from Westminster Hall appear clear, even it it had none of the congenial freshness of the new world. At the very least, English materials offered additional weaponry to be used in practice, and, with a real lack of treatises on purely American law, English texts filled a genuine need. There existed, then, something of a paradox. There was "universal sentiment" that the profession should discontinue its dependence on English legal materials, but, of necessity, English materials were almost universally used. This anomalous situation led to increased demands for the construction of an autonomous American jurisprudence.

Many professionals believed that the continued use of English law, whether of ancient or recent origin, was due to the uncritical obsequiousness of American judges to English jurisprudence and their excessive veneration to precedent and authority. Henry Dwight Sedgwick claimed that the extravagant deference paid to authority "retarded the improvement of law among us."[60] Given the felt need to be free from the uncongenial and regressive English legal science, this characteristic was particularly exasperating. Thomas Cooper, commenting on American "servility" to English decisions, complained that "we seem content to remain in perpetual infancy, and venture no step out of our imported go-carts."[61]

Men like Cooper and Sedgwick were caught in a contradiction. They perceived abuses, not only in the faithful cleaving of the judiciary to foreign doctrine, but also in what they considered to be the capricious and uncertain characteristics of the common law method of adjudication. Seemingly, the judiciary could not be capricious and at the same time unswervingly follow English precedents. Logically, a strict adherence to authority would prevent the use of discretion that made the law uncertain. In practice, however, judges often combined a selective borrowing from English jurisprudence and other sources with a free-wheeling rejection of other received doctrines. The repository from which a jurist could select his authorities was diverse enough to support a variety of discretionary options in a given case. Furthermore, as a logical contradiction, it was no worse than the orthodox common lawyer at once stressing both the malleability of the common law that allowed it to adapt itself to changing circumstances and the certainty it offered because of the rule of *stare decisis.*

Although the abuses perceived in the legal system focused largely on the problems arising out of the common law, serious defects were also recognized in the statute law. These, too, were specificially criticized. The complaints varied little from those already heard in the years before 1815, though there were a few variations still to be heard. Again, it should be stressed that, while none of these grievances were unique to the period, the exigent demands placed on the legal system by the developing society and economy and the continued rapid growth of the law worked to intensify persistent complaints.

David Hoffman, in a text book for law students, warned his readers tht "[n]o science is more recondite, no art more complex and difficult, than the art of sound legislation." Hoffman believed that the American legislators had not mastered the science. He declared that American "statutes are always exorbitant in words." As a result, "much time and attention are required to extract their meaning."[62] Other commentators agreed. Charles Humphreys, a Kentucky lawyer, in 1823 bewailed the fact that some laws were so "hastily drawn, and worded with such looseness as to leave it doubtful with the ablest jurist as to their precise meaning."[63] Thomas Cooper blamed legislators for contributing to the "evil" of capricious judge-made law "by enacting laws so vague, so voluminous, so wordy, so unintelligible" that judges were given the opportunity to assign to them whatever meaning they chose.[64]

Contemporary critics found it easy to offer specific examples of statutory abuses. A writer for the *American Jurist,* in an article entitled "Law Drafting," cited a Massachusetts law that was supposed to abolish the punishment of whipping in all cases in which it had not already been abrogated. "[B]ut," he said, "the act appears to abolish every species of punishment for all kinds of crimes, except a fine not over $200 and imprisonment not exceeding six months." The author believed it "a little singular," given "the practical curse of our legislation," that "so many persons should be ready to think themselves quite competent to draft a law."[65] Another writer, discussing the rapidly emerging corporate law in the United States, commented on the "slovenly manner" in which a Massachusetts corporate liability act of 1818 was written. The law, he said, made it uncertain, for example, what sort of writ could be served on a corporation in a suit and on whom. He declared subsequent statutes on the matter were "still more dark."[66] Such instances, multiplied many times over, created serious problems in the lawyer's practice as well as in the administration of the law.

The members of the profession also complained of a second persistent problem in dealing with the statutes. The statute book, they said, was artificially enlarged and mutable. This, too, spelled legal uncertainty. "The frequency of popular elections, the minute representation of sectional interests, and the Athenian fondness for novelty among us," an irritated William Gardiner declared, "have given rise to a very mischievous fertility of legislation."[67] Whether these factors were responsible for an ever increasing volume of statutes, or whether such growth was the result of meeting real legal needs through legislation, the burden of an expanding statute law was becoming onerous for practitioners. In Maryland, for example, the average size of session-law pamphlets in the decade and a half following the War of 1812 was nearly twice as large as those in the previous fifteen years.[68]

These circumstances would not have been so burdensome if the additions had been integrated into a systematically organized corpus of statute law, but this was not the case. "Our laws," explained one law writer, "after the first provision, are commonly enacted in detached parts, and by references from one act to another. This frequently embarrasses, not only the plain unlettered citizen, but the attorney and judges."[69] Furthermore, the law was frequently changed, often to fit particular circumstances. One law writer claimed this occurred with "notorious" frequency, and often had the effect of rendering the law "ill adapted" for any other situation.[70]

There obviously had been no real modification in the manner of promulgating or managing the statutory product on a regular basis to insure its easy accessibility and certainty since the Revolution. Before 1815, the situation was more tolerable, and, in some states, statutory revisions and similar traditional reforms had alleviated problems that arose. But the tremendous growth of the statutory law multiplied persistent difficulties, and men began to look about for other reforms that could deal with the problem.

The complaints of lay critics concerning the legal system often sounded similar to those of the legal profession. However, they were derived from a particular perspective—from having to pay a lawyer to secure justice and having to bear the burdens of the outcome of litigation or, to put it another way, from being consumers of legal services. The layman's interests were intimately involved in the working legal order, but he was only a highly interested observer, not an active participant in legal processes.

The expressions of lay dissatisfaction with the legal system resembled those that followed the Revolution. In fact, Benjamin Austin's diatribe against the law guild and the common law was republished in 1819. Generally however, the tenor of lay criticism in these later years was less vituperative, and the emphasis of the criticism appears to have shifted somewhat from the legal profession to the law itself.

One of the most interesting expressions of lay sentiment was James Kirk Paulding's *The Merry Tales of Three Wise Men of Gotham* (1826) a biting satire that not only took to task the common law, but also the pseudo-science of phrenology and the factory, which was then becoming visible on the American landscape. In the book, Quonomous, a self-proclaimed "martyr to the perfection of reason," described his native land as "a country where they have sufficient wisdom to make their own laws, but not quite enough...to understand them." Consequently, his countrymen "sent beyond the seas to get them explained." The result was a vast accumulation of contradictory interpretations. In the law, "everyman could find...a decision, or at least an opinion to suit his purpose." The system came to be called the perfection of reason "because it furnished every man, however, different his opinions might be, with reasons to support them," Typical of the workings of the legal order was the case of a counterfeiter

> caught with a bundle of counterfeit notes in his right breeches-pocket, when it appeared in evidence it was taken from his left breeches-pocket. After three days of hard argument, the court decided...that the prosecutor had mistaken the *locus in po* or the *hocus in quo,* and the prisoner must be acquitted.

Paulding conjectured, with tongue in cheek, that *hocus in quo* "is what we call *hocus pocus* in English."[71]

James Fenimore Cooper, in his novel *The Prairie* (1827), stressed the antagonism nicely between the layman's sense of justice and the formal law when the boarderer, Ishmael Bush, spoke of the difference between "legal law" and his own sense of right and wrong, as well as his belief that a just result in a dispute could best be achieved "without troubling a justice and twelve men."[72] Leatherstocking himself, Cooper's unadorned hero, was frequently at odds with the law and, toward the end of his life, went to the uncivilized prairie to escape the law's heavy and artificial grasp.[73] The popularity of the character and the theme suggests that the reader in the early nineteenth century found both of them appealing and relevant.

While there were no new tracts such as Jesse Higgins's *Sampson Against the Philistines* written for general consumption, newspapers were often laymen used to flay the legal system. "Examiner," writing in 1826 to the New York *American*, expressed his belief that the land laws of his state were "made for the rich and not the poor." He believed this was so because the law allowed unwarranted delays, and it was *"always in the power of the man who has money, to ruin his poor* opponent, by delays and expenses of the law," regardless of the justice of his cause. He observed that "right and justice" were often "sacrificed to the legal forms and quibbles," and went on to declare that lawyers were responsible for killing any reforms because the legal system conferred on the profession "powers and emoluments, which no body of men ever voluntarily parted with."[74]

"One of the People," in the same newspaper, expressed similar sentiments. He asserted that judges, lacking "unvarying rules of law and justice, make up their decisions as suits their pleasure." Consequently, the law was often "various and contradictory." Hence, lawyers "find but little difficulty in fortifying themselves with decisions in support of either side of the question which they may happen to be engaged upon."[75]

Many of the lay critics were not quite as prepared to indict the whole of the law guild as being a band of evil sharpsters who maintained the law in the present state for their own selfish purposes. Lawyers and jurists had become too pre-eminent in the social and political life to allow comprehensive censure of the whole profession. Popular political figures were frequently lawyers. Indeed, every president who held office between Washington and William Henry Harrison was an attorney, as were most state governors, members of Congress, and many state legislators. Even members of the judiciary, by their long public service and their demonstrated grasp of the difficult science of the law, were objects of popular veneration. Two ships plying the waters between Albany and New York City in the 1820s were named after Chancellors Kent and Livingston. This would have been unthinkable in the previous generation. Consequently, in criticizing the profession, lay critics often aimed their barbs at those mischievous and malevolent men who used a defective legal system for their own advantage, as opposed to the more respectable members of the bar who did not stoop to such dealings. The *National Advocate* in 1825 contrasted the respectable professionals with "those licensed pests called pettifoggers." The law, the writer claimed, allowed them to "resort to strategems the most vile and treacherous to kindle and keep alive the fuel and strife of litigation." It was their "mainstay." If the laws were reformed and made "plain," they would serve to check these men, as lawyers would be made "honest and the client safe."[76] But, regardless of whether one felt the whole of the profession was deserving of reprobation or only a select few, the message was the same: the law must be reformed.

The popular critic's most important goal was to simplify the law to make it accessible to the people at large. The Charleston *Courier* complained that the law was so intricate and complex that "[i]t becomes the study of a whole life" to master it. Furthermore, most of the law was found in books of reports that were "beyond the reach of the great body of the people." Not only were they expensive, but "the contents of one volume often contradicted the contents of another." As a result, "human reason is puzzled to know what is the prescribed rule of right."[77] The *National Advocate* in 1825 contrasted the recently approved New York constitution with the law in general. The former was "intelligible," while the latter was not; yet it should be because "all the laws...should be understood."[78]

However, something more was involved in the lay demands for legal reform than a desire to clean the Augean stable of the law in order to achieve a purified legal system where a person could be assured of receiving justice. Increasingly, the notion that the law must be a function of the people's will was heard. Jacksonianism was felt in the legal environment. When the *National Advocate* observed that the New York constitution was "intelligible," it declared that this was so because the new document was "bottomed upon the intelligence, virtue and affections of the people." The paper further declared that the law was "always safest in the custody of the people at large, but *that* custody can only be obtained or secured by unlocking its mysteries and its frauds." Once the laws were under popular control, it could be redeemed without fear because "*corruption* NEVER *begins with the people.*"[79] The following day, the newspaper editorialized that "the PEOPLE are the acknowledged source of power" in the state. Reemphasizing its belief that only when the law became a function of popular will would the legal system be acceptable, the *National Advocate* declared it could not "consider anything fair or honest, even in the law, which is not purely republican."[80] In the 1830s these notions would gain in prominence and emphasis in the popular interpretation of the legal system.

This democratic element separated the lay law reformers from their professional counterparts. Aside from the emphasis on the need for lay control over the law, the critics of each group sounded quite similar. Lawyers occasionally expressed a desire for greater lay understanding of the law, but it seemed quite gratuitous.[81] In the main, lawyers desired that the lay public gain an understanding of the legal process in order that the law would be accepted and respected. This would not give the layman any control over that process or allow any practical input into it; the system would continue as before. The layman would still have to depend unquestioningly on the profession to secure him his rights. The lay critics wanted, on the other hand, to reform the law in such a way that they would, not only understand the legal system, but also be able to control and regulate it to the advantage of the consumers of the law, not to its practitioners.

While many and different abuses were seen in the legal system, lawyers and laymen alike increasingly looked upon codification as the reform that would accomplish the reform goals they desired. After 1815, the ideas about improving the law through codification began to take root and blossom. But, like the sources of the reform impulse, its branches and the fruit it bore were many and varied.

NOTES

1. [William H. Gardiner], "Revision of the Laws of New York," *North American Review* 24 (1827): 199.
2. "A Digest of the Law of Maritime Captures and Prizes," *North American Review* 2 (1816): 218.
3. [Nathaniel Haven], "Greenleaf's Reports," *North American Review* 22 (1826): 29.
4. [Richard Rush], "American Jurisprudence," *Carolina Law Repository* 2 (1816): 349, 354, 359.
5. Ibid., pp. 543-45, 553.
6. For information on Virginia's several revisions and the contemporary belief in the importance of periodic revisions, see [Gardiner], "Revision," pp. 200-202.
7. Sir William Blackstone, *Blackstone's Commentaries: With Notes of References to the Constitution and Laws of the Federal Government of the United States, and of the Commonwealth of Virginia,* St. George Tucker, ed., 5 vols. (Philadelphia: William Young and Abraham Small, 1803).
8. Joseph Story, "Progress of Jurisprudence," in *Miscellaneous Writings of Joseph Story,* William W. Story, ed. (Boston: Charles C. Little and James Brown, 1852), pp. 212, 226, 237.
9. Ibid., pp. 218, 226.
10. [Caleb Cushing], "Law Reports," *North American Review* 18 (1824): pp. 375, 377, 387.
11. Nathan Dane, *A General Abridgement and Digest of American Law,* 9 vols. (Boston: Cummings, Hilliard & Co., 1823-29), I:vi.
12. William Griffith, *Annual Law Register of the United States,* vols. 3-4, 1-2 not published (Burlington, N.J.: D.Allinson, 1822), passim.
13. Dane, *General Abridgement.*
14. J. Willard Hurst, *The Growth of American Law* (Boston: Little, Brown and Co. 1950), p. 85.
15. George Bibb to William Sampson, n.d., William Sampson, *Sampson's Discourse, and Correspondence with Various Learned Jurists Upon the History of the Law,* Pishey Thompson, comp. (Washington, D.C.: Gales & Seaton, 1826), p. 111.
16. Peter S. Du Ponceau, *"Tesimon. Erudit. Viror," Journal of Jurisprudence* 1 (1821): 4.
17. "Johnson's Reports, Vol. XIX," *United States Law Journal* 1 (1822): 215.
18. James Kent, *Commentaries on American Law,* 4 vols. (New York: O. Halsted, 1826-30), I:442.
19. Quoted in David Mellinkoff, *The Language of the Law* (Boston: Little, Brown and Co., 1963), p. 141.

20. [Haven], "Greenleaf," p. 28.

21. Roscoe Pound, *The Formative Era of American Law* (Boston: Little, Brown and Co., 1938), see esp. chap. 1.

22. Morton J. Horwitz, "The Emergence of an Instrumental Conception of American Law, 1780-1820," *Perspectives in American History* 5 (1971): 317, 326.

23. Horwitz ably demonstrates this in his "The Transformation in the Conception of Property in American Law, 1780-1860," *University of Chicago Law Review* 40 (1974): 248-90.

24. "Provincial and Colonial Laws," *American Jurist and Law Magazine* 3 (1830): 117.

25. [Henry Dwight Sedgwick], "The Common Law," *North American Review* 19 (1824): 428.

26. Dane, *General Abridgement,* p. xiv.

27. Peter S. Du Ponceau, *A Dissertation on the Nature and Extent of the Jurisdiction of the Courts of the United States* (Philadephia: Abraham Small, 1824), p. 128.

28. "To the Public," *American Jurist and Law Magazine* 1 (1829): iii-iv.

29. Quoted in Griffith, *Law Register,* III:7.

30. [William H. Gardiner], "Pickering's Reports," *North American Review* 23 (1826): 314.

31. "Recent Reports," *American Jurist and Law Magazine* 3 (1830): 314.

32. [Cushing], "Law Reports," p. 378.

33. [Sedgwick], "The Common Law," pp. 428, 433.

34. Thomas Cooper, New York *American,* 14 Dec. 1824.

35. William Sampson to Isham Talbot, 4 March 1826, Sampson, *Discourse,* p. 107.

36. Charles Jared Ingersoll, "The Influence of America on the Mind," in *American Philosophic Addresses, 1700-1900,* Joseph Blau, ed. (New York: Columbia University Press, 1946), p. 40.

37. [Daniel Webster], "Wheaton's Reports, Vol. III," *North American Review* 8 (1818): 68.

38. Thomas Cooper to William Sampson, n.d., Sampson, *Discourse,* p. 68. Interestingly, Cooper himself had been removed from judicial office for allegedly being arbitrary on the bench.

39. Simon Greenleaf, *A Collection of Cases Overruled, Doubted, or Limited in Application* (Portland, Maine: Arthur Shirley, 1821).

40. Thomas Cooper to William Sampson, 4 March 1824, in *National Advocate* (New York), 31 July 1824.

41. New York *American,* 8 Oct. 1824.

42. Thomas Cooper to William Sampson, n.d, Sampson, *Discourse,* p. 71.

43. William Blackstone, *Commentaries on the Laws of England,* 4 vols. (Philadelphia: Robert Bell, 1771), I:71-72.

44. New York *American,* 8 Oct. 1824.

45. Edward Livingston, *The Complete Works of Edward Livingston on Criminal Jurisprudence,* 2 vols. (Montclair, N.J.: Patterson Smith, 1968 reprint edition), I:187.

46. Ibid., pp. 91, 181, 411.

47. See Thomas Hobbes, *Leviathan,* A.R. Waller, ed. (Cambridge: Cambridge University Press, 1904), p. 199.

48. Du Ponceau, *Dissertation,* p. 129.

49. "Johnson's Reports," p. 209.
50. Charles Watts to William Sampson, n.d., Sampson, *Discourse,* p. 93.
51. Sampson, *Discourse,* p. 32.
52. Ibid., pp. 25, 26-28, 33.
53. Ibid., pp.7-8.
54. Ibid., pp. 11-12, 32.
55. New York *American,* 8 Oct. 1824.
56. Charles Watts to William Sampson, n.d., Sampson, *Discourse,* p. 87.
57. [Sedgwick], "The Common Law," p. 424.
58. Sampson, *Discourse,* p. 35.
59. "To the Public," p. iii.
60. [Sedgwick], "The Common Law," p. 416.
61. Thomas Cooper to William Sampson, 4 March 1824, *National Advocate* (New York), 31 July 1824.
62. David Hoffman, *Legal Outlines* (Baltimore: E. J. Coale, 1829), p. 290.
63. Charles Humphreys, *A Compendium of the Common Law in Force in Kentucky* (Lexington, Ky.: William Gibbs Hunt, 1822), p. iii.
64. Thomas Cooper to William Sampson, 4 March 1824, *National Advocate* (New York), 31 July 1824.
65. "Law Drafting," *American Jurist and Law Magazine* 3 (1830): 182.
66. "Manufacturing Corporations," *American Jurist and Law Magazine* 2 (1829): 97.
67. [Gardiner], "Revision," p. 196.
68. Grace E. MacDonald, comp., *Check-List of Session Laws* (New York, H.W. Wilson Co., 1936), pp. 82-83.
69. Charleston *Courier,* 9 Sept. 1825.
70. [Gardiner], "Revision," p. 197.
71.. James Kirk Paulding, *The Merry Tales of Three Wise Men of Gotham* (New York: Harper & Brothers, 1826), pp. 105, 106, 108.
72. James Fenimore Cooper, *The Prairie* (New York: Airmont Publishing Co., 1964 edition), p. 35.
73. See esp. Cooper, *The Pioneers* (1823), available in a number of editions.
74. New York *American,* 24 Jan. 1826.
75. New York *American,* 1 and 5 April 1825.
76. *National Advocate* (New York), 31 March 1825.
77. Charleston *Courier,* 9 Sept. 1825.
78. *National Advocate* (New York), 5 April 1825.
79. Ibid.
80. Ibid., 6 April 1825.
81. See, for example, Charles Watts to William Sampson, n.d., Sampson, *Discourse,* p. 87.

4

NOTIONS OF LAW REFORM THROUGH CODIFICATION, 1815-1830

The widespread perception of defects in the American legal system quite naturally encouraged a broad interest in, and a demand for, legal reform, especially after 1820. One commentator in 1825 observed that "[a] general impression seems to prevail, that the system of civil and criminal legislation, and the procedure by which justice is administered... is far behind the improvement of the age." As a result, the "spirit of legal improvement" had become "widely diffused" and was "no longer confined to speculative philosophers."[1] For nearly three decades, law reform would remain a preoccupation of the legal profession. Few comparable periods exist in American legal history when reform was so prominent in professional life.

In many ways, this attempt to amend and improve the legal structure in the United States was a linear continuation of what had been going on since American independence, if not throughout the whole colonial period—the effort to rear an effective legal system on the foundation of the inherited legal tradition that was suitable to America's particular needs. What differentiates the period after 1820 from the preceding years was the manifest vitality and comprehensiveness that law reform activity displayed. In the earlier years, overt programmatic improvement of the law was episodic and localized, as was discussion of major legal problems. After 1820, a general American law reform movement could be said to exist. While the states necessarily remained the focus of reform efforts, agitation and debate concerning the improvement of the legal system transcended local boundaries.

The legal profession acknowledged a variety of deficiencies in the legal system. Of course, some saw defects where others did not. Despite lack of agreement about what specifically required the regenerating hand of reform, the corrective most vigorously promoted by lawyers during the early nineteenth century was codification. This does not mean that other, more traditional remedies were abandoned. Statutory revisions following the customary pattern were frequently undertaken, and courts continued to improve the content of the law in a piecemeal fashion. Nor did the crusade for codes preclude the emergence of other innovative proposals. Peter S. Du Ponceau in 1821 suggested the law journal, then a relatively new idea, as a partial solution to America's legal problems. He believed professional periodicals could disseminate sound juristic principles or a general jurisprudence that would bring a much-needed uniformity to American law.[2] A few years later, he, possibly self-servingly, recommended a national law school for the same purpose.[3] But it was codification that captured the imagination of the lawyer who was inclinded toward reform. Before the end of the decade, William H. Gardiner would write: "[t]here are few questions of internal improvement, upon which sound and liberal minds are more divided among us, than the expedience and practicability of substituting a general code for the whole of the common and statute law."[4]

Codification, as promoted in antebellum America, was, by and large, a lawyer's reform designed to remedy ills that practitioners and judges observed in the legal environment. The foot soldiers as well as the generals of the codification movement were recruited from the law guild. There are, however, substantial difficulties in analyzing the content of codificationist thought. There is no single person who can be considered the theorist of the movement. The codifiers significantly differed among themselves about the purpose and nature of the reform. Furthermore, because the discussion about codification took place largely in the public and professional press, and tended to be more promotional than analytical, it rarely moved beyond generalized statements to a detailed presentation of programmatic recommendations and a rationale. Few among the codifiers articulated fully developed reform designs. Most spoke in general terms, without thinking their ideas through. This situation led one anti-codifier to comment that "even among the most strenuous advocates of a code, there is not one who would not find himself awkwardly situated if called upon for a distinct and intelligible detail of his plan."[5]

Still more important was the intellectual nature of the codifiers themselves. Being, by and large, practical men of the common law, they were not comfortable with legal philosophy or theory, except in an elemental sense. These were men used to dealing with concrete fact situations who drew their law from experience. Consequently, when it came to the formation of abstract principles on which a proposed system of codified law would operate, they were quite noticeably out of their element.

Laymen often vigorously supported the reform and frequently suggested it as a remedy for the particular abuses they experienced in the legal system. But their notions of codification and how a codified system of laws would function in practice were even more superficial than those of the lawyers.

Codificationist thought was derived from no single origin. Inspiration for the reform came from existing and historical examples as well as from theoretical sources. Being working lawyers rather than legal philosophers, and knowing that they would have to convince their professional colleagues of the efficacy of the reform if it were to be implemented, the codifiers drew especially on the experience of other countries for their ideas and for support of their positions. For these reasons, the Code Napoléon occupied an important place in the writing of the codificationists. It suggested a mode for improvement that seemed to apply to American conditions, and provided an example that illustrated, at least to the reformers, that a code system could function with good effect.

Ample opportunity existed for American lawyers to study and consider the French code itself. Peter S. Du Ponceau had translated and published the French penal code in the *American Review* in 1811.[6] The *United States Law Journal* began republishing it in 1823, as well as its sections relating to bankruptcy.[7] A translation of the French commercial code was completed and printed by John Rodman of New York in 1811.[8] Moreover, copies of the entire code were widely available from England, which remained a more important source of legal literature throughout the 1820s than was the native American press.

Codifiers were fascinated by the French achievement. Even orthodox common lawyers found it engaging, although they were not seduced by its merits. Given the reality of the American legal environment, where the law reposed in a large and ever increasing number of books and contained innumerable contradictions, complexities, and archaisms, it was little wonder that the Code Napoléon was found alluring. The civil code comprised the whole of French private law in 2,281 paragraphs, each being, as codifiers frequently pointed out, "about as long as a Bible verse."[9] And the complete body of the French law was so brief that it was "often seen printed in one duodecimo volume."[10]

The content of the code appeared no less attractive. John Rodman declared that "pure morality...sound legal principles [and] enlightened reason...pervade every part of it." Its organization, he said, was marked by "lucid order, precision and method."[11] The French codifiers, another reformer declare had rejected "the subleties of the ancient schools" and revealed the law in "simple principles of right" written "in simple language."[12] Joseph Story, who was a consistent and strong advocate of codified law for nearly two decades, referred in 1821 to the Code Napoleon as "perhaps the most finished and methodical treaties of law, the world ever saw."[13]

Additional evidence of the appeal of the French system of law was provided in the form of expositions or commentaries used to elucidate the code. These were found in *L'Exposé des Motifs sur Chaque Loi,* a collection of discourses and discussions of the various titles and provisions of the code made prior to its final drafting by the Council of State and the Tribunate, and in the *Conference du Code Civil avec la Discussion particuliare du Conseil d'Etat et du Tribunat*... a compilation of the debates on each segment of the code during its final formulation. In these two collections, which comprised eighteen duodecimo volumes, a complete repository of commentary was apparently furnished to draw upon in order to determine the meaning of any part of the code. Edward Everett declared that he "did not know in what quarter, more can be learned of continental and general law; where a more ample collection of important facts, sound reasonings, ingenious views [and] powerful illustrations are to be found."[14] It appeared that all the books the French advocate needed were the codes and these expositions, a situation American lawyers could only envy.

The Anglo-American legal system thus stood in stark contrast to the French system of codified law. John Rodman, in comparing the codified French commercial law to the law of commerce found in common law jurisdictions, observed that the latter did not exist "in any definite and distinct form. It must be sought in the voluminous pages of the statute book, and still more in the countless volumes of elementary treatises and in reports of adjudged cases, which encumber the library, and distract the mind of the judge and lawyer." There was little question of where Rodman's preferences lay. "If the law be indeed a moral science," he declared, "its principles should not only be pure, but its rules precise and easy of comprehension."[15] The Code Napoléon was law reduced to a system and, from that standpoint alone, was thought worthy of emulation. The codifiers did not suggest that the content of French law should be embraced in the United States; rather, they proposed that the French methodology of expressing the law should be adopted.

The existence of a systematic, succinct, and perspicuous body of law, together with a limited, but seemingly sufficient, collection of expository materials, did not alone oblige men to become codifiers. The French experience also offered practical evidence of the viability of the concept of codified law and its relevance to the United States. This, as much as the abstract beauty of the code, attracted men to the cause of codified law. "Experience," wrote Henry Dwight Sedgwick approvingly, had demonstrated the viability of the French code and its beneficial results. "[I]t matters not," he added, "that the experience is not our own."[16] It was incontrovertible that the French legal system worked. Codifiers frequently pointed out, with special emphasis, as did David Hoffman, an early disciple of the cause of codified law in America, that the brief code Napoléon was "the instrument which regulates the tribunals of a populous and enlightened kingdom with effect and advantage."[17] Sedgwick offered what must have been for many a convincing piece of evidence that the French code, with its briefly expostulated precepts, worked well. He pointed out that in France, "law suits relating to the title of real estate are very infrequent." He added that "[t]his affords a fruitful theme for reflection and inference." Given the frequency and complexity of real-property litigation in the United States, largely because of an artificially intricate and anachronistic land law, the point was well taken.

The factors that led to codification in France seemed to parallel the features of the American legal environment. Edward Everett referred to the "cartloads of ancient jurisprudence" that weighed so heavily on the French legal system before codification.[19] Another pointed out that before the code was promulgated, France was divided by numerous jurisdictions, and no one had the power to resolve the morass of legal problems created by the divergence of law. But, he affirmed, "the jurisprudence of France was ameliorated by the substitution of one code, simple and uniform...in lieu of the fifty systems of ancient government."[20] Charles Watts of Louisiana stressed, in a letter printed in the common law states, a different aspect of the French experience pertinent to the United States when he asserted that the reworking of French law into a code was found necessary following the revolution, "when a new state of society rendered necessary the adoption of extensive modifications of former rules of rights, and the abolition of inapplicable laws and maxims."[21] For Watts, as well as for other codifiers, the American Revolution would remain unfulfilled until the United States worked a similar revolution in its own legal system by declaring its independence of English law.

The civil law tradition, of which the French experiment was a part, was viewed as being an inappropriate repository to draw from as it was the law of despotism, in contrast to the common law, or the law of freedom. The codifiers rejected this notion as "erroneous and absurd." John Rodman insisted that "[h]owever arbitrary a government may be, it can never be its interest or policy to make laws, by which the bonds of society may be slackened, and the relative rights of individuals left at the mercy of accident or force." Rather, he continued, "the laws of even a despotic state are quite as likely to be framed, so as to afford protection and security to private rights, as under the government of the freest republic."[22] One law writer, in an introduction to a translated portion of the Code Napoléon, looked at the problem from another angle. The United States, he said, "are making a grand and eventful experiment," and "it becomes us to borrow light and knowledge from every quarter of the globe" to aid in reaching the goal of legal perfection.[23] Similarly, Henry Dwight Sedgwick, in referring to the Napoleonic Code, reiterated the ancient maxim of Ovid, "*fas est ab hoste doceri*" (it is allowable to learn even from an enemy).[24]

The codifiers labored under no illusions about the autocratic rule of Napoleon. His government, one of them asserted, was "stained with the crimes of political fanaticism and mad ambition."[25] But when the codifiers spoke of Napoleon as a law reformer, they spoke with unrepressed admiration. He was a "modern Justinian," who stood "infinitely beyond those narrow minded contemporary princes who have stigmatized him."[26] His code was far more important than his military victories and his attempt to establish a European empire. "When his wars and his ambitions are forgotten or forgiven," said one law writer, his code "will rise upon the memory, and consecrate his name."[27] While no one proposed the creation of a dictatorship to solve America's legal problems, there was a certain longing among codifiers for the individual efficiency with which Napoleon consummated a thorough reform of the legal chaos he had found. Legal reform in America, seen as generally ineffective by the codifiers, had been achieved in the past only at the whim of slow-moving democracy and never seemed to reach the ideal. The French dictator's redemption of the law was unequivocal, rapid, and seemingly effective. Furthermore, Napoleon appealed to the romantic spirit of the age, to which lawyers were certainly susceptible.[28]

The French codification achievement, contemporary and timely, was the greatest source of tangible inspiration for the codifiers. But the codifiers also drew on other codification efforts. Justinian's Code and the legal environment that made it necessary, as well as the other numerous codes in Roman legal history, were well known and frequently referred to. Also the codes of contemporary Louisiana provided pertinent examples of the possibility of codification of American law. As a sister state, her success seemed especially worthy of consideration. While the codification experience of none of these governments was completely transferable to the American legal environment, each exhibited a methodology of reform from which to borrow.

The speculations of Jeremy Bentham on codification were another source of inspiration for the American codifiers. However, it is difficult to determine his actual influence. Among the codifiers of the early nineteenth century, only Edward Livingston and Thomas Cooper openly claimed to be his disciples, and Cooper did not avow himself a Benthamite until the 1830s, after the codification movement had failed in his native South Carolina.[29] Few credited Bentham as a source of their ideas and proposals concerning the law reform. One wing of the movement probably borrowed heavily from Bentham's concept of codification, but chose to be silent about it because the association of Bentham with codification was a serious promotional liability.

From the very beginning, and throughout the struggle for codified law in America, those opposed to the reform directed much of their criticism specifically at Bentham and his concept of codification in an effort to connect the entire law reform movement with him and to disparage it. Typically, one orthodox common lawyer claimed that Bentham approached the problems of law reform "with the usual adventurousness of those who have no practical knowledge of the subject." Bentham's "speculations" that the law could be completely codified, he asserted, "are such as might be expected from a closet philsopher." While his ideas were "certainly beautiful in theory," they "were not fit to be applied to the practical operations of the law."[30] Following the literary conventions of the day, most critics did not attack Bentham by name, but he was clearly their target. Isaac Parker, for example, cautioned a Massachusetts audience to trust the common law and its authentic craftsmen "instead of... the fancy and inexperienced projectors" and "visionaries" who believed that a complete body of law could be put into a code.[31] In other words, Bentham was a mere theoretician with no practical experience in working with the law. Thus, he could make only unrealistic speculations for its improvement. As such, his law reform proposal—codification—should be positively rejected as dangerous.

The argument that Bentham was a visionary and consequently that codification was unworkable was designed to appeal to working professionals. As a result, the codifiers greatly feared being tarred with a Benthamite brush. There is an almost total absence of favorable references to the English utilitarian in the literature of the codification movement. Many codifiers made overt attempts to disassociate their own proposals from the most objectionable elements of Bentham's codification concept and to demonstrate the practical relevance of their own.

Nonetheless, Bentham's works on codification probably initiated discussion of the reform in America, and it is reasonable to assume that they did much to set men thinking about codification as a solution to problems they perceived in their legal system. The anti-codifiers' critical emphasis of Bentham suggests that he was widely read. Furthermore, although Benthamism is associated with the most radical elements of the codification movement, even moderates could acquire extra ammunition for their position by selectively borrowing from his tracts. After all, who could disagree with the principles Bentham laid down for legal draftsmanship to the end of making the law precise and clear? Bearing this in mind, it will be helpful to outline briefly the Benthamite concept of the law and codification, to understand better the intellectual content of the American codification movement.

The major focus of Bentham's writings on law reform were directed at the English legal system, although he was quite prepared to undertake the improvement of the law anywhere. This emphasis on English law made his ideas applicable to the United States, a fact appreciated by Bentham. If anything characterized the Anglo-American legal system, it was its well-developed corpus of judge made, or common, law. To Bentham, allowing judges to develop the law was "tyranny, the most all comprehensive, most grinding, and the most crying of all grievances" in the English legal system. The common law method was oppressive because its "very essence" made the law uncertain. Judges made the common law, he declared, "as a man makes laws for his dog. When your dog does anything you want to break him of, you wait till he does it, and then you beat him for it." Being *"ex post facto law,"* the common law was "pregnant with insecurity" for the individual and his rights. It was, however, impossible to determine what the law was even after the judge laid down his decision. The whole corpus of the common law, as found in the decisions and opinions of the courts, was "[c]onfused, indeterminate, inadequate, illadapted and inconsistent." In short, the common law was a "shapeless mass of *merely conjectural* and *essentially uncognizable* matter." In this situation, it was little wonder that "[s]carce any man has the means of knowing a twentieth part of the laws he is bound by."[32]

If the methodology of the common law was difficult, so was its content. It was riddled with antiquated rules "pronounced in this or that barbarous age." The common law had been produced piecemeal in "random decisions... pronounced in a multitude of different generations," each of which had different legal requirements. As a result, because it had never been pruned of its archaisms, much of the law governing people's lives had little real applicability to their situation or needs. This made the law artificially complex, overly technical, and arbitrary. It was a labyrinth. Only lawyers understood it, but even they were in frequent disagreement about it. Legal fictions, which were adopted to make the old law workable, received special censure from Bentham. To him, they were simply lies. "In English law," he observed, "fiction is a syphilis which runs into every vein and carries into every part of the system the principles of rottenness." Procedural law was especially singled out for criticism. Justice, he asserted, was subverted by the rules of practice as they stood. Procedure was filled with archaic and perverted technicalities and fictions that produced nothing but delay, expense, and vexation. Too often, he submitted, a just cause was lost because of the failure of counsel to follow some formal punctilio of practice.[33]

Bentham blamed the legal profession, or "Judge and Co." as he called them, for the condition of the law. It was they who created and maintained the existing legal structure for their own selfish interest. The profession could not be expected to work to change the system because "the power of lawyers is in the uncertainty of the law." Practitioners used the law as a "hook to lead the people by the nose, and a pair of shears to fleece them." But change, Bentham believed, must come. The law was too important to the individual to be unknown to him. Law reform, consequently, should have the goal of making the law cognizable, certain, and rational, with the end of making every man his own lawyer.[34]

Bentham viewed codification—a word of his own invention—as the appropriate vehicle of reform. Most important to Bentham, codified law was written law. Indeed, only written law was "deserving the name of law." Furthermore, codes should be comprehensive. The purpose of codification was to make the law known, because "laws are a snare for those who are ignorant of them." Therefore, he saw "no reason for omitting anything." The natural corollary of this rule was the principle that "[w]hat ever is not in the code, ought not to be law." To allow recourse to customary law, foreign law, or natural law would "corrupt the whole code" by rendering it incomplete.[35]

A code, Bentham declared, ought to be "addressed to the people, and to the least intelligent portion of the people." To achieve this objective, a code's contents must be drafted as succinctly, clearly, and precisely as possible. To assist further in the common understanding of the law, Bentham believed the whole of the code should be systematically and scientifically arranged. Once a code were developed by using these elements of style and construction, the law "would not require schools of explanation," or "casuists to unravel subtleties. It would speak the language familiar to everybody; each one might consult it at his need." Bentham insisted that a code must be so plain that a father might "without assistance" instruct his children in all the knowledge of the law that they needed.[36]

In matters of form, a Benthamite code would quite obviously have revolutionized the law. Bentham's tracts point to a similar revolution in the content of the law. It would be new law, not the old restated. However, he did not believe that the substance of the common law was totally void of merit. "As in a dunghill," he said, no doubt choosing his metaphor with care, "here and there a grain of corn, so in a volume of common law here and there a genuine reason...may be found." But the draftsmen of the code, of course, would admit "none of the excrement...no fictions; no technicalities, sound grain nothing else."[37]

In formulating a code, legislators would apply a doctrine of utility—the "greatest happiness principle," as Bentham preferred to call it. Each rule of law would be empirically tested to see if it provided the greatest happiness for the greatest number of citizens. Happiness was vaguely defined as the maximization of pleasure and the minimization of pain. Thus, the law would ostensibly be created by a system of moral mathematics based on a people's actual needs, which was in keeping with Bentham's notion that government existed for the greatest happiness of the people. Although he failed to explain how this process would work in practice, it certainly implied that the law should be carefully and scientifically created, not haphazardly developed, to meet the needs of the citizenry.[38]

The last element in the Benthamite codification scheme was the preservation and conservation of the code against the threat of judicial interpretation and the creation of an authoritative body of law outside the confines of the code itself. It was not enough to destroy the existing unwritten law; its potential reemergence as an interpretive tool must be positively prohibited. Bentham was well aware of human frailties and the inadequacies of language; no code could be perfect. But the subsequent improvement of a code was an inviolable function of the legislature. Judges were only to apply the law as it existed; they were not to interpret it.

New cases would, of course, occur for which the code made no provision. In this event, Bentham suggested that "the judge may point it out and indicate a remedy," but he was emphatic that "no decision of any judge...should be allowed as law," even if it were meant to improve the code and remedy its defects. Similarly, portions of a code might prove defective, even though great care had been taken in its drafting. Again, the judge could only inform the legislature of these imperfections. To insure further against authoritative judicial interpretation creeping into the legal system, Bentham declared that a code should be revised every one hundred years "for the sake of changing such terms and expressions as by time may have become obsolete."[39]

Implicit in Bentham's works on codification is the concept of law as a sovereign command intended to promote human happiness. Law was a social tool in the hands of the community at large to utilize for its own benefit. It was something to be consciously created and implemented with care and with a fixed purpose. Law was too important as an instrument of social improvement and stability to be allowed to develop without direction.

While Bentham was probably the most important philosophical source of the American codifiers' thought, others existed. Sir Francis Bacon, as lord chancellor, had proposed to James I to reduce the common law to a written form and had accompanied it with his rationale for the scheme. Some years later, Matthew Hale in his preface to Henry Rolle's *Abridgement,* a text often used in America, had made a similar recommendation. Both men were known to the codifiers. The fact that Hale and Bacon were closely associated with the common law tradition made their proposals potent evidence of the practicability of the scheme. William Sampson, for example, asserted that "[i]f no wise jurist had ever recommended the digesting and new ordering of the law," there would be "temerity in the proposal." However, he noted, "Hale and Bacon have not only approved, but offered their views and plans." Significantly, this New York codifier used neither Bentham's name nor the English utilitarian's term—"codification"—in this or other statements in support of codified law.[40]

It is likely that most codifiers developed their notion of codification from no single source. None of the sources to which they had access were directly applicable to the American legal environment or entirely appealing to the lawyers who comprised the movement. The codifiers improvised their own concept of codification by borrowing selectively and, with equal discrimination, by rejecting a variety of elements found in the sources available to them.

In developing his distinctive notion of codification, of course, an individual was not limited to those tangible examples of codified law or to speculations about it. The reformers frequently pointed out the relevance of legal configurations not usually considered codifications. The most imporant of these in the American legal setting were the country's numerous written constitutions. Thomas Grimke, for example, called the American constitutions "nothing more than the political Common Law, reduced to the simplicity and order of a code, with all the improvements, derived from practical wisdom and experience." He asked what would be the difference "between the reductions of the civil Common Law to form a system, and that, which has been thus accomplished, with our written codes of political law?"[41] Similarly, in the Anglo-American legal experience, there was a strong tradition of reform of specific areas of the law through legislation. The celebrated English Statute of Frauds and the Statute of Uses and Trusts, as well as a variety of native ordinances passed with the intention of consolidating and improving selected portions of the law, were among the numerous illustrations of this sort of reform format. These were seen as limited codifications that suggested the possibility of a similar, but far more sweeping, reform of the law.

Aside from these overt influences, the codifiers of course drew on their own professional experience. Almost without exception, they were men who had much practical experience at the bar or on the bench. This is the element that gives the intellectual content of the codification movement its great variety of expression and that, consequently, precludes the possibility of generalizing very much about codificationist thought as a whole. There were no typical codifiers.

Yet, codification did not mean all things to all people. There were certain common denominators among the codifiers who were members of the legal profession. On the issue of who should actually draft the code and control the process of codification, the codifiers were in complete agreement. It should be someone learned in the law. Henry Dwight Sedgwick, for example, was emphatic on the matter. He declared that the "principle actors," as he called the prospective jurisconsults, should be "chiefly lawyers and common lawyers ... men whose minds had been cast in the molds of Littleton, Coke and Blackstone." Further, they should be "grave and experienced men, for none but those who had attained a high station in the profession should be entrusted with such a task."[42] Charles Watts suggested that codification of the law should be carefully "entrusted to proper hands, and made with due deliberation." Stressing the need to reform the content of the law, Watts thought that "[t]hose who, from ancient prejudices and by long habits, cannot be brought to think favorably of any changes" should be excluded. But he also objected to appointing "rash theorists, who would overturn foundations and rear up a rickety and ill proportioned edifice," to undertake the task. The reform, he concluded, should be effected in "a wise and prudent manner."[43]

Behind such recommendations lay the elitist assumption that only lawyers had the knowledge and training to reform the law properly. If codification were undertaken by individuals consumed by selfish motives or visionary goals, it was feared that the existing law would undergo a radical transformation that would upset the legal equilibrium, property rights and all. Sedgwick emphasized professional control of codification to prevent the possibility that "all the elements of jurisprudence would be confounded and remodeled" and "everything would be thrown into confusion."[44] Watt's caution about commissioning "rash theorists," which appears aimed at Bentham and his concept of codification, also expressed this anxiety. In being so explicit on the matter, the codifiers were also attempting to reassure a skeptical legal profession gripped by tradition, and which associated codification with the impractical speculations of Bentham, that they had nothing to fear from the reform. This position also suggests that these codifiers were opposed to any democratization of the law. While a properly elected assembly would have to approve of a code in the end, the emphasis on learned jurists as the draftsmen minimized the extent of serious direct popular input into the codification process.

This universal agreement among codifiers on the need for professional control over the business of reform manifested a latent element of legal conservatism that runs thoughout the codification movement among lawyers, at least in matters of private law. These codifiers by no means viewed codification as an instrument to turn the working legal order on its head; rather, it was seen as a method of improving the legal system to secure better and preserve its benefits, chief among them being the protection of property. One would expect this to be true of a codifier like Joseph Story, a veritable personification of the legal status quo. But those with a more radical predilection showed no penchant for sweeping changes in the existing legal order. William Sampson, a flamboyant codifier who castigated the common law and urged the need for America to declare its independence from English jurisprudence, was no less desirous of maintaining legal stability. Concerning the codification of what he called "our laws," Sampson declared that "it is one thing to change, and another to reform them with a tender, patient, kindly, and experienced hand; and God forbid that they should be touched or meddled with, by any other than the wise and honest." He explained his attachment to "[o]ur law" by declaring that "it is the law of a free people, and has freedom for its end; and under it we live both free and happy."[45] Even Edward Livingston, who swallowed Benthamism nearly whole, when he helped to recodify Louisiana's civil law, undertook only the clarification and rationalization of the existing law of Louisiana and made only relatively minor changes in its substantive content. These men were common lawyers, proposing the legal change in a nonrevolutionary context, not men bent on upsetting the legal order. Consequently, the codification movement was quite compatible with the essentially conservative nature of the American law reform tradition.

To be sure, many contemporaries did not see it this way. Indeed, a majority of the legal profession, by the codifiers' own estimate, rejected the reform because they believed it would be profoundly counterproductive of reform and would turn the legal order into a shambles. Even among the codifiers, who all argued that authoritatively clarifying and digesting the law would have the salutary effect of making it more certain, there was a profound disagreement over how far they should go in reforming the content of the law and in changing the existing means by which it was expounded and construed. On these two issues, it is possible to classify most codifiers as either moderates or radicals, though some cannot be easily pigeonholed. Whether an individual was a radical or a moderate depended upon his perception of the nature and degree of abuse within the legal order, and upon the consequent function he assigned to codification as a vehicle of reform.

The moderates' critique of the legal system focused largely on problems arising out of the diversity and magnitude of the American legal product and, to a lesser extent, on the particularly confused and careless state of the statute law. They viewed the objective body of the law as disorderly and overgrown, which resulted in the law being inaccessible and uncertain. In sum, what the moderates desired, and what they believed codification could achieve, was greater explicitness in the law as it existed. The reform process would not only greatly reduce the bulk of the law, it would also clarify and systematize it, but it would go no further. A writer for the *American Jurist* described the moderates' objective by saying that the law had become a "dark forest, where the most intrepid lawyer never thinks of exploring beyond the margin." As a result, it was necessary to render the law more accessible and comprehensive through codification, or, as the writer said, maintaining the metaphor, the "territory" must be "surveyed and laid out anew... to let in a little light."[46].

The reform applied to the common law would exclude the useless cases, those turning on special facts, those subsequently overruled or limited or obsolete. Conflicts and doubts would be resolved as far as possible to fix the existing law. Thus, the thousands of cases that made the law confused and overly large would be removed from consideration. Of necessity, for purposes of clarity and explicitness, the case law would be rewritten so as to form a set of concisely and clearly stated principles or axioms. The whole would then be systematically integrated with a revised and similarly rewritten statute law to form a comprehensive code.

The purpose of the moderates was to rationalize and systematize the law, not to reform it. "Sufficient for us," declared Joseph Story of the ends that should be achieved through codification, "will be the achievement to reduce the past to order and certainty."[47]. The moderates made special efforts to extol the virtues of the common law and to disclaim any intention of demolishing it in favor of an analytical system. Thomas Grimke, in discussing the need for codification, made a representative assertion when he registered his protest "emphatically and anxiously" against the view that the common law was a "chaos of absurdity and injustice; of antiquated rules, inapplicable to modern society, and even hostile to progressive improvement." Instead, he expressed his "admiration" for the "Common Law, and the singular excellence of its standard rules and maxims."[48] Instead of being a tool of destruction that would tear down the edifice of the common law, the moderates conceived of codification as a means of better expressing, fixing, and actually strengthening the common law by putting it into a more permanent and exacting form. If the form were new, the content would largely remain the same; the old familiar landmarks of the common law and their traditional applications would still be visible.

In the process of restating or codifying the law, changes and improvements would be made: conflicts would be resolved, and the obsolete would be pruned away. Defects, which Story called "blemishes," would be remedied. But Story emphatically insisted that "[s]uch interference ought... to be made with caution, prudence, and deliberation."[49] Another moderate, George Bibb, made the point somewhat differently. Concerning "the modifications of old principles" through codification, Bibb observed that "[b]efore the old law should be abolished and a new rule submitted, it should be assiduously weighed, whether the inconvenience which would result to the community from suffering the old rule... is so great as to justify the requisition upon society to learn a new rule which is put in its stead."[50] As one might suspect, the moderates greatly downplayed the need for substantive reform to adapt the inherited legal tradition to American conditions. Instead, they emphasized the progress that had already been made in that direction.

The jurisprudence of the moderates was of the historical genre. Law, to them, in its most visible and appropriate form, was created through the slow accumulation of precepts formed through the actual experience of society. The law gained its strength and vigor from its organic growth. "[E]very good system of laws," Story declared, was "slow... in consolidating." The common law, being the accumulated wisdom of generations, perfectly fitted this notion of legal development. It was natural that they opposed any thoroughgoing reform in the law administered by the legislature lest, in Story's words, "the rashness of an hour may destroy what ages have scarcely cemented."[51] The "grand revolutions in the law" that were appropriate and had real utility, according to David Hoffman, did not come about through "accident" or "individual opinions in its makers and interpreters" but from "the gradual expansion of men's minds on the subjects most allied to their felicity as men, and their freedom as citizens."[52]

Given this jurisprudential philosophy, the moderates believed that no code could ever be designed that would be complete and meet all future needs of a society. Such notions, Story asserted, were the "theoretical extravagances of some well meaning philosophical jurists," which were "absurd" in practice. At best, codification would provide a statement of the law "more or less comprehensive, to regulate many or few concerns, to supply defects, or give symmetry and order to the law over particular subjects."[53]

Being good common lawyers, the moderates had a natural predilection against legislatures. The courts were the proper agencies to orchestrate basic legal change. If the legislature had any role to play in dealing with the fundamental system of private law, it was "to supply defects, and cure mischiefs in systems already existing" and not to create new rights and duties.[54] In the moderates' conception of codification, the courts were not reduced to being mere triers of fact in the Benthamite sense. Rather, a code would be treated as a clear and systematic, but perforce incomplete, statement of the common law that judges could authoritatively interpret, expound, and correct as they had before the law was codified. In other words, the decisions of the courts would continue to be creative and have the same obligatory force.[55] Of course, this meant that a corpus of decisional law would develop subsequent to codification that could potentially rival the size of that which had originally been codified. This was a problem that the moderates believed could be easily resolved. The law should be recodified at periodic intervals. Story, for example, suggested every fifty years.[56] As the law was periodically codified anew, it would, according to Story, eventually "acquire scientific accuracy."[57]

As one might expect, the moderates did not believe that judge-made law was inherently capricious. Their thinking on the matter was quite orthodox. The rule of *stare decisis*, one of their number declared, "controls the arbitrary discretion of judges, and puts the case... beyond the peculiar opinions and complexional reasoning of a particular judge," and therefore "has the advantage of producing certainty as to rights, privileges and property." New rules were laid down with great care because of the judicial "consciousness, that the decision will form a permanent precedent, affecting all future cases," which "introduces necessarily great caution in giving it."[58] If the common law appeared unstable, it was not because of "the obscurity and fluctuation of decisions, as the vulgar erroneously suppose," but rather because of "the endless variety of human actions," which made the law "to a certain extent... ever... subject to uncertainty and doubt."[59] Furthermore, "[t]he changes which have been wrought in the fabric of the laws, have not so much arisen from mis-application of principles by courts, as from the new state of society having rendered the old institutions and laws inexpedient and inconvenient." Law, where common law methodology prevailed, was actually much more certain than in civilian countries. In the latter,

> the celebrity of a particular jurist may introduce a decisive change in the rule, or at least in the administration of the law....Precedents have not...a fixed operation and value; and judicial tribunals consider, that a prior decision governs only the particular case, without absolutely fixing their principles involved in it.[60]

In summary, one discerns a strong element of traditionalism among the moderate codifiers. Their concept of codification carried with it no revolutionary import for the existing law or the workings of legal institutions. They only desired to make the existing law more accessible and certain by rationalizing and restating it. So limited were the moderates' goals and so strongly attached were they to the common law and its institutional machinery that they frequently sounded like the anti-codifiers. Indeed, the gap that separated the moderates from the orthodox common lawyers was not large. However, the anti-codifiers did not believe they could step across the distance that separated them without placing the whole of the legal order in jeopardy.

The radicals' perception of defects in the legal system included the same abuses that the moderates discerned. The law, one radical angrily complained, fell upon the legal profession "in overwhelming showers of printing."[61] Like the moderates, the radicals believed that codification would result in a beneficial reduction in the size of the objective body of the law through the elimination of the "accumulated rubbish of years proceedings" and the condensation of the law to a system of succinct principles.[62] But when the radical codifiers spoke of "the good work of reformation," they had a broader purpose in mind, because their perception of legal wrong extended far beyond that of the moderates.[63] The content of the law, they claimed, required thoroughgoing reform, and the discretion allowed judges in the common law, they also asserted, had to be bridled.

The radical codifiers believed that American law needed to be severely pruned of much of its English content, which they claimed was created for a feudal and aristocratic society and was consequently ill adapted to the country's legal needs. They disagreed with the suggestion of many moderates that the abuses of the English legal system had been eliminated from American usage. While improvements had been made, William Sampson declared, "it cannot be denied that many strange and grievous absurdities still disgrace our laws."[64] These, Sampson remarked elsewhere, make American jurisprudence "intricate and thorny" and give it "the air of occult magic."[65]

Special pleading, legal fictions, many of the forms of action, the separation of common law and equity, and all manner of technicalities were among the things the radicals would have abolished outright in the process of codification. Other portions of the law marked by convolution, artificiality, and refined distinctions, such as limitations, conditions, contingent remainders, uses and trusts, and executory devises, would be greatly simplified. And what Cooper called "the metaphysics of real property" would be similarly rendered less complex and intricate. Those perennial litigants, John Doe and Richard Roe, the fictitious characters necessary to an action of ejectment, would forever be banished from the courtroom. In contrast, Joseph Story of the moderates extolled the virtues of ejectment.[66] Such overly subtle distinctions as those between actions of trespass and trespass upon a case would meet the same fate. In short, according to Charles Watts, codification would greatly simplify the legal system by stripping the law of "its unnecessary intricacy, absurd fictions, obsolete and inapplicable maxims, rules and forms."[67]

For the code's content, the radicals would go back to unadorned first principles of the law, or what Cooper called "plain, undeniable, legal principles."[68] William Sampson put it somewhat differently, but the import was the same. He said a code should be based on "natural reason, universal justice, and present convenience."[69] It is manifest that if the radicals continued the process of reform, many of the pre-eminent identifying features of the common law would be eliminated. However, as it has already been suggested, they did not desire to revolutionize the existing legal equilibrium by completely remodeling the fundamental rights and obligations sanctioned in the existing legal order. The radicals' criticism focused on procedural aspects of the law and the complexity with which substantive rights were stated rather than those rights themselves. Care would be taken in the reform process so as not to upset prevalent relationships. The propertied classes would not be victims of codification. Rather, the radicals believed that, once the law were properly codified, the legal system could better guarantee existing rights and secure the performance of existing duties. Codification, according to Sampson, would abolish "all forms that impede the march of justice and firmly [establish] those which are meaningful to its ends."[70]

The radicals, not wanting to appear as revolutionaries, declared they found much in the common law that met with their approval. Sampson asserted "that the English reports contain, amidst a world of rubbish, rich treasures of experience, and those of our own courts, contain materials of inestimable worth." In fact, most radicals lauded the common law, but when they did, they were referring primarily to its fundamental rules and maxims alone. Sampson claimed "[o]ur law is justly dear to us."[71] Another radical, Henry Dwight Sedgwick, declared that if he had to choose among the legal systems of the world, he would "certainly decide in favor of the common law."[72]

To the orthodox common lawyers, it seemed a baffling inconsistency to condemn the common law, as the radicals did, and then express a preference, if not an admiration, for it. The orthodox did not believe it possible to separate the substantive rights and rules of the common law from its total configuration. They could not, for example, separate the concept of ownership of property from the forms of action. Further, they placed great emphasis on the need to maintain the traditional format of the inherited law (that is, case law) if the common law were to be preserved. In contrast, the radicals believed it possible to distill from the law a basic series of precepts and to codify them. The moderates would have agreed. However, for the radicals, codification would not have meant putting old wine in new bottles, as the moderates desired to do. They would have purged much of what the moderates would have maintained. The common law, Sedwick said, would be "divested of its Gothic costume" through codification.[73]

Implementation of the radicals' concept of codification would have resulted in the creation of a distinct, legal self-identity for the United States, presumably making a continued dependence on English cases and legal texts unnecessary. Almost no one objected to the notion that America should assert its legal individuality, but the radicals' demand for legal independence had a trenchant and uncompromising quality about it. "[B]eing of full growth and stature," William Sampson declared, "we should no longer go in leading strings, but manfully take upon us the burden of our own concerns."[74]

The radicals believed that codification was the only mechanism by which the law would be sufficiently improved. Without reducing all the law to a code, Charles Watts declared, "you *can never get rid of principles no longer applicable, of cumberous forms, of maxims founded on ignorance, barbarism and a different state of society.*"[75] Partial legislative reform would be insufficient, as it would only result in a patchwork when comprehensive reform was needed. Nor could the courts be depended on to reform the law deliberately by degrees. "[G]radual reformation" in the law by the courts, Sampson declared, depended too much on the "accidental occurrence of doubtful litigation."[76] Elsewhere, this New York codifier expanded his reasoning on the matter. If the courts are to be depended on, he remarked, the country must "wait till a sufficient number of litigated cases may enable the judges of last resort, to liberalize, overrule, and new model, by a series of arbitrary decisions and new construction the *wisdom* of their predecessors."[77] Direct regenerative intervention into the legal system—codification—would be far more effective, to say nothing of having a certain intellectual integrity that overruling and limiting allegedly well-founded case law could never have.

In contrast to the historical jurisprudence of the moderates, the radicals had an instrumentalist conception of the law. Law, Sampson insisted, "subsists" for the use of the people. Being a "human, not a preternatural institution," it was "a creature of their power; the work of their own hands." Quite properly, it should be shaped and transformed at will according to "the test of reason in the open light of day" so that it "will advance with a free and unimpeded step towards perfection."[78] This view of the law seemed, to Sampson, more in keeping with the moral and political foundations of a democratic society.

The radicals' notion of the effect of a code on the workings of the legal system was likewise quite different from that held by the moderates. The radicals conceived of codification as a means of checking what they considered the unwarranted discretion allowed the judiciary by the common law, which, they believed, created profound legal uncertainty. Once formulated, a code would provide a complete statement of law to the exclusion of all others. The courts would no longer have a limitless repository of case law to draw upon at will. Under the radicals' proposed system of codified law, the adjudication of disputes would be governed by well-established and clear principles, a science of "general jurisprudence," as Thomas Cooper called it.[79] Once the law were codified, according to Sampson, "[t]he law will govern the decisions of judges, and not the decisions of the law."[80] The role of the courts would be reduced to that of a fundamentally uncreative one of applying the law mechanically to given fact situations. The legislatures would thus replace the courts as the major agencies of legal development. This was the most revolutionary aspect of the radical concept of codification. It meant making a complete break with the common-law tradition through the acceptance of civilian methodology.

Like all responsible codifiers, the radicals did not believe it possible to formulate a code for all time that was free of defects. They considered that it "would be a vain attempt" to try to do so. "[A]ll that is proposed," one of their number declared, "is, to embody and lay down all the rules and regulations for the government of society, as far as can be devised, to suit the general habits, modes of life, and the present nature of property."[81]

However, none of the radicals, without exception, actually developed a mechanism that would perfect a code, once written, and keep it current to the legal needs of society. While they vehemently criticized the role of the courts as law makers in the legal system, only Edward Livingston devised a replacement. Many of the radicals borrowed from Livingston's ideas, which were found in the projected Louisiana Civil Code of 1825. In that proposed system, courts were bound to do justice in all cases that could not be brought within the purview of the code according to the dictates of natural equity. However, no decision involving a case of first impression would be authoritative unless subsequently sanctioned by the legislature and added to the code. Judges were required to inform the legislature of defects in the code and to propose remedies in reports that they submitted to the legislature at regular intervals. This information would enable the legislature to correct and improve the code as the need arose and would insure the ongoing effectiveness of the legal system. Thus, according to Sampson, "decisions may be the means of improving legislation, without being themselves laws. The departments of government [are] to be thus kept in their respective spheres—the legislature not judging, nor the courts making laws." Cooper remarked of the proposal that while he might be "too short sighted to discern difficulties," he believed the "experiment may be safely made."[82]

As Livingston had recognized when he formulated the scheme, the courts had to resolve existing litigation speedily, without waiting for legislative action whenever the code appeared deficient or defective. In order to "prevent individual rights from being infringed, or to grant compensation for any encroachment upon them," he declared, "there is an absolute necessity of deciding a case not provided for by positive law."[83] In giving the courts a "power of construction" to decide a case according to "equity," Livingston was adopting a traditional civilian formula found in the French civil code. But his proposal went beyond the French system by specifically providing for the mandatory reporting of defects to the legislature. He believed that the "advantages to be derived from the wisdom of judges," as well as the much-praised malleability of the common law, could be incorporated into a code system without the legal uncertainty that normally accompanied common law methodology. Bentham had proposed a similar idea, but Livingston had apparently devised the solution on his own.[84]

The emphasis on legislative control of the legal system and the concomitant reduction of the courts to a largely mechanistic or advisory function was probably too short-sighted. While many of the radicals recognized the weakness of a codified system in meeting day-to-day legal needs, their hopes that the problem could be solved without giving the courts broad interpretive powers were exaggerated. They placed too much faith in the ability of a jurisconsult to state the law so as to admit no judicial discretion in its application, and too much faith in legislative maintenance of an effective system of law. Many of these same men had frequently lamented the maladroitness of American legislators, to say nothing of their dilatory habits in matters of great moment. Livingston himself complained of the "procrastination prevalant...in most legislatures," which "put off from day to day" important business.[85] How could they be expected to manage a codified system effectively? Furthermore, the radicals thought not at all how the proper and uniform application of a code could be guaranteed.

Undoubtedly, in the end, greater responsibility than the radicals had envisioned would have been abdicated to the courts, as in civil law countries.

Both the radicals and the moderates, as well as orthodox common lawyers, had complained of the growing amount of legal diversity among the states. The reformers suggested that codification would improve the situation. Their ideas do not seem to reflect a radical or moderate inclination. Many suggested that the federal government should codify those areas of the law over which the Constitution had given it pre-eminent control, such as bankruptcy and commerce. This would create a much-needed degree of legal uniformity in some of the most important matters in interstate affairs. However, this was not something desired by the codifiers alone. It was a widespread demand among contemporaries, although the actual term "codification" was not used by non-codifiers.[86]

Of course, federal power under the Constitution did not extend to very many vital areas of law. The codifiers recognized and accepted the constitutional limitations that, of necessity, made the states the principal theaters of reform. Some codifiers, like Joseph Story, likewise realized that doctrinal variety was a characteristic of the federal structure in a diverse nation that would continue. "American jurisprudence," he declared, "can never acquire a homogenous character; and ... we must look to the future for increasing discrepancy, [rather] than coincidences in the law and the administration of justice." But codification would help by making American law, with all its internal dissimilarities, more accessible to the profession. By "reducing to a text the exact principles of the law," Story remarked, "we shall, in great measure, get rid of the necessity of appealing to volumes which contain jarring and discrepant opinions."[87]

Other codifiers were more hopeful that the reform would bring legal uniformity. Sampson, for example, asserted his belief that codification could remedy the "evil of divergence ... by creating the standard of simple wisdom, to which all may rally; for there is nothing so uniform as truth, nor so simple as wisdom."[88] Thomas Cooper implied much the same thing when he affirmed that the uncertainty that arose "from *conflicting principles of law*" could be corrected by the formulation of "plain and honest legal principles and rules."[89] Elsewhere, Cooper spoke of the need for a science of "general jurisprudence."[90] Statements such as these suggest an element of natural law logic in the thinking of these codifiers. Similar notions were also found in the common law theory, which stressed that the law's content was comprised of transcendent and enduring legal principles. Compare Sampson's statement with that of Peter S. Du Ponceau, a staunch defender of the common law against codes: "Those who wish to see uniformity of jurisprudence in this widely extended union, ought to remember that nothing is uniform but sound principles, and false theories and false logic lead inevitably to contradictory decisions."[91] In retrospect, Sampson's and Cooper's confidence in the triumphant march of reasonable principles seems visionary. Certainly, given the immense variety of conditions in the United States, no system of laws, no matter how much unadorned wisdom it enshrined, would have been universally applicable to all the states.

Henry Dwight Sedgwick argued that codification could diminish legal diversity in a more realistic way, though perhaps Cooper and Sampson had the same thing in mind. He proposed that "at least some of the larger and more wealthy states of the union should cause their laws to pass under general revision, and be formed into *written codes.*" These innovative states would thus set an example and offer models for other states to adopt. The idea had a traditional ring, as it had become a well-established practice among the states to borrow legal designs from one another and especially from the "larger and more wealthy states" like New York.[92] Sedgwick's proposal was prophetic, as this is indeed what happened with certain of the New York codes in the years to come.

By improving the law and the legal system through codification, all the codifiers believed that the country as a whole would benefit from the reform. The law would be made more accessible and certain; consequently, individual rights would be better served and guaranteed. The legal fraternity would also profit directly from codified law, as it would make the law more professionally functional. Indeed, most codifiers strongly implied that the advantages that would accrue to the legal order would come about by meeting the occupational needs of the legal profession. A more accessible and certain law would make their tasks easier, and they could better serve their clients' needs.

Joseph Story spoke of the work-related advantages of codification in a letter to Henry Wheaton in 1825. Complaining that "[h]alf our [the profession's] time is now consumed in examining cases," he suggested that if the law were codified, "it would greatly abridge the labours; and exhausting researches of the profession.... What a great gain it would be for us to have a starting point—something irrevocably fixed as settled principle." Not only would the lawyer's labors be greatly reduced, but, as he pointed out, "certainty [would] exist where darkness before overshadowed his mind."[93] He considered it "no small gain to have a positive text, which should give...the true rule, instead of leaving it open to conjecture and inference by feeble minds."[94] No lawyer believed that codification would do away completely with the onerous tasks of the profession, but all the codifiers felt that they would be greatly abridged as a result of the reform. As Charles Watts told his fellow attorneys, "it is not to be supposed that by the formation of a code, all other books are to be dispensed with." He added, however, that their numbers would necessarily be "very small."[95]

Most lawyer-codifiers asserted that a code would enable the general public to understand better the laws governing society, but all overtly rejected Bentham's claim that the law could be stated so clearly that every man could become his own lawyer. Charles Watts suggested that "the degree of complexity necessarily attendant upon any system of laws which adjust the rights of individuals in a complicated society" made the latter idea "weakly theoretical" and impossible to implement.[96]

The literature of the codification movement is replete with such statements. They reflect, not only professional elitism, but also a desire to quiet any fears the legal fraternity might have that the reform would be detrimental to their pocketbooks. Occasionally, the codifiers unabashedly attempted to mitigate these concerns. "The gentlemen of the bar," Cooper certified, "may rest assured, that their business and clients will not be annihilated by any improvement in the code or digest."[97] The codifiers did suggest, however, that if codified law could not make every man the master of his own legal affairs, it would enable the layman engaged in public affairs to discharge his duties better. These were the "educated" or "intelligent" men, said Thomas Cooper, who "are constantly acting as jurymen, arbitrators, and commissioners; as legislators and public officers; and guardians, executors, administrators and agents."[98]

Codification, the reforms suggested, would nonetheless have a favorable impact on the general public from the lawyer's point of view. "None will deny," Thomas Grimke contended, "that the law has been exposed to much odium, contempt, and ridicule" because of its "confused and uncertain state" and "its vain repetitions, awkward circumlocutions, uncouth phraseology and obsolete provisions." Codification, he claimed, "must exercise a happy influence on the character and usefulness of the Law. The former will be elevated and dignified.... latter will be extended and simplified." But the legal profession itself would be a beneficiary of improved popular opinion concerning the law. Once the law became "respectable in the opinion of the community at large," Grimke told a meeting of the South Carolina bar, "it seems a fair conclusion that the Legislators, the Judges, as well as the Professors of the Law, would rise in a correspondent ratio in public estimation."[99] William Sampson put the idea somewhat differently. Once the law were properly codified, litigation would be resolved by an appeal to "natural reason, universal justice, and present convenience," instead of the mummery of English law. This would build popular confidence in the legal system, as justice would be better served. Alluding to the odium that was perennially heaped on the profession, he stated his belief that had the law been previously reformed, as he suggested now be done, "lawyers would have been the ornaments of our country.[100] This was an argument seemingly bound to appeal to a profession that was sensitive about not being held in high public esteem.

A predilection for the type of legal improvement codification seemed to offer had long been latent in popular reformist thought. Simplification of the law into a written system had been a frequent lay demand. Laymen seem to have borrowed the specific idea of legal reform through codification from the legal fraternity, which they adapted to meet their own needs and desires as consumers of the law. Predictably, the lay reformers did not articulate fully developed programmatic conceptions of codification. Their notions of the reform are often only sketchy declarations of what they considered desirable changes in the legal order. Nonetheless, an outline of their thought can be discerned.

Too often, it seemed to laymen, just causes were lost in the maze of the law or because of some technicality or exotic form that had nothing to do with common sense. Furthermore, the law, in its existing condition, allowed the unscrupulous attorney to twist and bend it for his own greedy purposes. But once the law were properly codified, the "stream of justice would flow purely and freely," and the country would be "exempt from the vexations of pettifogging." In addition, "the administration of justice would be speedy without oppression and safe without chicanery."[101]

Lay thought continued to exhibit a simplistic notion of right and wrong, which was badly offended by jarring legal inconsistencies and the debates over what the law actually was on a given point. Because of these things, one layman wrote, a cause depended "more on the skill of lawyers retained for a favorable result" than on its merits or the law itself. The legal system "must remain imperfect, whilst justice is susceptible to perversion and intellectual ingenuity." Instead of this, a "rule of right" ought to be "distinctly laid down, free from all ambiguities" in a code. Then the law would be applied "without doubt or hesitation."[102] A citizen's rights, another wrote, "will be much better decided by a judge, under the silent administration of [a] code, than by all the metaphysical jargon, the acute construction, or overbearing declamation of the ablest hireling."[103] "One of the People" spoke of the need for "certain and unvarying rules" or "fixed rules" so that the decisions of the courts would not be "various and contradictory." As it was now, the law allowed judges to "make up their decisions as suits their pleasure."[104]

The statements of the lay reformers are too vague to identify any specific improvements they would have made in the law. They probably did not know themselves, but their intent was clear. They desired a legal system that met their needs as consumers of the law and that would reject those things that worked against that end. This is especially seen in their desire to break the professional mastery over the legal process by rendering the law simple enough for the common man to understand.

One lay codifier made a representative assertion when he spoke of the "people, to whom all law, even in its principle or embodied mind, should be understood, and by whom it will be understood, when the *profession* ceases to be a *craft*. We think the law is always safest in the custody of the people at large, but *that* custody can only be obtained or secured by unlocking its mysteries and frauds."[105] Another suggested that, once codified, the law would be "simplified, in substance and in form," and as a result, "the people at large would be enabled to comprehend the provisions of the law necessary for the security of property and person."[106]

The system the lay reformers envisioned went far in the direction of the Benthamite ideal of a lawyerless legal order, though few, at least in the 1820s, actually suggested that goal was possible. Rather, they wanted the law made clear enough for lay comprehension so that they would no longer be hapless victims of a legal process they did not understand. Then they could know that justice was not being subverted by chicanery, that the attorney was properly representing his client, or that a judge had correctly decided a case. The lay reformers considered the legal profession different from any other set of craftsmen they depended on. "If we could send our estate or character, as we send a watch, to be mended," one layman remarked, there would be no compelling reason to understand its workings. He continued, "because the law is not exactly a manual art, though not free of slight of hand tricks... we wish to preserve to the community at large, some little judgement, as well as concern in their own affairs."[107]

In short, codification would offer the layman a means to check on the proper workings of the legal system. "An observer," writing in the New York *Statesman* in 1824, put it succinctly. Once the law were reduced to a code, "we shall have nothing to fear from the profession."[108] Only Cooper, among the lawyer-codifiers, voiced any sort of agreement. While he did not believe that the legal profession could be eliminated by a code, he declared, "the plainer and more intelligible the principles of all trades and professions can be made, the less chance will be there be of imposition on the public."[109] Of course, Cooper was alone among the professional codifiers, as a nonpracticing attorney. The others, by implication, rejected the idea. Like all other craftsmen, they had no desire to allow the uninitiated to penetrate the mysteries of the calling lest they impose restraint and control upon a profession they did not truly understand.

NOTES

1. "Uniacke's Letter to the Lord Chancellor of England," *New York Review and Atheneum Magazine* 2 (1826): 126.

2. Peter S. Du Ponceau, *"Tesimon. Erudit. Viror." Journal of Jurisprudence* 1 (1821): pp. 4-5.

3. Peter S. Du Ponceau, *A Dissertation on the Nature and Extent of the Jurisdiction of the Courts of the United States* (Philadelphia: Abraham Small, 1824), pp. 169-70.

4. [William H. Gardiner], "Revision of the Laws of New York," *North American Review* 24 (1827): 193.

5. "On the Substitution of a Written Code in Place of the Common Law," *Atlantic Magazine* 1 (1824): 295.

6. "Penal Code of the French Empire," *American Review of History and Politics* 2 (1811): appendix, pp. 1-69.

7. "Constitution and Penal Code of France," *United States Law Journal* 1 (1823)' 405-45.

8. John Rodman, *Commercial Code of the French Empire Translated for the American Review, With Explanatory Notes of Commerce in General* (Philadelphia: C. Wiley, 1811).

9. David Hoffman, *Legal Outlines* (Baltimore: E.J. Coale, (1829), p. 471.

10. [Edward Everett], "Code Napoléon," *North American Review* 20 (1825): 400.

11. *The Commercial Code of France with the Motives or Discourses of the Counsellors of State, Delivered Before the Legislative Body, Illustrative of the Principles and Provisions of the Code*...[John Rodman, trans.] (New York: C. Wiley, 1814), pp. vi, vii.

12. "Jurisprudence of Louisiana," *American Quarterly Review* 4 (1828): 55.

13. Joseph Story, "Progress of Jurisprudence," in *Miscellaneous Writing of Joseph*

Story, William W. Story, ed. (Boston: Charles C. Little and James Brown, 1852), p. 238.

14. [Everett], "Code Napoleon," p. 403.

15. *Commercial Code of France,* pp. x, xiv.

16. [Henry Dwight Sedgwick], "The Common Law," *North American Review* 19 (1824): 435.

17. Hoffman, *Legal Outlines.*

18. [Sedgwick], "The Common Law," p. 425.

19. [Everett], "Code Napoléon."

20. "Scott's Life of Napoleon," *Southern Review* I (1828): 184-85.

21. Charles Watts to William Sampson, n.d., William Sampson, *Sampson's Discourse, and Correspondence with Various Learned Jurists Upon the History of the Law,* Pishey Thompson, comp. (Washington, D.C.: Gales & Seaton, 1826), p.77.

22. *Commercial Code of France,* p. vii.

23. "Constitution and Penal Code of France," p. 405.

24. [Sedgwick], "The Common Law," p. 436.

25. "Jurisprudence of Louisiana," p. 56.

26. Hoffman, *Legal Outlines,* p. 469.

27. "Scott's Life," p. 186.

28. On the romantic appeal of Napoleon, see ibid., pp. 184-86; "Jurisprudence of Louisiana," pp. 55-56; Hoffman, *Legal Outlines,* pp. 469-72; New York *Statesman,* 25 Jan. 1825.

29. Dumas Malone, *The Public Life of Thomas Cooper* (New Haven: Yale University Press, 1926), p. 370.

30. "Codification," *American Quarterly Review* 6 (1829): 109.

31. Isaac Parker, "Inaugural Address Delivered in the Chapel of Harvard University, by the Hon. Isaac Parker, Chief Justice of Massachusetts, and Royall Professor of Law," *North American Review* 3 (1816): 25.

32. Jeremy Bentham, *The Works of Jeremy Bentham,* John Bowring, comp., 11 vols. (New York: Russell and Russell, 1962 edition), V: 235; IV: 459, 460.

33. Ibid., IV: 446; X: 92.

34. Ibid., X: 429; X: 236.

36. Ibid., III: 205, 206.

36. Ibid., p. 209.

37. Ibid., IV: 494.

38. Ibid., I: 271n.

39. Ibid., III: 210.

40. Sampson, *Discourse,* p. 37. See also Charles Watts to William Sampson, n.d., ibid., pp. 92-93.

41. Thomas Grimke, *An Oration on the Practicability and Expediency of Reducing the Whole Body of the Law to the Simplicity and Order of a Code* (Charleston, S.C., 1827), p. 13.

42. [Sedgwick], "The Common Law," p. 431.

43. Charles Watts to William Sampson, n.d., Sampson, *Discourse,* p. 93.

44. [Sedgwick], "The Common Law."

45. Sampson, *Discourse,* p.36.

46. "Dane's Abridgement," *American Jurist and Law Magazine* 4 (1830): 66.

47. Story, "Progress of Jurisprudence," p. 238.

48. Grimke, *Oration,* p. 8.

49. Joseph Story "Law, Legislation and Codes," in James McClellan, *Joseph Story and the American Constitution* (Norman: University of Oklahoma Press, 1971), p.370.

50. George Bibb to William Sampson, n.d., Sampson, *Discourse,* p. 114.

51. Joseph Story, "The Value and Importance of Legal Studies," in *Miscellaneous Writings of Joseph Story,* William W. Story, ed., (Boston: Charles C. Little and James Brown, 1852), p. 515.

52. David Hoffman, *A Course of Legal Study* (Baltimore: Coale & Maxwell, 1817), p. xix.

53. Story, "Law, Legislation and Codes," p. 363.

54. Ibid., p. 366.

55. See Joseph Story, "Digests of the Common Law," *North American Review* 20 (1825): 61.

56. James McClellan, *Joseph Story and the American Constitution* (Norman: University of Oklahoma Press, 1971), p. 94.

57. Story, "Progress of Jurisprudence," p. 237.

58. Story, "Law, Legislation and Codes," p. 359.

59. [Joseph Story], "Hoffman's Course of Legal Study," *North American Review* 6 (1817): 43-44.

60. Story, "Law, Legislation and Codes," pp. 358-59.

61. Sampson, *Discourse,* p. 33.

62. Thomas Cooper to William Sampson, n.d., ibid., p. 53.

63. Ibid., p. 32.

64. William Sampson, "The Common Law," *Atlantic Magazine* 2 (1825): 281.

65. Sampson, *Discourse,* p. 38.

66. Story, "Progress of Jurisprudence," p. 217.

67. Charles Watts to William Sampson, n.d, Sampson, *Discourse,* p. 87.

68. Thomas Cooper to William Sampson, n.d., ibid., p. 54.

69. Ibid., p. 32.

70. Ibid., p. 38.

71. Ibid.

72. [Sedgwick], "The Common Law," p. 429.

73. Ibid., p. 413.

74. Sampson, *Discourse,* p. 13.

75. Charles Watts to William Sampson, n.d., ibid., p. 88.

76. Sampson, "The Common Law," p. 292.

77. William Sampson to Thomas Cooper, n.d., Sampson, *Discourse,* p. 64.

78. Ibid., pp. 5, 6, 10.

79. Thomas Cooper, New York *American* 14 Dec. 1824.

80. Sampson, *Discourse,* p. 38.

81. Charles Watts to William Sampson, n.d., ibid,. p. 92.

82. William Sampson to Thomas Cooper, n.d.; Thomas Cooper to William Sampson, n.d., ibid., pp. 61, 74.

83. Edward Livingston, *The Complete Works of Edward Livingston on Criminal Jurisprudence,* 2 vols. (Montclair, N.J.: Patterson Smith, 1968 reprint edition) 1: 16.

84. Edward Livingston to Jeremy Bentham, 1 July 1830, Bentham, *Works,* XI: 51.

85. Ibid.

86. See "Kent on American Law," *American Quarterly Review* 1 (1827): 175-85; "Uniacke's Letter," p. 130; Charleston *Courier*, 12 Nov. 1825, 9 Jan. 1826.

87. Story, "Progress of Jurisprudence," p. 237.

88. Sampson, *Discourse*, p. 39.

89. Thomas Cooper to William Sampson, 4 Mar. 1825, *National Advocate* (New York), 31 July 1825.

90. Thomas Cooper, New York *American*, 14 Dec. 1824.

91. Du Ponceau, *Dissertation*, p. 127.

92. [Sedgwick], "The Common Law," p. 430.

93. Joseph Story to Henry Wheaton, 1 Oct. 1825, quoted in McClellan, *Story*, p. 93.

94. Story, "Law, Legislation and Codes," p. 369.

95. Charles Watts to William Sampson, n.d., Sampson, *Discourse*, p. 89.

96. Ibid., p. 87.

97. Thomas Cooper to William Sampson, n.d., ibid., p. 53.

98. Ibid., p. 30.

99. Grimke, *Oration*, pp. 27, 32.

100. Sampson, *Discourse*, p. 32.

101. Charleston *Courier*, 9 Sept. 1825.

102. Ibid.

103. *National Advocate* (New York), 20 Aug. 1826.

104. New York *American*, 5 April 1825.

105. *National Advocate* (New York), 5 April 1825.

106. Charleston *Courier*, 9 Sept. 1825.

107. *National Advocate* (New York), 19 Aug. 1825.

108. New York *Statesman*, 10 May 1824.

109. Thomas Cooper to William Sampson, n.d., Sampson, *Discourse*, p. 70.

5

DEBATING CODIFICATION, 1815-1830

As a historical phenomenon, the American codification movement manifested a diffused expression of reformist energy rather than a picture of tightly knit organizational activity. In its early years, the movement was embodied in debates over the utility of the reform, largely among lawyers, in pamphlets, periodicals, and newspapers. Discussion of codification in these forums gave it widespread publicity and encouraged a national interest in the possibility of legal reform through codification. It was, however, a national movement only in the sense that the intellectual controversy over codified law transcended local boundaries, for the states alone had the authority to codify effectively the bulk of America law. Consequently, agitation for codes ultimately became focused in the state legislatures and, to a lesser extent, in state constitutional conventions. There, either success was achieved or failure was endured.

Before 1815, there were expressions of interest in the idea of codified law, but nothing existed in the way of a sustained reform movement. Interest was occasionally displayed by small numbers of individuals and, then, with no real impact. James Wilson and Hugh Henry Brackenridge, as we have seen, separately encouraged a reluctant Pennsylvania to take up law reform through comprehensive legislation. Both, however, were protocodifiers, who apparently had developed their ideas independently of any general reform movement. While their proposals and accompanying rationales were similar to those of later codifiers, having been designed to remedy similar abuses, neither had any real connection with the later effort.

Preceding the War of 1812 and throughout the second decade of the nineteenth century, interest was manifested in the civil law, especially in the French legal system, and specimens of the French civil law were available in the United States. Thomas Cooper translated Justinian's *Institutes* and published his work in 1812.[1] In the initial numbers of the first legal periodical in the United States—*The American Law Journal*—begun in 1807 by John Hall, there were translations of civil law codes and texts.[2] The publication of French law did not necessarily represent a developing interest in codification. Content rather than form was the focus of attention. Contemporaries were cognizant of the fact that the United States was engaged in developing a legal system. Many practitioners suggested, as Jesse Root had some years before, the merit of borrowing selectively from the world's legal systems in the process of creating an American legal product. As Peter S. Du Ponceau remarked, this "disposition to extend the bounds of our science, and to improve our jurisprudence by the study of that of other nations" was evidence of "the inclination of our professional men to cultivate jurisprudence as a philosophical science."[3] Nonetheless, professional readers were struck by the simplicity with which French law was expressed, as well as by the order and system of the civil law codes.

John Rodman, who translated the French commercial code for the *American Review*, exhibited an early fascination with what he described as "the lucid order, precision and method with which matter is arranged and exhibited" in the French system of codified law. The French codes, Rodman continued, were "splendid monuments of jurisprudence," which contained "all the general principles of civil and municipal law." The form of the French law of commerce, Rodman asserted, was superior to its English counterpart. Indeed, he declared, "[s]uch a body of mercantile law, condensed in so small a compass, its various parts arranged and exhibited in so able a manner, is not to be found in the jurisprudence of any other nation."[4] Rodman stopped short of advocating that the United States should follow the French lead. Such a recommendation would have fallen on deaf ears in any event, given the radical departure from the established law that the adoption of a code format represented, coupled with the atmosphere of general satisfaction with the legal system that existed in the United States in 1815.

It was through the efforts of Jeremy Bentham that the idea of law reform through codification was first disseminated in the United States in the years following the War of 1812. While he failed to generate a significant favorable interest in or response to his proposals at that time, he did convert some disciples to the cause of codified law and, more importantly, planted the idea so that it could be later harvested.

Bentham had long considered the United States a likely and proper environment in which to implement his ideas, believing they had a better chance of success there than in his native tradition-bound England. Having no ready disciples in the United States to encourage law reform along the lines he proposed, Bentham wrote to President James Madison in 1811 offering to formulate a code of American law or, as he said, "*a complete body* of proposed law, in the form of Statute law; say, in one word a Pannomion... including a succedaneum to that mass of foreign law, the yoke of which, in the... shapeless shape of *common,* alias unwritten law, remains still about your necks." Once given "the necessary encouragement" in the form of a letter "importing *approbation,*" he promised to "forthwith set about the task." Bentham declared he would do this work for nothing; he even offered to pay the costs of printing.[5]

In his letter to Madison, which was in fact an abbreviated version of his concept of codification, Bentham told the American president that the proposed code would be small. "[T]he quantity of space occupied" by the code, he promised, would be "rendered much less than could readily have been imagined." But the code would be as complete a statement of law as possible. "[N]o case that can present itself," he asserted, "shall find itself unnoticed or unprovided for." Elsewhere in his letter, he reaffirmed that his would be "a *complete* body of law, in which saving the requisite allowance to be made for human weakness, every imaginable case shall be provided for, and provided for in the best manner." As for the content of the proposed body of law, Bentham declared that every effort would be made to simplify the law and to state it as clearly as possible to secure "the maxim of *cognoscibility.*" Once the codification were completed and implemented, the law would be comprehensible, known, and certain, and, as a result, the rights of individuals would be more secure. Furthermore, the United States would be freed from dependence on foreign law.[6]

In contrast to his projected system of codified law, Bentham described to Madison, in a biting critique, the existing legal system of the United States. "[E]very man's dearest and most important interests," he declared of the common law, "stand, or rather fluctuate... [o]n some random decision or string of frequently contradictory decisions, pronounced... almost without any intelligible *reason* under the impulse of some private sinister interest." The common law was no more than a "shapeless mass of *merely conjectural* and *essentially uncognizable* matter." It was "[c]onfused, indeterminate, inadequate, ill-adapted, and inconsistent"; a "species of mock law," which left rights insecure.[7]

Anticipating the sort of objections that the legal profession would make to his scheme, Bentham suggested that "an enterprise of this sort" might engender fears that rights and property would be thrown into confused uncertainty. Property rights under existing law, he declared, were already in a state "of perpetual and universally extending disturbance" because "*uncertainty, uncognoscibility, particular disappointment* without end" and a "general sense of insecurity" marked the workings of the common law. "So far as the *disturbance* to existing rights is the disorder in question, the proposed operation... presents not only the sure, but the only possible remedy."[8]

Since Bentham's proposal came to Madison on the eve of the War of 1812, the president was necessarily tardy in responding to the offer. In fact, Madison waited until May 1816 to reply, when, in a guarded way, he acknowledged the appeal of Bentham's reform scheme. "[A] digest of our laws on sound principles with a purgation and reduction to a text of the unwritten part of them," he declared, "would be an invaluable improvement." He doubted, however, whether codification could be practically done "within the space...contemplated." Furthermore, he suggested that the proposed codification of the common law would only "partially" cure the problems inherent in unwritten law, as the terminology of the code's text would "necessarily" require "a resort for definition and explanation to the volumes containing that description of law." In the end, even though he found "much to admire in the comprehensive and profound views" expressed by Bentham, Madison refused to give him the desired encouragement he wanted to commence codification. The president simply asserted that it "would not be in the scope of my proper functions" to act on the proposal.[9]

Bentham had not remained idle while waiting for Madison's reply. In 1814, he discussed his letter to Madison with Albert Gallatin, one of the peace commissioners sent to Europe to bring an end to hostilities with England. Gallatin suggested to Bentham that he had tendered his offer to codify American law to the wrong official, as the states were the only jurisdictions that could mechanically take up the reform. He further indicated that his adopted state of Pennsylvania might respond positively to Bentham's proposals. Gallatin had been a member of that state's legislature in 1793 when James Wilson had proposed to reduce the laws to a written text. He suggested to Bentham that he might realize the ends that Wilson had envisioned.[10]

Taking Gallatin's advice, Bentham wrote to Simon Snyder, the governor of Pennsylvania, proposing that he be authorized to codify the state's laws. He included a printed copy of his letter to Madison as the basis of this project, without drafting a new rationale. Optimistically believing that his offer had "a chance more or less considerable of obtaining acceptance at the hands of the legislature," Bentham requested that the governor send him, as soon as possible, the requisite materials and documents needed to undertake the project. He further requested that he be informed at once of the authorization so that not a moment would be lost. Bentham, then sixty-seven years old, was anxious to undertake and complete the actual formulation of a code, something he had been suggesting for years, before he died.[11]

Gallatin wrote a letter of introduction to Snyder to accompany Bentham's proposition. In it, he expressed his own predilection for codified law. He asserted his belief that while the difficulty of the project was "almost equal to its importance," Bentham appeared "particularly fitted for the undertaking." He suggested that the state could "without risk or expense" greatly benefit from the codification of its laws. Gallatin also pointed out that while Bentham's work contained "peculiarities,both of matter and style, and some suggestions, which you will condemn as inadmissible or inapplicable," any proposed code would have to meet the approval of the legislature, which could make changes that were felt necessary. Pennsylvania, he concluded, had the opportunity "to take the lead" in this matter and complete the variety of legal reforms already implemented in the state with "this most important general improvement."[12]

For some unexplained reason, nearly two years passed before Bentham's letter reached Governor Snyder. A representative of the backwoods democracy, Snyder had earlier worked successfully for law reform in the state, dealing with the simplification of the judicial process. However, while he evidenced sympathy for Bentham's plan, he appeared less than enthusiastic when he presented it to the state legislature in December 1816. Calling Bentham's letter a "philanthropic communication," he merely passed it along with accompanying documents sent by Bentham to the legislature for its consideration, with no recommendation on his part. Snyder left it to the legislators to "determine whether, under the circumstances of our as yet unconsolidated system of civil and criminal policy, we can, in the prosecution of this important work, be benefited by the labours of the benevolent Mr. Bentham."[13]

Snyder expressed privately that he thought it best to submit the proposal "untrammelled by any suggestion or presumptions" to the legislature, as he believed it would have a better chance of passage. "[E]xecutive suggestion," he had learned by experience, "proves not always a recommendation for the adoption by a free legislature." More often than not, such recommended proposals were "passed over with silence, than acted upon by practical men."[14]

Unfortunately, that is exactly what happened to Bentham's offer. The legislature simply did not act on the matter. Possibly it was unwilling to entrust a matter so important as this to an unknown foreigner. A more likely explanation is found in the general satisfaction of the contemporary legal profession with the legal environment. Lawyers in the legislature were simply not interested in codification because they believed it was unnecessary. While the legal system was not free of defects, no abuses were experienced at that time that could encourage an enthusiastic desire for the revolutionary transformation that Bentham proposed.

Convinced by Gallatin that the states were the proper instrumentalities to approach with this codification proposals, Bentham, before he heard of Pennsylvania's disinclination to take up the reform, sent a letter to each one of the state governors offering to codify their laws. He included, under the title *Papers Relating to Codification,* all his correspondence with American officials on the matter of law reform, as well as "testimonial evidence," which comprised a similar offer to the czar of Russia to codify Russian law and the czar's reply. This information was accompanied by sets of Bentham's published works. He prevailed on John Quincy Adams, then ending his tenure as ambassador to the Court of St. James, to transmit these materials (twenty-five sets in all) to the governors and to several other prominent Americans, including Thomas Cooper.[15] The following year, realizing that he would have to generate public support for the measure, he penned a series of letters addressed to the people of the United States in which he examined at length the evils of unwritten law and the advantages of a codified legal system.[16]

Contrary to Bentham's expectations, only one governor, William Plumer of New Hampshire, expressed any enthusiasm. Soon after receiving Bentham's communication in September 1817, Plumer wrote to the English utilitarian expressing his strong assent to the proposal. He declared that he had considered for some time a code that would "supercede the *unwritten law*... a great desideratum in legislation," and asserted that if it were implemented, "it would in a great measure, not only correct the numerous errors and gross absurdities, but destroy the great *uncertainty* of what is called the *common law* and render our government, more emphatically... *a government not of men but of laws.*" Plumer expressed his apprehension that the proposal would encounter "a host of prejudices," chiefly among the "body of lawyers, many of whom *here*... dread *reform,* fearing it would diminish their individual profits." As governor, he declared, he had "no power... to request you to draw a code of laws for this state," but he promised to communicate Bentham's proposal as well as the "papers of codification" to the legislature in the "hope they will receive that candid consideration which their high merit demands."[17]

When the next legislature convened in June 1818, Plumer duly presented Bentham's proposal to that body, stating that "a complete code of laws focused upon enlightened principles of legislation" was "a subject worthy of your mature consideration."[18] The legislators were not caught by surprise. Previous to their meeting, several newspapers had reported on Bentham's proposal as well as Plumer's communication to him.

The Boston *Daily Advertiser* printed the Plumer letter with the critical comments of a correspondent. This opening salvo from the anti-codificationist ranks had none of the earnest intellectual flavor that the opposition argument took on in the 1820s. The writer was so contemptuous of the idea of codification that he refused to consider it seriously. However, underlying his remarks was a notion inherent in common law thinking—that a well-functioning legal system could not be formed as easily as the idea of codification might suggest. Rather, it was the result of years of experience. Thus, a mere written code, being only the production of a moment, could never replace the common law. He concluded his derisive commentary on codification and on Bentham by suggesting that New Hampshire should adopt the reform so that other states could profit from its inevitable failure.[19]

Not all commentators were critical in their appraisal of codification. The Republican papers of the state republished a portion of the *Edinburgh Review's* favorable notice of Bentham's *Papers* and of the codification project. Plumer's son, also a convert to codified law, wrote letters to the New Hampshire *Gazette* defending the reform. He observed that the question at issue was whether the common law of England was "best adopted of any system that can possibly be devised, to preserve order...and to guard the lives, the liberty, and property" of the citizens of the state. Challenging the common law tradition, he noted that even the "most learned and experienced" practitioners often became involved in "inexplicable difficulties" in trying to explain the law because of the "multiplicity of contradictory decisions" the common law contains. It was "manifest absurdity" to use "the abstruse subtleties of feudal law and the barbarous and antiquated system of property" that flourished in England "to illustrate and explain" American institutions. He declared that the choice for the state was between "the heterogeneous collection of Gothic customs eked out by civil and statute law" or "a systematic code, whose provisions are consistently adopted to each other and the present state of things, and the whole of which is founded upon philosophical principles."[20]

In another letter, he declared that attempts had been made to improve the content of the common law in the state, but such efforts were usually initiated at "the discretion of judges who have thus blended legislative functions with their own." Furthermore, these reforms only ameliorated limited areas of the law. Consequently, "the design and superstructure" of the common law was unchanged. In contrast, a properly formulated code would "obviate the confusion" found in the state's written law and "reduce the uncertainty and contradiction inherent in" the common law, emanating, as it does, "from the peculiar opinions of individuals." Citing the Code Napoléon as an example,he asserted that if the law were codified, the legal system would be grounded "upon rational principles of mutual dependence."[21]

Bentham's proposal did not fare well in the hands of the legislators. If it had been a party issue in the state's newspapers, it was not such in the legislature. As one New Hampshire politician later wrote to Bentham, "all the lawyers of both parties...were decidedly opposed to passing any other resolve on the subject than a general one—that it was inexpedient to accept your proposal." He suggested that some legislators, having studied the common law all their lives, had come to think of it as needing little improvement, "least of all, so entire and radical a change as that proposed by you." Others were convinced that the reform "would prove *injurious to the profession* by rendering the law more *clear* and *explicit* and thus diminishing the *profits* which are at present derived from its *uncertainty* and *obscurity*." They denounced the scheme as "visionary, impracticable, and unnecessary." This opposition, as well as the novelty of the idea and the press of other business, he went on to say, led the legislature to postpone consideration of the matter until its next session, which would meet a year hence. Bentham's correspondent related that he had "very little hopes of any favorable result." His foreboding proved correct, as the matter was not taken up again by the succeeding legislature.[22]

No other state seriously considered Bentham's offer.[23] There were several reasons for his lack of success. William Plumer, Jr., cited one cause some years later to Joseph Story. "The idea...that an old man in London," he related, "of whom few...had ever heard, should be employed" to formulate a code "struck most...as improper, not to say absurd."[24] Bentham appeared as an inappropriate jurisconsult for other reasons. He was considered a closet philosopher, not a practitioner of the law. Academics and theoreticians have never been held in high regard by common lawyers. Their guidance could not be trusted, it was believed, as they had no experience in the practical affairs of the law. The reform might have fared better had it been applied only to the statute law, but the codification of statutes was only auxiliary to Bentham's main purpose.

Codification was promptly attacked by the orthodox common lawyers as it appeared on the American scene. However, their arguments differed little from Joseph Hopkinson's rebuttal a decade earlier to Hugh Henry Brackenridge's recommendation that the common law be rendered into a written text. These early anti-codifiers took Bentham literally when he said that it was possible to form "a complete body of law" through codification. Daniel Webster in 1818 called the idea one of the "idlest and weakest theories of the age" because it was not possible to "provide beforehand, by positive enactment, and in such manner as to avoid all doubts and ambiguities, for all questions to which the immense variety of human concerns gives rise." Webster declared that "legislation can do no more than establish principles," which the courts, in keeping with their proper role, would combine and apply to the "infinite variety" of human actions that no legislator could comprehend.[25]

Theron Metcalf, a Massachusetts lawyer, observed that a real danger would befall the legal order if the common law were replaced by legislation. Because "no collection of legislative wisdom is competent to embody into a system the rules, which are to govern the multifarious, the infinitely diversified affairs of men," the courts would have to decide "arbitrarily" each time a lacuna were discovered in the code. The established and certain rules of decision found in the common law would be replaced by the "moral obligations of judges." As a result, "[a]ll would be uncertainty," and there would be "no liberty and no security." The common law system, however, did not have this limitation. It was

> a system which has been formed and nurtured by the experimental wisdom of the ages, and which finds its highest eulogy in its practical effects. It is a system of principles; and the new points which arise and are decided, are merely the application of those principles to new combinations of facts for the purposes of attaining justice.[26]

These orthodox practitioners believed that only courts using common law methodology—that is, applying custom, equity, analogy, precedent, and construction to legal problems as they arose—could meet the day-to-day legal needs of society. Without such inherent adaptability, no legal system could properly function to satisfy the demands made upon it. While this idea was latent in the thought of the early anti-codifiers, their argument was not fully developed. However, in a few years, it would become an essential element in the case against codes.

Webster also attacked codification from another angle. Bentham said that the common law was so complex and contradictory that it was uncertain. In rebuttal, Webster declared that "experience does not teach us, that legal subjects are always plain in proportion to the quantity of legislation bestowed upon them. Statutes themselves are often ambiguous and uncertain." Moreover, he asserted, there were "important branches of the law, resting almost entirely on precedents and decisions," that were clearer and more certain than others "founded in a great number of statutes." He cited the law of bills of exchange and bailments as examples. In contrast, he charged that the English law of bankruptcy, based on legislation, created boundless sources of controversy and litigation. Because even "the most skillful legislation" will give rise to questions of interpretation, statutes must remain uncertain until the courts rule on their meaning; but with no common law, no collection of decisions, such legislative meaning must remain forever uncertain.[27]

Considerations such as these no doubt were factors in the lack of success that Bentham experienced in America. Not only did lawyers who had a commanding say in legal reform consider common law the best possible legal system practically achievable, it was also the system they had studied and understood. A writer for the *Edinburgh Review* in 1817 came to a similar conclusion. While he considered the prospects of codified law in the United States "[d]azzling and alluring," he concluded that "they will never be realized" because of "the influences which practicing lawyers are said to have in all the States of America." He declared that the "spirit and tendency of their education" and their "habits and modes of thinking" contracted in practice rendered the profession "adverse to all innovations, and, above all, to an innovation of such magnitude as that of subverting the whole system, which [it]... has been the business of their lives to study and give effect to."[28]

If conditions were not propitious for a codification movement at this time, however, there were signs that they would soon become so. Joseph Story reflected a changing state of affairs that led to a concerted attempt to achieve the codification of American law when he declared in 1817 that while great advances had been made in American jurisprudence, "a profound and comprehensive knowledge of it never was more difficult of attainment." While numerous aids for legal study existed, it was "a task of vast labor and difficulty" to become an "eminent lawyer." "The most diligent study and practice of a long life," he declared, "are scarcely sufficient to place any gentleman beyond the necessity of continual exertions to keep pace with the current of new opinions and doctrines."[29] In 1817, Story was among the few common lawyers who had made such a pessimistic analysis, but soon a large portion of the profession would echo it.

Upon his first exposure to codification, Story, like most common lawyers, opposed the reform. In 1817, he declared uncategorically that

> [i]t is impossible to provide by any code, however extensive, for the infinite variety of distinctions as civil justice, arising from the imperfections of human language and foresight, from the conflict of opposing rights, from real and apparent hardships, and from those minute equities, which are often found in different scales, adding somewhat to the weight of each, but rarely forming an exact equipoise.

Since it was impossible "to realize those utopian dreams," he suggested that "the upright and enlightened administration of justice" could best be achieved by diligent legal studies and the support of liberal salaries for the judiciary,which would encourage the independence and integrity of the bench.[30] While Story persistently held the view that it was not possible to reduce the entire law to a code, he soon began to see the efficacy of a limited codification. He was among the first to modify the Benthamite codification formula to make it compatible with the common law system.

In his address to the Suffolk bar in 1821, Story appealed for the codification of American law, though Bentham's term, "codification," was noticeably absent from his discussion.[31] This was one of the first times since the unsuccessful espousal of codified law in New Hampshire by William Plumer that the reform was publically advocated. While Story expressed a degree of satisfaction with the progress of jurisprudence in the United States since the Revolution, he also related his apprehensions about the prospects of the law if it continued on its present course. First, he declared, the decentralization of the lawmaking institutions in the United States under the federal system was replacing the relative uniformity of the common law with doctrinal confusion and diversity. This made the task of administering justice "very laborious and perplexing" and threatened to split the profession "into distinct state bars" that would be "devoted to mere state jurisprudence." Directly related to this was a problem that had a more ominous import to Story—the runaway growth of the objective body of American law.[32]

Story declared that there was "but one adequate remedy" for these problems: "a gradual digest, under legislative authority, of those portions of our jurisprudence, which under the forming hand of the judiciary, shall from time to time acquire scientific accuracy." Once the "exact principles of law were reduced to a text," the legal profession, "in a great measure," would be "rid of the necessity of appealing to volumes which contain jarring and discordant opinions; and thus we may pave the way to a general code, which will present, in its positive authoritative text, the most material rules, to guide the lawyer, the statesman, and the private citizen." Story was careful to disassociate his proposal from Bentham's concept of codification, although the English utilitarian was not mentioned by name. According to Story, the profession should not "indulge in the theoretical extravagancies of some well meaning philosophical jurists, who believe that all human concerns for the future can be provided for in a code, speaking a definitive language." It would be, Story asserted, a "hopeless labor" and an "absurd project" to attempt to write a definitive code. Only the law as developed by the courts could be reduced "to order and certainty." Citing the successful codification of Roman law by Justinian and French law by Napoleon, Story declared that codification was not "a matter of doubtful speculation." He concluded by saying, "[i]t is left to the future jurists of our country and England to accomplish for the common law, what has thus been so successfully demonstrated to be a practical problem in the jurisprudence of other nations."[33]

Story's discourse has a more important place in the development of the intellectual content of codification in the United States than in the actual dynamics of the codification movement. It was the earliest statement of the moderates' position on codification, and it was a position that Story would persistently espouse over the next two decades. The address appears to have gone largely unnoticed at the time. It was not reprinted and widely disseminated until the end of the decade. Nonetheless, it can be taken as evidence that codification was in the air, even if it had yet to coalesce into a genuine reform effort.

It was not until 1823 that the American codification movement was actually set in motion by William Sampson's "Anniversary Discourse" to the New York Historical Society. The address encouraged codification as a reform formula in a manner that insured that it would not go unnoticed at a propitious moment. The rapid development of a national debate over codified law following its publication suggests that the contemporary condition of the changing American legal environment made the United States extremely ripe for a law reform effort. Within a year, ferment for legal change through codification convulsed the legal profession.

The great bulk of Sampson's talk was a caustic critique of the content of the English common law, designed to demonstrate its inapplicability to American conditions. In fact, in the first thirty-two pages of his thirty-six page address, reform through codification was not even mentioned. Sampson had long advocated the necessity of creating a national jurispdence, but this was the first time he actually suggested codification as a vehicle to achieve that end. Citing Louisiana's appointment of Edward Livingston to formulate a penal code for the state, Sampson called upon his audience to "hail this happy augury, and prepare for a still nobler effort, which imperious necessity will force upon us, and which cannot and ought not to be long delayed"—the formation of a general code of American law.[34]

He asserted that this was no visionary scheme; successful codes had been drafted in the past. Codified law, Sampson declared, "has been the first glory of the greatest sovereigns, and the best policy of the wisest people." No doubt realizing that codification was usually associated with civil law, a legal system frequently depreciated in the Anglo-American legal tradition, to say nothing of its connection with Jeremy Bentham, Sampson cited Bacon and Hale, giants in the common law, as authorities who had testified that the reform was necessary and practical. Bentham's name was entirely absent from the address, as was the term "codification" itself.[35]

Sampson appreciated his profession's attachment to the existing legal order as well. While he was intensely critical of the common law, he did not desire to leave his audience with the impression that he would revolutionize the legal environment by replacing the content of the common law with a theoretical code. Sampson asserted emphatically that the common law contained "rich treasures of experience," which required "little more than regulation and systematic order." Codification would abolish only those "forms which impaired the march of justice," and it would also firmly establish those existing rules "which are needful to its ends."[36]

The picture Sampson painted of the reformed, codified legal system was alluring. "[G]eneral law" rather than "particular cases" would be resorted to by the attorney and jurist. The implication was that, not only would the work load of the legal fraternity be lessened, but also that the law would become more certain. He suggested that the size of the body of the native law would be greatly diminished and promised that codification would free the legal profession from dependence on "those ever increasing swarms of foreign reports and treatises, which darken the very atmosphere, by their multitudes" and threaten to smother the congenial freshness developed by indigenous law. Jurisprudence "will be no longer intricate and thorny." Legal fictions, which gave the law "the air of occult magic," as well as "awkward contrivances," which rendered the law "ridiculous" and diminished "its dignity and efficacy," would be abolished. "We shall be delivered from those odious volumes of special pleading, which cannot be used without degrading and lowering the tone of moral sentiment." Sampson concluded his remarks by declaring that, through codification of its laws, the present generation could fulfill the effort begun by the previous generation of American revolutionaries by creating a truly indigenous legal product suitable to America's peculiar destiny. Not only would the resulting "untrammelled jurisprudence...expand to the measure of our growing fortunes," but "all regenerated nations" would be given "a model of judicial polity equal to that already exhibited in our political institutions."[37]

Not all Sampson's auditors agreed with his evaluation of the common law, nor were they seduced by his depiction of the reformed legal environment that would result from codification. Among the toasts that followed the discourse, one of the society's members, the Recorder of New York, expressed his apprehension of the reform and, in so doing, suggested one of the strongest obstacles within the legal profession to codification—a firm attachment to the common law and the fear that codification would destroy it. "Our common Law," he declared, "may it not fall beneath the *blind* strength of our Sampson."

Undaunted, Sampson, in reply, sought to allay anxiety: "The Recorder of New York and the Common Law—may he like Sampson take the *honey* and leave the *carcass*."[38]

While part of Sampson's audience may have disagreed with the ideas he enunciated, the historical society nevertheless believed the address important enough to be published in pamphlet form. This secured a wide audience for the reform message that Sampson proclaimed at a time when the legal profession was becoming increasingly restive about the legal environment. The result was a widespread discussion and debate of law reform through codification. According to one contemporary observer, the discourse "electrified the public mind."[39] Sampson himself was pleasantly surprised at the wide interest in his talk and the controversy it engendered. Somewhat more than a year after the address was published, he remarked to his friend David B. Warden that "[i]ts success has been beyond my anticipation."[40]

The discourse was widely received and discussed in a variety of literary periodicals as well as in the newspapers of a number of cities. Few were dispassionate in their analysis. Many were sharply critical. "Jay," in a stinging review in the New York *American*, considered the address a "feeble production," which had the object of bringing into "ridicule among us the common law of England, and to introduce codes for guides in judicial decisions." He declared, in what became a familiar analysis of codified law, that no code could ever replace the common law in giving "a permanent, uniform and certain rule of conduct in the various transactions of life."[41]

Another critic, writing in the newly founded *Atlantic Magazine*, believed the discourse was written "in a very unphilosophical spirit." Sampson, he declared, "has undertaken a work which is too mighty for him.... The character of true reform calls for the most sublime exertion of human intellect." He said that Sampson made but "loose charges" and that, instead of treating his topic philosophically, he indulged in an objectionable "satirical strain."[42]

Even the most censorious commentator, however, did the cause of codified law the favor of giving the reform increased publicity and of encouraging debate. That Sampson's address engendered a good deal of interest in the reform is evidenced, not only by the notice given it, but also by a sizable correspondence that developed between its author and a number of lawyers throughout the United States. Sampson used this as a means of promoting the reform by encouraging the publication of communications relating to codification in newspapers. He declared: "If discussions of important topics be of any use, their utility is greatly increased by the extensive and rapid circulation of a daily newspaper."[43] A selection of this correspondence, together with the discourse and certain state papers relating to codification, was published in 1826 by Pishey Thompson, who declared that the "great interest" generated in codification "at home and abroad" encouraged him to print the collection.[44]

By mid-decade, debate over codified law was common throughout the United

States. William Gardiner declared in 1827 that "[t]here are few questions of internal improvement upon which sound and liberal minds are more divided among us, than upon the expediency and practicability of substituting a general code for the whole mass of common and statute law." He believed the day was not far off "when codifiers and anticodifiers will wage a war as fierce and interminable, as that which raged in yore between the Doctors of Admiralty and his Majesty's servants of King's Bench."[45] Almost every law writer after 1825 felt compelled to include his views on the reform in his works of whatever sort. Some chose to treat codification with mocking disdain, without really coming to grips with the issue. One writer, for example, refused to give "full credit for sincerity" to "that set of men who are forever worrying us with their tiresome letters... in newspapers, and the long dull articles in magazines, about civil law and codification." He attributed their interest in reform to "coxcombry and affectation."[46] Sampson replied in kind that such critics were fanatics in their attachment to the common law who were "altogether incorrigible, and truth only heightens their distemper."[47]

On the whole, however, the analysis and discussion of the reform was far more intelligent and sophisticated than that which surrounded any serious law reform effort in American legal history. Yet, this debate over the merits of codified law left something to be desired. Part of the reason has already been suggested. American lawyers were never at their best in discussing jurisprudential theory. Furthermore, like all advocates of strongly held views, both the codifiers and their opponents tended to exaggerate the defects of the legal system they opposed while understating the deficiencies of the system they promoted. This was especially true of the anti-codifiers. Edward Everett was prompted by this situation to observe correctly that while codification was "a question on which different opinions would be entertained, after it was reduced to its simplest and most abstract statement," the antagonists in the law reform debate "would think much more nearly alike than they now do, if they 'understood' each other precisely, as to the terms of the controversy."[48]

Reflecting on the impact of his discourse, Sampson once mused that "[w]hen it came out it scared the night birds."[49] Typical of the sort of reaction to codified law that Sampson was referring to was the observation of a writer for the *American Quarterly Review*. "[N]othing," he said, "can be more unwise and dangerous than a wild ungoverned spirit of innovation in the law."[50] This contemporary was expressing a widely shared fear of the radical codifier's desire to simplify the substantive content of the law. While a good deal of the opposition to codified law focused on the matter of substantive reform, especially in the earliest years of the codification movement, this issue was never really at the crux of the debate over codification. The methodology of the common law, not its content, was the essential issue. However, concern over innovation in the substance of the law nevertheless had an impact on the codification movement and affected its outcome.

Sampson appreciated what he called "a prudent fear of innovation" and the "apprehension that the work of reformation might fall into rash and unskillful, perhaps dishonest and unworthy hands." He believed, however, that too often the orthodox common lawyer's opposition to codification was not based on judicious concerns but rather on a belief "that there is an exquisite and occult virtue in the common law, transcending all human wisdom, and that it is the only source of truth and light."[51] Sampson possibly overstated the opposition's position. Nonetheless, the codification debate encouraged the anti-codifiers to stress the advancements and improvements made in the common law in the United States and to de-emphasize its remaining defects. For example, John Porter, in a major article on codification for the *North American Review,* claimed that the common law on this side of the Atlantic contained only "a few slight errors," which were largely innocuous.[52] Similarly, Peter S. Du Ponceau passed off as "mere inconveniences... the numerous fictions with which it [the common law] abounds," emphasized that English jurisprudence was "gradually correcting itself" in the United States, and suggested that "common law appears more dignified with American features." Indeed, he declared that the common law in America was a highly reformed version of the English law that Sampson condemned for being artificially complex and abstruse. "[T]he true spirit of the *American* common law," Du Ponceau asserted, "abhors unnecessary forms" and stresses cheap and simple justice.[53]

In other words, Porter, Du Ponceau, and the other anti-codifiers rejected the radical codifiers' analysis as irrelevant because the inherited legal system had already been regenerated since the abuses cited had already been abolished. This was merely a reiteration of the theme articulated by Richard Rush in 1815, but it was now enunciated with greater force since the preservation of the common law as a legal system appeared at stake.

The emphasis placed by the anti-codifiers on the improved state of the common law in the United States was only one element of their opposition to substantive reform through codification. A second component of their argument stressed their fear of precipitous and radical change in the content of the legal system. This, they believed, would turn the established legal order topsy-turvy. As one law writer wrote in 1826, the inherited legal system was "woven in all our institutions and systems of jurisprudence," and "to demolish it would break up the very foundations of society."[54]

Some anti-codifiers were so imbued with this sentiment that they were even opposed to discussion of supposed abuses in the legal system. A writer for the *United States Law Journal,* reacting to the increasing debate over the state of the American legal structure, declared that "[p]ublic discontent with existing institutions, and particularly with the administration of justice, is in itself a source of great and numerous evils." He suggested that "tampering quacks" and "unskilled meddlers" could excite "causeless dissatisfaction" that might cause "a nation which is actually doing well, and is in truth prosperous, flourishing and happy...to go positively wrong."[55]

One lawyer with a penchant for poetic expression related his concern for the safety of the legal system and the society as a whole in a rendition of Hamlet's soliloquy, modified for the occasion and entitled "Codification."

> A code, or not a code—that is the question!
> Whether 'tis better in the law to suffer
> The flaws and defects of numerous practiques,
> Or to take arms against a sea of troubles,
> And, by revising, end them!—To Prune—to change—
> No more! And by a code to say we end
> Abuses, and the thousand natural pests
> That law is heir to: 'tis a consummation
> Devoutly to be wished.—To prune—to change—
> To change, and perhaps destroy! ay, there's the rub!
> For in that sleep of law what ills may come,
> When we have shuffled off the dreadful plague,
> Must give us a pause...
> [T]hat the dread of something after change—
> (Those undiscovered evils, from whose ruin
> No government returns)—puzzles the will,
> And makes us rather bear those ills we have
> Than fly to others that we know not of.
> Thus *Wisdom* does make cowards of us all.[56]

The anti-codifiers were not intrinsically opposed to change in the law. After all, they lauded the numerous reforms of the English legal science carried out in the United States. For them, however, reform of the law ideally came, not through conscious effort, but "gradually and insensibly" so as not to be disruptive.[57] "The true genius of the common law," one orthodox common lawyer remarked in a review of Sampson's discourse, "is that of perpetual reform." He declared that "inherent in its very constitution" was "a sort of vis medicatrix" by which "it uniformly accommodates itself to the existing exigencies of the times."[58]

Such notions reflected the legal philosophy of the anti-codifiers—historical jurisprudence. Most did not, however, see themselves as part of a specific school of juristic thought. Rather, they simply believed that the common law mode of legal development, which embodies the historical method, was the best possible legal system for the United States. Many were nonetheless aware of the contemporary philosophical debates among continental legal theorists, and they expressed their agreement with the historical school. James Kent, for example, declared unreservedly, "I am altogether with Savigny."[59]

Increasingly, after 1825, the matter of juristic philosophy dominated the codification debate. John Porter, as severe a critic of codification as there was, noted this change in emphasis when he expressed his belief in 1828 that the issue of substantive reform had largely been settled, with the codifiers conceding the point. "The only question," declared,

> now actually at issue between the writers on this subject [codification], we believe to be this. Is it expedient for us to undertake to analyze the whole of the common law, select the most valuable principles, digest them, arrange them, embody them into a code, give them the sanction of some direct legislative act, and by the same act declare all the residue to be void or of no validity?[60]

Porter possibly overstated the disappearance of debate over substantive reform, which continued in a muted form. However, the debate over codes within the American legal profession focused more and more on the science of the legal process, or the relative merits of a legal system based on unwritten or customary law as opposed to one where the only true source of the law would be written rules. For Porter and the other anti-codifiers, the replacement of common law methodology with that of codified law, even though the content of the law would be retained, was an ill-advised scheme, being not only latent with danger for the legal order but impracticable and inexpedient. "Other systems have been wise and ingenious, in theory," declared one orthodox common lawyer, "but for plain and sound sense, and real practical wisdom and utility, for the true and permanent security of life, and the great source of national prosperity, the common law surpasses by vast odds, all the systems that were ever contrived."[61]

Such statements reflect one of the reasons that the anti-codifiers believed should impel continued adherence to the existing system of unwritten law. The common law, they argued, was superior because, by its very nature, it was a practical system of laws built on long experience and actual need, whereas codified law, they believed, was essentially abstract and speculative. Orthodox common lawyers were fond of quoting Sir Matthew Hale's expression of admiration for the common law because it was "not the product of the wisdom of some one man, or society of men, in any one age; but the wisdom, counsel, experience, and observation of many ages."[62]

However, the common law was more than the accumulation of sage tradition. The nature of this organic growth, the orthodox lawyers argued, guaranteed that the common law could better meet the actual legal needs than a codified system. The methodology by which the common law was developed was not essentially artificial, contemplative inquiry, or, as one orthodox lawyer put it, the common law was "not derived merely from an abstract consideration of the human mind." Rather, it originated and evolved through the adaptation of "rules and action to the precise character, situation, and wants of those whom it governs" in actual cases and controversies.[63] The common law, then, to its defenders, was law declaratory of social experience in the administration of justice, and, as such, it naturally corresponded to genuine needs. Codified law, on the other hand, reflected only those needs and wants perceived by the codifiers. As a result, "Henry" declared in the New York *American* that codified law "never can be more perfect than the ideas of justice presented" by its authors.[64] Because of the limitations of the human intellect, one anti-codifier claimed, "[n]o code ever had been or can be framed to meet the ever varying cases of human life."[65] While the known law might be codified to meet known needs, another, pursuing this familiar theme, asserted that "[n]ew and unrecognized cases will forever come up, for which no legislative provisions could have been made," which would render any code inadequate to meet the legal exigencies of any developing society. Indeed, it was "not in human foresight to anticipate even the various classes of cases that may arise."[66]

The essential characteristic of the common law that enabled it to be responsive to unforeseen demands was said to be its malleability. The common law was judge-made law (through the anti-codifiers would have been loath to use that term), which was perpetually formulated in the actual process of litigation. It was customary law and written only insofar as the judicial opinions that expounded it were reduced to writing. It is not fixed as legislation. Thus, it was capable of "infinite expression and improvement."[67] Where the codifiers saw uncertainty arising out of judicial discretion, or its malleability, the anti-codifiers saw a healthy flexibility.

Possibly the rapidly multiplying demands placed on the legal system in those years by the developing American society made the orthodox common lawyers particularly sensitive to the need to preserve what they considered the intrinsic adaptability of the common law. It was frequently declared to be a system of law, as one said, particularly "suited to our growing wants and circumstances."[68] Another echoed this appraisal by saying that codified law was suitable for "despotic countries," where "the investigations of jurists are chiefly confined to existing law; but where the mind expands itself in freedom," law "may assume a wider range, and impart its aid to the important subject of improvement."[69]

These orthodox common lawyers asserted that while change occurred in the common law, it took place without causing legal disruption. Essentially, the system was stable without being rigid. Unlike legislators, who were only limited by the letter and the spirit of the constitution and who could change the law at will, the common law judge must, it was asserted, develop the law in relation to the existing body of common law doctrines. As one New York judge put it in 1825, "[t]he flexibility of the common law consists, not in change of principles, but in the application of old principles to new cases, and in the modification of the rules flowing from such cases as they arise, so as to preserve the reason of the rules and the spirit of the law."[70] And, as the courts continually applied the rules of the common law in more and more cases, the law moved toward certainty and perfection. "[T]he more numerous the decisions," "Jay" declared of the common law in the New York *American,* "the more accurate will be the rule."[71]

In clearly settled cases, the judge was bound by the rule of *stare decisis* to follow an established precedent. On the whole, the orthodox lawyers believed that this gave stability to the common law. If there were any uncertainty, it arose from the novel legal situations with which courts often had to deal. But here there was really little to fear. The judges made their decisions after deep, unbiased reflection, knowing that they were, according to John Porter, "sharply and unremittingly watched from every side" by "the shrewdest and most intelligent men [read "lawyers"] in the community."[72] Willard Phillips, a well-respected Boston lawyer, enunciated the same idea with more professional modesty: "A judge, who knows that his decisions, with their reasons will be recorded and made public, and compared with each other, and tested by those of other judges and courts of former and after times" would be "indifferent to his own reputation and public opinion" if he did not act cautiously.[73] It was through the prompt publication of faithful reports that the common law was submitted "fairly to public examination." As a result, "false principles will be laid aside, and the truly valuable ones have the force of law," and the faithful administration of justice would be preserved.[74] For these reasons, the orthodox common lawyers saw the increasing numbers of reports, not as harmful, but as beneficial to the legal system.[75]

In contrast to the nice balance of stability with adaptability and flexibility in the common law, the anti-codifiers saw only an unhealthy rigidity in written law. "A code of laws," asserted a law writer in the *North American Review,* "is a coat of mail, which however perfectly made, admits but few movements, and can fit but one person and that for a short period."[76] James Kent, a perfect model of common law orthodoxy, opposed written law for similar reasons. "The great objection to legislative rules, and to all kinds of codification," he declared, "is, that the rules are not malleable; they cannot accommodate to circumstance; they are imperative."[77] Such notions reflected common law thinking about statutory law. Common lawyers, as Roscoe Pound once correctly observed, look upon statutes as fixed rules for defined situations and not something to be reasoned from by analogy.[78] It is little wonder that they opposed codification.

This conceptions of written law led to a foreboding analysis of legal systems where codes were the sole source of law. Declaring that human foresight could not, in a code, provide for all the different cases that would arise in the future, John Porter observed that "we should be in a state infinitely worse than despotism; a state where there are innumerable and continually multiplying violations of right, for which, however, there can be neither redress nor remedy."[79] To those who would argue that unforeseen legal needs could be met by merely changing the code, another anti-codifier claimed that any changes in the code "will not be enacted until the evil becomes general and generally felt. A system of statute law must always be behind the actual state of society, instead of keeping pace with it."[80] Because of a code's intrinsic rigidity, one orthodox common lawyer declared, in order to embrace codification, "either we must go back to a natural state of society, when wants are few, and all the complications of commercial intercourse are unknown, or we must wait till the millennial period, when... men will act with strictest justice, and live in perfect beatitude."[81]

A legal system grounded entirely in written law, then, was thought simply unworkable. Every advanced society, the orthodox lawyers claimed, must resort to a judge-formulated, or common, law if its legal system were to be at all effective. This, John Porter declared, was "an incontrovertible truth," which arose from "the uncomprising nature of things."[82] "Do what you will," Peter S. Du Ponceau declared, "legislators will never be able to provide for every possible case, and much will still be left to the sound discretion" of the courts.[83]

While the codifiers saw the Code Napoléon as evidence that proved the efficacy of codification, their opponents, conversely, cited the French experience to support their position. The French code, they said, had not obviated the need for unwritten law, nor had it created certainty. It was with not a little smugness that one anti-codifier declared in 1824 that the Code Napoléon "has already given birth to fifty volumes of reports."[84] These were the *arrêts* (decisions) of the *Cour de Cassation,* the highest French appellate court, which insured a uniform interpretation of the code. And another critic in 1829 declared, with no less self-satisfaction, that the *Repertoire de jurisprudence* (a digest of French law) arising out of the French codified system had reached nineteen volumes. He remarked that Dane's *Abridgement,* which filled only nine volumes, was "pigmy size" by comparison. He also pointed to "numerous supplementary enactments" that attempted to rectify mistakes and insure the code's relevance to existing conditions as "endless commentaries and expositions" on the code by civilian writers.[85]

For the orthodox lawyers, all this was potent evidence that a codified system would not operate as the codifiers asserted it would. The codifiers had suggested that codification would result in greater clarity and certainty and would lessen the labors of the profession. However, in France, as one anti-codifier declared, "the community at large are... puzzled to know the exact bearing and extent of the *two thousand two hundred and eight one* concise and perspicuous laws of their code."[86] He saw the numerous volumes of *arrêts* as a conclusive answer to the question whether the Code Napoléon "silenced all the doubts, and fixed all the uncertainties of their jurisconsults and judges? Whether litigation of purely legal question is anything more rare or unheard of in the... tribunals of France, than our own?" The point was clear: the French code did not materially reduce the labors of French practitioners. If anything, their toil was greater. The experience of France, which had one of "the most precisely worded and cautiously constructed" codes, led an anti-codifier to suggest that if the law was codified in the United States, the legal system would "be bridled, in a few years, to as many commentaries and glosses as the common law is at present."[87]

This statement reflected the anti-codifiers' fear that the reduction of the common law to a code would result in a legal uncertainty and instability and would threaten the legal order. It has already been suggested that the orthodox common lawyers feared reform of the substantive content of the law lest it disrupt the legal status quo. Changes in form would be no less disruptive than changes in substance, and established rules would, of necessity, be stated differently. There was no guarantee that the courts would derive from the same meaning and application from each restatement of the law. As one anti-codifier declared, "the change of a word might produce the most alarming uncertainty." Reducing the common law to a code, he asserted, was "a change so vital" that it "would shake our institutions to the center, and create an amount of litigation almost intolerable as intestine war."[88]

Certainly the anti-codifiers had no faith in the ability of American legislators to codify the law so as to minimize its disruptive effects. "The business of fully codifying our law," John Porter declared without reservation, "never could be accomplished by one of our free legislatures." While lawmakers might appoint a jurisconsult to formulate a code, "[t]hey think it their duty to place implicit confidence in none." Consequently, the final product would bear their unmistakable mark. "We can imagine the innumerable alterations, amendments, and substitutions," Porter remarked, "which almost every member thinks himself capable of introducing." Not only did legislatures have a reputation for making "bad laws," but they were considered an intrinsically poor agency to be utilized in undertaking so fundamental a change as codification. "[F]action and the views of self interest... reign in them," and many members were elected on "poor principles of qualifications."[89]

The onus of rectifying, interpreting, and construing the code would, of course, ultimately devolve on the courts. But this, too, was latent with the danger of legal uncertainty. Because, in a codified system, the code is the only source of law, the decisions of the courts would not have a binding effect. With no rule of *stare decisis,* only the "breast of the judge" would be controlling. Any case, no matter how similar it might be to its predecessors, could be decided capriciously. Thus, "B" declared in the New York *Statesman,* a codified system would "be productive of endless uncertainty."[90]

The case made against codified law by the orthodox common lawyers contained some good points, but, like the argument of the codifiers, it was not indisputable. Their evaluation of the condition of the substantive content of the American common law, as opposed to its English parent, was sensible. Sampson and the radical codifiers had pointed their sharp arrows at an English, and not necessarily an American, target. Marked improvement had been made in nearly every aspect of the law. And if many anachronisms appeared to be part of the living law, many had fallen into disuse and were not to be resurrected. Much of the reform had taken place as the anti-codifiers declared legal change should come about—gradually and insensibly. However, the common law's ability to adapt to changed circumstances did not work with the automatic ease that was suggested by the orthodox lawyers. The malleability of the common law was supposed to be balanced by the rule of *stare decisis,* with a healthy tension existing between the two. The scale, however, was heavily weighted in favor of stability. As a result, if much had been reformed, much remained to be done. There were unnecessary archaic complexities and intricacies in nearly every branch of the law. For some years following the anti-codifiers' claim that the American common law was an improved form of its English antecedent with few remaining defects, American courts and legislatures were engaged in a necessary process of reform, or Americanization, of the common law. This piecemeal reform was naturally unsatisfying to many practitioners who saw the need for a variety of changes. Instead of malleability, they saw rigidity. Furthermore, changes made in the law were somewhat inaccessible due to the welter of American reports and statute books, and this was naturally vexing to the attorney who was looking for sound answers to the problems that arose in his practice.

Edward Everett was correct when he declared that codification was the sort of issue "on which different opinions would be entertained, after it was reduced to its simplest and abstract issue."[91] Whether a system of laws based on unwritten or common law, as opposed to one grounded in written sources, was more stable and provided more legal certainty was then, and remains today, largely a matter of conjecture. Essentially, what the orthodox lawyers were saying when they criticized the civilian system and upheld the common law was that they were not at all amenable to any major change in the system of law they practiced. They were familiar with the workings of the common law and even with its defects, whose existence they would admit in a nonadversarial situation. However, they were unwilling to abandon it for something that was so different and, to their minds, inherently speculative in nature and therefore potentially disruptive. And less virtuously, they had no desire to surrender their profitable knowledge and proficiency in working with the settled legal system.

Of course, the orthodox common lawyers' argument did not go unanswered. In response to their opponents, the codifiers engaged in clarifying their position. They found it necessary to take great pains to stress their conception that codification was not a chimerical, Benthamite millennium. Codes, they said, would not result in a lawyerless society, nor could they make the law so clear that the need of law books to explain the law would be obviated. As far as they were concerned, the Code Napoléon appeared to prove their case for codes. In France, they asserted, the law was clearer and more certain than under the common law. The fact that there were *arrêts* and treatises on the code proved nothing except that it was impossible to write a perfect code, a point with which they agreed. The French code, William Sampson declared, had not been "superceded or lost sight of, as is gratuitously asserted; it is so firmly fixed that in France...it is still looked to as a polar star."[92]

The orthodox claim that codified law would destroy the necessary malleability embodied in the common law, of course, posed no problem for the moderate codifiers, as they agreed that the judicial discretion of a common law judge should remain untouched. The orthodox common lawyers, however, never came to grips with codification as the moderates proposed it. Then, criticisms were invariably aimed at the radicals. Perhaps they were so frightened by the reform that they failed to discern differences in the notions of codification as held by the proponents of the reform. The issue of malleability and the need for some sort of judicial discretion gave the radicals some difficulty at first. Reconciling codification with what they agreed to be a necessary element in any legal system—that of finding some form by which flexibility could be institutionalized in a codified system—was no easy task. They had no real answer until many adopted the not altogether satisfactory format proposed by Livingston in Louisiana.[93] Even if they were to concede all the arguments presented against codification, which they were not about to do, they felt that the sorry condition of the law still justified an attempt at reform. Thomas Cooper put it this way: "If we cannot do everything that is wished for, are we to abandon all improvement in despair and do nothing?"[94]

NOTES

1. Justinian I, *The Institutions of Justinian,* Thomas Cooper, trans. (Philadelphia: P. Byrne, 1812).
2. See "Civil Law," *The American Law Journal* 1 (1807): 491-96, 2 (1808): 462-71; "Il Consolato Del Mare," 3 (1810): 21-56.
3. Peter S. Du Ponceau, *A Dissertation on the Nature and Extent of the Jurisdiction of the Courts of the United States* (Philadelphia: Abraham Small, 1824), pp. xix-xx.
4. *The Commercial Code of France with the Motives or Discourses of the Councellors of State, Delivered Before the Legislative Body, Illustrative of the Principles and Provisions of the Code*... [John Rodman, trans.] (New York: C. Wiley, 1814), pp. vii, ix, x.
5. Jeremy Bentham to James Madison, Oct. 1811, Jeremy Bentham, *The Works of Jeremy Bentham,* John Bowring, comp., 11 vols. (New York: Russell and Russell, 1962 reprint edition), IV:453, 457, 459.
6. Ibid., pp. 455, 456, 561.
7. Ibid., pp. 459, 460.
8. Ibid.
9. James Madison to Jeremy Bentham, 8 May 1816, ibid., p. 467.
10. Albert Gallatin to Simon Snyder, 18 June 1814; Jeremy Bentham to Simon Snyder, July 1814, ibid., pp. 468, 469, 470.
11. Ibid., pp. 469-74.
12. Ibid., p. 468.
13. Ibid., p. 476.
14. Simon Snyder to David Mead, 31 May 1816, ibid., pp. 475-76.
15. See Bentham's circular letter to the governors, ibid., pp. 476-77.
16. Ibid., pp. 478-507.
17. William Plumer to Jeremy Bentham, n.d., ibid., p. 577.
18. New Hampshire *Gazette,* 9 June 1818.
19. Boston *Daily Advertiser,* 20 May 1818.
20. New Hampshire *Gazette,* 9 June 1818.
21. New Hampshire *Patriot,* 21 June 1818.
22. ? to Jeremy Bentham, n.d., Bentham, *Works,* pp. 578-79.
23. Ibid.

24. William Plumer, Jr., to Joseph Story, 28 Dec. 1841, *American Jurist and Law Magazine* 27 (1842): 62-63.

25. [Daniel Webster], "Wheaton's Reports, Vol. III," *North American Review* 8 (1818): 63.

26. [Theron Metcalf], "Tyng's Reports, Vol. XIV," *North American Review* 7 (1818): 185-86.

27. [Webster], "Wheaton's Reports," pp. 65-66.

28. "Bentham on Codification," *Edinburgh Review* 29 (1817): 235.

29. [Joseph Story], "Hoffman's Course of Legal Study," *North American Review* 6 (1817): 63.

30. Ibid., p. 49.

31. It was not until the 1830s that the term "codification" had lost its detrimental Benthamite connotations and came into general use.

32. Joseph Story, "Progress of Jurisprudence," in *Miscellaneous Writings of Joseph Story*, William W. Story, ed. (Boston: Charles C. Little and James Brown, 1852), pp. 213-14.

33. Ibid., pp. 237-39.

34. William Sampson, *Sampson's Discourse, and Correspondence with Various Learned Jurists Upon the History of the Law*, Pishey Thompson, comp. (Washington, D.C.: Gales and Seaton, 1826), p. 37.

35. Ibid.

36. Ibid., p. 38.

37. Ibid.

38. Ibid., p. 120.

39. Ibid., p. 122.

40. William Sampson to David B. Warden, 25 April 1825, David Bailey Warden Papers, Maryland Historical Society, Baltimore, Maryland. I am indebted to Professor Maxwell Bloomfield of the Catholic University for this citation.

41. New York *American*, 16 Jan. 1824.

42. "Common Law," *Atlantic Magazine* 1 (1824): 24, 29-30. For a favorable review, see [Henry Dwight Sedgwick], "The Common Law," *North American Review* 19 (1824): 411-39.

43. William Sampson to John L. Wilson, n.d., Sampson, *Discourse*, p. 103.

44. Ibid., preface, n.p.

45. [William H. Gardiner], "Revision of the Laws of New York," *North American Review* 24 (1827): 194.

46. "Verplanck on Contracts," *United States Law Journal* 2 (1826): 91.

47. William Sampson to Charles Watts, n.d., Sampson, *Discourse*, p. 154.

48. [Edward Everett], "Code Napoléon," *North American Review* 20 (1825): 413-14.

49. William Sampson to David B. Warden, 27 April 1825, Warden Papers.

50. "Doctrine of Contracts," *American Quarterly Review* 1 (1827): 106.

51. William Sampson to Charles Watts, n.d., Sampson, *Discourse*, pp. 151, 154.

52. [John Porter], "Necessity of the Common Law," *North American Review* 27 (1828): 171.

53. Du Ponceau, *Dissertation*, pp. xiv, xxiv.

54. "Doctrine of Contracts."

55. "Verplanck on Contracts," pp. 73-74.

56. "Codification," *United States Law Intelligencer and Review* 2 (1830): 268.

57. Du Ponceau, *Dissertation,* p. 112.

58. "On the Substitution of a Written Code in Place of the Common Law," *Atlantic Magazine* 1 (1825): 295-96.

59. James Kent to Gustavus Schmidt, 31 July 1841, *Louisiana Law Journal* 1 (1841): 159.

60. [Porter], "Necessity of the Common Law," p. 170.

61. "Johnson's Reports," *United States Law Journal* 1 (1822): 208.

62. See James Kent, *Commentaries on American Law,* 4 vols. (New York: O. Halsted, 1826-30), I: 439-40.

63. [Nathanial Haven], "English Common Law Reports," *North American Review* 21 (1825): 380.

64. New York *American,* 1 April 1825.

65. "On the Substitution," p.291.

66. [Porter], "Necessity of the Common Law," p. 169.

67. [Haven], "English Common Law Reports," p. 380.

68. [Porter], "Necessity of the Common Law," p. 167.

69. "Codification," *American Quarterly Review* 6 (1829): 105.

70. *Rensselaer Glass Factory v. Reid,* 5 Cowen (New York) 586 (1825).

71. New York *American,* 16 June 1824.

72. [Porter], "Necessity of the Common Law," p. 170.

73. [Willard Phillips], "Pickering's Reports," *North American Review* 20 (1825): 182.

74. [Porter], "Necessity of the Common Law," p. 175.

75. Ibid., p. 179.

76. [Haven], "English Common Law Reports," p. 389.

77. Kent, *Commentaries,* IV: 275.

78. Roscoe Pound, "The Development of American Law," *Law Quarterly Review* 67 (1955): 50.

79. [Porter], "Necessity of the Common Law," p. 169.

80. [Haven], "English Common Law Reports," p. 382.

81. "Common Law," p. 27.

82. [Porter], "Necessity of the Common Law."

83. Du Ponceau, *Dissertation,* p. xix.

84. "Common Law," p. 30.

85. "The Civil Law," *American Jurist and Law Magazine* 2 (1829): 55.

86. Ibid.

87. "Common Law," p. 30.

88. "Codification," *American Quarterly Review,* pp. 110, 115-16.

89. [Porter], "Necessity of the Common Law," pp. 171-73.

90. New York *Statesman,* 7 April 1825.

91. [Everett], "Code Napoléon," p.413.

92. William Sampson to Thomas Cooper, n.d. p. 66. See also Cooper to Sampson. n.d., Sampson, *Discourse,* pp. 52-54, 68-72, 73-75.

93. See esp. Thomas Cooper to William Sampson, ibid., p. 53, for the original reaction of the radicals to this issue.

94. Ibid.

6

WORKING FOR CODIFIED LAW: SOUTH CAROLINA AND NEW YORK, 1820-1830

The debate over codification in the public forum was only preliminary to the actual efforts in the states aimed at securing legislative sanction to reduce the law to a codified form. Louis Real, a French jurisconsult who had helped formulate the Code Napoléon, warned the American codifiers that "[t]ill you have something done, something actually reduced to writing, it will be useless to talk of it [codification]."[1] Realizing this, the codifiers directed their energies toward getting legislative support for the reform in the states. Before 1830, their efforts resulted in two states, South Carolina and New York, taking up serious discussion of the reform. In South Carolina, they failed utterly; but in New York, a limited degree of success was enjoyed.

In many ways, South Carolina seemed the most likely to endorse codification. Few states, and certainly none among the original thirteen, rivaled the Palmetto State in the deplorable condition of its laws, particularly its statute law. In 1822, Benjamin James, a lawyer-farmer who had recently undertaken to compile the state's statutes in a single volume, claimed that the ordinances were "couched in language scarcely intelligible to the most learned in the professions as to be wholly out of reach of an ordinary capacity."[2] However, these deficiencies were greatly magnified by the fact that the statutes had never been authoritatively revised. For this reason, it will be recalled, John F. Grimke in 1790 declared that the written law of the state had become so inaccessible and uncertain as to be "wrapped up in...a profound confusion and sibylline obscurity."[3] A generation later, his son, Thomas Grimke, made a similar observation: "[I]t is often next to impossible, on account of the actual condition of our laws, to ascertain what the law is."[4] Because new laws had continued to be piled onto the heap of statutes, the situation confronting the younger Grimke was worse than his father had experienced. Compared with the other states, there were only a tiny number of privately executed compilations available in South Carolina to help relieve these burdens. For the twenty-four years following the publication of John Grimke's *Public Laws* in 1790, recently enacted law was available only through individual session law pamphlets or irregularly published collections of the pamphlets. In 1814, Joseph Brevard, one of the state's foremost jurists, published a digest of the state's statutes,[5] and Benjamin James published another in 1822.[6] No other compilations of South Carolina laws were printed for the next fourteen years. In all, only a dozen volumes of compiled state statutes were printed from the Revolution to 1836, and these were frequently defective and not generally available. By way of contrast, Virginia, in the same period, benefited from thirty-three volumes of state statutes, which included several definitive revisions. Pennsylvania, whose laws, like those of South Carolina, had never been revised, had no less than thirty-eight.[7] In both Virginia and Pennsylvania, these compilations were readily available in the 1820s, making access to all of each state's statutes relatively easy.

The availability of decisional law in South Carolina seemed to compare favorably with other states. Since 1804, reports of South Carolina's common law court decisions had been published continuously. Initially, these reports were privately compiled, but in 1824, an official reporter was appointed. By 1828, fourteen volumes of common law reports existed, which included cases from as early as 1783. Seven volumes of chancery decisions also existed, but they were published with less regularity.[8]

The nature of the judicial structure in South Carolina gave her case law a special sort of uncertainty. Since 1808, two separate appellate courts existed in the state—one for common law and one for equity. Each was jealous of its powers and prerogatives. Consequently, two bodies of law, frequently in conflict, developed. Governor John L. Wilson reflected the discontent and vexation of the state's legal profession when he declared in 1823 that the dual court system was "an anomaly in the science of legislation never before met under any circumstances." Citing many examples of conflicting discrepancies in the law as expounded by the two courts, he asserted that without some agency to give it uniformity, certainty in the law would continue to be elusive and "justice will be perverted."[9]

A variety of individuals in South Carolina complained about the inaccessibility of the content of the decisional law. In 1823, Wilson noted that there was a "great contrariety of opinion" within the profession and on the bench as to what the law of the state was.[10] A year later, expressing no less concern about the "undigested state" of the law, he called the common law a "chaotic mass" where rules of conduct were "buried beneath the unfathomable piles of folio, quarto, and octavo."[11] Benjamin James declared in 1822 that to gain a knowledge of the common law required "leisure, learning and pecuniary resources far above the means of ninety-nine hundredths of our citizens."[12] Thomas Grimke, calling the common law "confused and scattered," said that "[a]ll are deeply sensible of the exceedingly confused and imperfect state of our law; and none can be more thoroughly convinced of these truths, than the Judges and members of our profession."[13] Laymen also made complaints about the inaccessibility and uncertainty of the law from their own particular perspective.[14] The lay movement for law reform in South Carolina was not strong, however, it was the sentiments of the profession that were of real consequence.

The inaccessibility and uncertainty of South Carolina's law, especially its statutes, would have created an impossible situation in most other states. However, South Carolina had a relatively stable socio-economic structure, that placed no heavy demands on its legal system. The state could better tolerate the imperfect condition of its law, although it was quite vexatious and occasionally caused serious problems.

Some South Carolina professionals remonstrated against what they considered the unreformed content of the law. Thomas Cooper for example, spoke out in the Columbia *Telescope* against the "minute dexterity of the special pleader" and the habitual reverence for obsolete and unnecessarily difficult forms and maxims that enshrouded the law in a "veil of mystery."[15] Cooper also reflected what feeling there was in the state that favored limiting the discretionary power of the judiciary. Judge-made law, he asserted, varied "with the knowledge, talents, and temper of individual judges." It was "certain at no time [and] less now than any other period."[16] Possibly the activity for the state's equity courts, especially at the appellate level, encouraged a sensitivity to this problem. The appellate court often appeared to act arbitrarily in making new law and in overruling the decisions of the appellate court of the common law jurisdiction. Governor Wilson complained in 1824 that "[t]he courts of Equity go on to legislate at will, and the citizen is wholly unable to say by what tenure he holds anything that is his." He accused the equity courts of deciding "the same case, according to different rules, and no precedent governs them, when they choose to be untrammeled."[17]

While the content of the law and the seemingly unregulated discretion of the equity courts were considered vexatious, the undigested state of both the common and the statute law was more frequently decried as a serious abuse. The legal profession, almost to a man, complained about the condition of the statute law. Although censure of the common law on these grounds was heard less frequently, there existed enough sentiment for its reform in the state to sustain a significant effort aimed at codification.

The condition of the state's law was annually presented to the legislature by South Carolina's governors as a matter to be remedied. In 1821, Governor Thomas Bennett asked the legislature to provide for a "general revision of the laws of the state, embracing such principles of the common law as have received the sanction of judicial decision." Citing the example of the Code Napoléon, he suggested that this reform would give to each citizen "a correct knowledge of his rights and the means of maintaining them." Bennett also criticized what he considered to be an unhealthy reliance on English legal science as manifested by the tendency of the legislature to adopt English laws wholesale without careful analysis. This, he said, gave to the content of the state's laws much that was inapplicable to South Carolina's circumstances and needs.[18]

Former governors had encouraged the consolidation of the state's statutes, but this was the first time that the common law was recommended as an object of revision. The idea of codification, of course, was latent in Bennett's suggestion but not articulated as such. An active codification movement was still three years away. But certainly his encouragement of a general digest of the state's laws and his questioning of the use of English legal materials in the state reflected a growing concern with these problems. The judiciary committee of the house of representatives agreed with the governor and gave its approbation to the idea of a digest of law that would incorporate the decisions of the courts. However, the matter was not taken up by the legislature as a whole.[19]

There were several reasons for legislative inactivity in this and subsequent sessions. The length of time the legislature met annually was always short—rarely lasting more than a month. To take up a matter so momentous as this required a great deal of time and careful deliberation. The propertied, slave-holding aristocracy that dominated both houses of the legislature had neither the inclination nor the vocation for the sort of statecraft needed for such a significant reform. Even though the bulk of the work would devolve upon an individual or a small committee, it would still be necessary to examine any such compilation clause by clause to insure its completeness and accuracy. Then, there was the difficulty of finding someone of ability to undertake the task, which was universally agreed to be Herculean. The drudgery involved, coupled with the probably small stipend that might be granted by a traditionally parsimonious legislature, hardly encouraged anyone with the type of expertise needed for the task to step forward and offer his services. Furthermore, there was a certain fear, which attends all such calls for reform, that if a digest were completed and authoritatively sanctioned, it might cause greater legal uncertainty than already existed, thus disrupting existing rights and duties. Lastly, there was unadorned inertia—always a potent force in almost every legislature—that stood in the way of action.

In 1822, Governor Bennett once more attempted to impress on the legislature "the necessity and practicability of forming a Digest of the Statute Laws of this state, and the importance of condensing with these the principles of the Common Law which essentially govern the transactions of society." He informed the legislators that copies of the state's laws were not available even to the district courts and could only be found "in the libraries of the learned and affluent, where they are accessible to a very small portion of the community." Bennett suggested that the "magnitude" of labor involved in formulating any such digest had "long operated to deter us from any serious attempt." The very difficulty of the project, he declared, attested to the "necessity... of engaging in a general and extensive plan of reforming the jurisprudence of the state." He proposed the criminal law as a place to begin, as it had "the greatest possibility of success" and presented "the strongest claims of humanity."[20]

The legislature did not seriously consider Bennett's proposals, being absorbed in dealing with the repercussions of the Denmark Vesey slave conspiracy plot discovered during the previous summer. Not everyone was happy with the absence of action on the matter of law reform. "Cassius," writing in the Charleston *Courier,* complained bitterly of legislative inaction and "useless and frivolous debate." Claiming that the legislature was filled with tradition-bound old men, he called on the voters to elect a new crop of youthful lawmakers so that the needed reforms would be undertaken.[21]

The following year, a new governor, John L. Wilson, again raised the issue of law reform to the legislature. Condemning the "undigested situation both of the Common and Statute law" in the state, he asserted that "[n]one but the scientific lawyers can point out... the laws that are in force, upon many... important subjects." Even among them, "a great contrariety of opinion" existed on these matters. Calling for the appointment of an individual to digest the statute and common law of the state, he declared that the need for such a project "must be obvious to all."[22]

A bill was introduced providing for the revision of the civil and criminal law of the state that would exclude such "statutes and decisions [that] are repugnant to the spirit of our institutions and the provisions of our laws" and would "avoid as much as possible all technical words, and... make the system plain and intelligible to the common man."[23] The bill was referred to the judiciary committee in the house of representatives, where, probably to no one's surprise, it died as the session ended.

By the time the legislature met again the following year, the state had become thoroughly familiarized with the idea of codification. A significant movement aimed at reform through codification was afoot, as evidenced in a public debate over the reform. This was largely due to the efforts of Thomas Cooper, who published a series of articles on codification in the Columbia *Telescope.* In these essays, which, according to one contemporary, were written in a "clear masterly style," he "insisted upon the necessity of a written code, that the law might thenceforth be more intelligible, less burdensome, less tedious, and less expensive, by condensing, reforming, and arranging the rude and disordered mass of which is now composed."[24] Cooper also began a lengthy correspondence with William Sampson, in which both underscored the need for codification.[25] Others besides Cooper published their ideas on the matter.[26]

Cooper himself attributed the rapidly unfolding interest in codification to Sampson's *Discourse.*[27] The address and Cooper's efforts to give publicity to codification encouraged discussion of the reform in the state, but these were only catalysts that activated interest. The messages of Governors Bennett and Wilson evidenced a latent concern with the condition of the law, which was the actual foundation on which interest in codification rested. However, the nature of concern over the law and proposed reforms changed to reflect the emerging excitement about codification and its critical emphasis on the common law's inaccessibility. Whereas Governors Wilson and Bennett had previously stressed the need to digest both the statute and case law of the state, with no clear idea of the form the consolidation would take, Wilson in 1824 specifically underscored the need to codify the common law.

Wilson expressed to the legislature his "great satisfaction to see the opinion gaining strength, that the rules of the common law are susceptible of written form." The codification of the common law, he declared, "is a desideratum anxiously desired." Because knowledge of the common law was hidden in "a thousand books of black letter and Norman French," he asserted that "[n]one but professional men ever attempt to reach the fountain of the common law, and but very few of these arrive at the same source." Because of its inherent inaccessibility and uncertainty, judges, who were supposed to expound the true law, were "often at variance, and in some cases the bench is equally divided in opinion." Indeed, so deplorable did he consider the situation that Wilson suggested "it would be better at the present moment, that an act should be passed declaring the common law not in force, than to continue it longer as it now exists."[28]

To relieve the legislature of any notions that he was proposing some visionary scheme, he asserted that "[i]t is impossible to write the law of every case that may occur, and no such Utopian project ever entered into the imagination of anyone." But he also insisted that codification of the common law was practicable and he offered the Code Napoléon as evidence on this point. The laws of France, he observed, had been two thousand years in the making before they were codified. Despite their number and variety, the French codifiers were able "to educe symmetry from chaos, light from darkness, and order out of confusion." Given this fact, Wilson saw "no reason why a State like ours, where all are equal, a government in possession of every political and civil right, at peace with all the world, united in sentiment, opinion and interest, should not succeed in a similar undertaking." If the codification of South Carolina's laws were provided for, Wilson told the legislature, "it will yet be one of the most acceptable gifts to the people, which can emanate from your wisdom, and endear your memory to the latest prosperity."[29]

The legislature did not share Wilson's enthusiasm for the project. As he told William Sampson some months after the close of the session, "the judiciary committee of the house of representatives reported that it was *inexpedient* to write the common law. Why inexpedient, this enlightened committee did not deign to say." Wilson, who was no longer governor, did not despair. He still believed that the reform might be successfully promoted in the state, especially by Thomas Cooper, whose "able pen may yet do much good."[30]

The general discussion of codification continued in the state, with Cooper using the skills at his command to encourage adoption of the reform. Wilson also continued to express his views on codification and the common law, and Sampson praised him for following "the example of President Cooper, in giving publicity to your sentiments."[31] Throughout 1825, there were a growing number of articles on the topic of law reform in several South Carolina newspapers. While many of these carried the message of reform, others also dissented from the idea.[32] The opinions and sentiments expressed in these essays were typical of the debate over codes in the United States—little new was added.

When the legislature met in November 1825, the new governor, George Manning, did not call upon the legislators to undertake a general codification as his predecessor had. Rather, he stressed the need to improve the antiquated and barbaric criminal law of the state.[33] Possibly he was not then convinced of the efficacy of codification, or he might have believed that the criminal law was the place to begin the reform without raising the highly controversial issue of codification of the common law. Nevertheless, despite the absence of any urging on Manning's part to take up codification, the reformist feeling was strong enough that the house of representatives passed a resolution calling for the codification of particular portions of the law. However, the senate refused even to consider it.[34]

Manning clearly advocated codification in his message to the legislature the following year. Expressing the sentiments of a true codifier, he told the legislature that

> the time is...at hand...when the advances of improving society, and the accumulated wisdom and knowledge of man, will give a resistless call for such a digest [or] code...as will bring laws into such a form that contradictions, fictions and many unintelligible technicalities, may be superceded by rules of written reason and plain common sense, that they may be more easily understood and more happily adopted to the essentially varied condition of human society at the present day.

He criticized the English content of the law, saying that much of it was formed "when the human mind was yet in the dark," and these antiquated rules were still in force "with all their unsuitableness and encumbrances about them." Codification was necessary for other reasons. "All the elements of moral and natural justice," he said, "are...diffused through a thousand gloomy unmanageable volumes." In "this bookmaking age," it was necessary that "human laws...be reduced to their essences" if the law were to be accessible and certain. As it then stood, the bench and the bar were "very often...divided in opinion" as to what the law actually was.[35]

Manning, who was not a lawyer, blamed the legal fraternity for the sorry condition of the law. "The array of the Bench and Bar," he declared,

> among whom there is power, have stood up against it [legal reform]; the veneration of forms and laws, to which they have been... long instructed; and unreasonable fear that the spirit of innovation may tear down an antiquated and valued structure, and long cherished feelings not unlike those which arise from beholding some venerable monument of ancient grandeur, which has endured for ages, have kept back reforms and valued improvements.[36]

On the day following Manning's message, the legislature appointed a special joint committee, chaired by Hugh Swinton Legare, a champion of common law orthodoxy, to examine the issue of codification.[37] His chairmanship guaranteed something less than an enthusiastic report favoring codification.

The committee's report strongly recommended reformation of the statute law of the state, but registered strong disapproval of any codification of the common law. While stating that it was not insensible to the desirability of enlightening citizens on their rights and duties, the committee recommended that the legislature should "not... undertake for the present, a work so extensive, so difficult, and (notwithstanding the many plausible reasons that are urged in its favor) of such questionability." The report further cautioned the legislature, saying that "so great an undertaking ought not to be ventured upon but upon the weightiest reasons, and after much reflection and inquiry."[38]

The committee did express a desire that the statutes be radically revised, noting that "it is expedient to reduce the Statute Law to a form of a Code, with such additions and improvements as may arise out of the Common Law, the decisions of our Courts and legal experience, so far as these are concerned with or incident to the Statute Law." Such a codification, they declared, "cannot fail to do much good." Obviously, the codification movement had made a significant impact. Of course, the statute law, being already written in the general form that it would be in a code, seemed especially to lend itself to reform without the perils involved in the codification of the common law. However, the matter was not free of risk. The committee urged that great caution be taken in restating the acts in a simpler and more direct form lest, "by multiplying new expressions, we multiply doubts, and criticisms and increase the uncertainty which we wish to remove."[39] The report was cautious and fell far short of what the codifiers wished, but it was the strongest statement ever made by a committee of the South Carolina legislature on the matter of law reform.[40]

The report was taken up in the senate, where John Wilson urged that the resolution submitted by the joint committee be expanded to include the common law. Referring to the importance of the common law in the legal life of the state, Wilson told that body that "[i]t would be an idle, if not an useless act of legislation to reduce the shadow to form and symmetry, when the substance remained in all its present deformity."[41] The upper house, in the past, had been an unmovable obstacle to law reform. But now, spurred on by two irrepressible codifiers, Wilson and Thomas Grimke, it warmed to the idea. On the issue of "whether codification should be extended to the Common Law, or be confined to the statute law only," a majority of the senators voted in favor of the extension. The chance of achieving the same result in the house seemed less likely, a fact that contemporaries well realized.[42]

Reacting to the senate vote, Legare offered a simple resolution in the house: "That it is inexpedient to attempt the codification of the common law." After "considerable debate," the resolution carried almost unanimously, and the house went on to approve the original resolution submitted by the special joint committee. It called for the appointment of two commissioners "to test the practicability" of the codification of the statutes by codifying certain portions of them for the consideration of the legislature at its next session.[43] Unfortunately, the two houses could not agree on either plan and refused to compromise.[44] As a result, nothing was done.

"No Quack," writing in the Charleston *Courier,* and reflecting the sentiments of common law orthodoxy, commended the house for arresting "the wild scheme of codifying our Common law." He called "half learned" those who "imagine they can make *General Rules,* which ordinary men will easily apply to every case." Expressing his fear of the reform, he declared it would "set afloat all that is stable; and after amusing the people with hopes, leave them prey to an endless host of Quack Lawyers. Quackery in law produces the same effect as in medicine; it makes work for those who understand the business."[45]

In the months before the meeting of the next legislature, codifiers were busy promoting the reform. Their partial success in 1826 had given them the scent of victory, and they pursued it avidly. Thomas Grimke tried to convince the legal profession to take up the banner of reform in a speech to the South Carolina Bar Association in March 1827. In order to reach a great audience, the address was printed.[46] His fellow codifier, John Wilson, published a speech he had made before the senate on the reform together with a sample code.[47] And a senate committee appointed under Grimke's chairmanship to examine the reform in greater depth before the meeting of the next legislature took pains to insure that its report would have the widest possible circulation by taking the almost unprecedented step of having it reprinted.[48]

In his address to the legislature in 1827, the new governor, John Taylor, merely observed that the issue of codification was still pending. The senate went through Grimke's "voluminous and interesting report," which was largely a rewrite of his speech before the bar association. However, both the senate and the house failed to act on the reform. Subsequent legislatures followed suit, and the South Carolina codification movement died a quiet death. The debate over codes did continue, but in a muted form.[49] It was some years before South Carolina took up any sort of law reform. Then, it was a limited and cautious effort—the publication of the state's statutes at large beginning in 1836. On the very eve of the Civil War, the state did undertake a codification of its laws, but it was limited to its statutes, and, in the end, the code was rejected. It was not until 1872, under a Republican reconstruction government, that South Carolina's statutes were authoritatively revised and codified.

In examining the reasons for the failure of the codification movement in South Carolina, one might first suggest that the legislative struggle of 1826 demonstrated the intransigent opposition of the orthodox common lawyers to the scheme. Further action by legislators who, aside from men like John Wilson and Thomas Grimke, were not totally committed to the reform seemed pointless. Perhaps contemporary events accounted for the sudden demise of the reform. In 1825, John Wilson wrote to William Sampson, suggesting that "no time can be more propitious than the present for codification." He remarked that this was an especially stable period in which there was little that could distract or harmfully influence any law reform effort.[50] If this were the sort of environment required to undertake codification successfully, conditions changed as the end of the decade approached. The national economic policy favoring a protective tariff seemed, to South Carolinians, to have depressed their economy and threatened the social system of the state. Concern over these problems became focused on the nullification struggle beginning in 1828. The state became totally consumed by its constitutional test of wills with the national government. The state's three leading codifiers—Wilson, Cooper, and Grimke—were completely caught up in the crisis.[51] Certainly this sort of changed environment discouraged any talk of law reform and overshadowed domestic affairs almost entirely. As we have seen, it was not for some years after the resolution of the nullification crisis that the state did something about the really critical problem of inaccessible law.

But something still more fundamental stood in the way of codification in the state. It was suggested at the outset that given the unreformed state of the law in South Carolina, it was a likely candidate for a law reform movement. Paradoxically, the factors that created that situation probably obviated the success of any law-reform effort as radical as codification. Simply put, the state had absolutely no tradition of legal reform, which makes the codification movement appear as an aberration in its legal history. Indeed, the state had no reform tradition whatsoever. It was the most conservative of all the states, and its lawyers embodied its traditionalism. The legal fraternity has always been reluctant to undertake reform. But, as Donald Senese, a careful student of the South Carolina legal mind in the antebellum years, has pointed out, Carolina practitioners were more hostile to change than most. They saw law as a vehicle to preserve the status quo, and looked upon its reform as something potentially disruptive. "Each time reform was urged, the South Carolina lawyer took recourse to a plea to allow society to progress as a slowly developing organism, to oppose rapid unreflective change, and to resist anything which would threaten the stability of society."[52]

Contemporaries assessed the situation similarly. Governor Manning claimed that lawyers prevented reform because they harbored an "unreasonable fear that the spirit of innovation may tear down an antiquated and valued structure."[53] John Wilson also blamed a conservative legal profession for the failure of reform in the state. He claimed that lawyers were "adverse to reform" and used their "prevailing influence" in the legislature to quash it.[54]

The conservatism of the state and of its legal profession in matters of reform was borne out of in nearly every facet of the political-legal life of South Carolina. While the rest of the southern Atlantic states engaged in constitutional reform in the early antebellum years, South Carolina continued to live under an archaic constitution written in 1790. The governor was elected by the legislature. Presidential electors were selected by the same body, which bore little relationship to the population patterns of the state. Imprisonment for debt existed in the state until 1868, about thirty years after it had been abolished elsewhere in the country. It took a reconstruction government—the very antithesis of the antebellum regime—to do away with that abuse. Similarly, the criminal law, marked by the barbarisms of its English parent, remained unreformed until after the Civil War. Only with great reluctance and hesitation did the state undertake to rectify the impossible situation of its dual court system. With such a record of reaction, South Carolina could have hardly been expected to set about codifying its laws.

The socio-economic environment that produced a codification movement in New York was markedly different from that in South Carolina. Whereas South Carolina exhibited a relatively stable society and undiversified economy that experienced only indifferent growth after 1820, New York presented a picture of progressive activity, growth, and change. The country as a whole was undergoing significant development in nearly every phase of life in the early nineteenth century, but it was especially pronounced in the Empire State. The population of the state nearly tripled between 1800 and 1820. No other state, except those emerging in the West, experienced a greater rate of growth.[55] Other indices of development were equally impressive. In 1800, New York banks had a capitalization of $3.42 million. By 1821, the figure had ballooned to $21.1 million. The combined value of the import-export trade of New York was $8 million in 1791. Thirty years later, the figure was $36 million, and, by 1825, the state had captured over half of the nation's import trade. These figures suggest that by the 1820s, New York was becoming the pre-eminent commercial center of the nation, and the completion of the Erie Canal in 1825 happily sealed that fate. Of course, commercial New York rested on a solid rural foundation. Comparable growth was experienced there, too. Between 1784 and 1821, the amount of improved farm land in the state increased from about one million acres to five and one-half millions.[56]

This spectacular growth and development placed heavy demands on the legal system and manifested itself in the equally impressive expansion of the size of the objective body of the law. The annual session law pamphlets of New York were rarely less than three hundred pages in length, with some exceeding five hundred pages during the first three decades of the nineteenth century.[57] Each contained a dizzying multitude of of separate acts. Following one especially productive session, the New York *American* noted that it had received "a list of laws, 343!!! in number, passed" during the recent session of the legislature.[58] No state had a comparable outpouring of written law. In this same period, by way of comparison, the South Carolina legislature produced only about 125 pages of law annually.[59]

The enlarged size of the statute book, together with the knowledge that it contained much "useless rubbish," seemingly necessitated relatively frequent revisions. Since the Revolution, New York had undertaken no less than three revisions at intervals of about a dozen years.[60] New York had apparently developed a genuine reform tradition in dealing with its statute law. Only Virginia had made a more concerted effort to insure the accessibility and certainty of its written law.

Even with these almost regular revisions, printers had little trouble selling privately done compilations of the state's session laws. By 1828, nineteen such volumes had been published, some in several editions. With one exception, each was a massive book exceeding five hundred pages, with some approaching a thousand pages. It was only with such tools that the New York attorney could keep abreast of the statutory growth and changes in his state.[61] But the very mass of the law stymied its easy accessibility and certainty. As the idea of codification became popular, New Yorkers began to see its adaptability to their situation.

The growth of the objective body of the decisional law of New York rivaled its statutory counterpart in its own way. Between 1799 and 1823, thirty different volumes of New York common law and seven of chancery decisions had been printed.[62] In no other state was a comparable repository of native case law available.

The advent of written reports, as we know, did not guarantee legal certainty. Occasional problems arose from the extrinsic properties of the reports themselves. One New York lawyer, for example, believed he had won a case, only to find, on appeal, that the decision on which he had based his argument was incorrectly printed as a majority opinion when, in fact, it was the dissent.[63] More important than typographical errors was the uncertainty inherent in the common law. It was through the rule of *stare decisis* that a necessary certainty was supposed to be brought to the common law. Once a decision had been made, in James Kent's words, "the community have a right to regard it as a just declaration or exposition of the law, and to regulate their actions and their contracts by it." If these decisions were "lightly disregarded we should disturb and unsettle the great landmarks of property." But Kent also urged that when settled law appeared to be in error, it should be overthrown "without fear, and reversed without reluctance, rather than to have the character of our law impaired" by its perpetuation.[64] Kent's remarks pointed up the basic problem in common law methodology—the difficulty of balancing continuity with the need for change.

The common law could not come to a doctrinal standstill if legal needs were to be met, but change in the law, however necessary, brought perplexity and doubt.

The developmental state of the law only exaggerated this basic problem. Kent once observed that "[e]ven a series of decisions are not always conclusive evidence of what is law; and the revision of a decision very often resolves itself into a mere question of expediency."[65] It seems likely that he was referring to the necessary process of adopting English law to American circumstances. No area of law could be considered settled until this process were completed. However, the courts in New York followed anything but a consistent pattern of legal development. In some cases, courts dictated adherence to a well-established English rule, while in others, the judges abandoned what had been considered a secure line of decisions. What developed, according to a scholar who studied the decisional patterns of the New York courts in the early nineteenth century, was "a crazy quilt patchwork as far as certainty is concerned."[66]

The rapid pace of socio-economic development in the state heightened such dilemmas for the New York jurists, who were on the cutting edge of American legal development. Because other states frequently used their decisions as evidence of what American law should be, New York reports were among the most respected authorities throughout the country. But to the New York attorney faced with the problem of determining what the law was in a given case, the reports often gave murky answers, and their very numbers only added to the problem. Increasingly, codification was proposed as a remedy for the problem of inaccessibility and uncertainty encountered in dealing with New York's common law.

It has been suggested that the New York courts followed an uneven path in moving away from the substantive content of the inherited legal system. Some were not at all happy with the Americanization that was taking place. One law writer no doubt had New York especially in mind when he declared that it would be "unmanly squeamish to pretend that the jurisprudence of the northern states is not an unhopeful condition." The case law of "every state north of Pennsylvania will show that there has been a gradual departure from the old highways of the common law; a disposition to decide on principles of natural equity and imaginary convenience, rather than to pre-established rules and legal conformity."[67] Not everyone made the same analysis. Men like William Sampson were also little encouraged by the doctrinal developments of the state, but for different reasons. Instead of a free-wheeling abandonment of established rules of English jurisprudence, he and others saw an unhealthy aherence to what they considered obsolete and unnecessarily abstruse English law. Consequently, they desired sweeping changes aimed at simplying the law and adapting it to local circumstances.

Sampson, in his *Anniversary Discourse,* was not the first to suggest the need for legal change in New York. Two years before, Henry Dwight Sedgwick had published *English Practice,* a biting critique of English law, in an effort to encourage reform.[68] Sampson himself had long suggested the need to Americanize the English legal tradition in the state.[69] Indeed, the notion that the law required doctrinal regeneration had been an element, varying in intensity, in the American legal system since the Revolution. But in New York in the 1820s, the felt need for legal reform was especially strong among both lawyers and laymen, and codification seemed to be a hopeful avenue by which to approach it.

The operation of the courts also nourished a codification movement in the state. Complaints directed against the judiciary arose from the problems already discussed. For example, the frequent uncertainty encountered in the common law was taken as evidence of the courts' unwarranted use of discretionary powers. A more widespread, and probably more sharply felt, abuse was the lengthy delays in the administration of justice experienced in the superior courts of the state. Laymen often grumbled about the slow workings of the law, but, in New York, the complaint was very strong among lawyers, judges, and laymen alike.

The problem arose from the fact that the work of the courts increased as the population multiplied and as the society became more complex, whereas their institutional machinery and practice remained the same. During the decade between 1811 and 1821, the number of cases doubled, and, while the court terms were extended, onerous delays were still incurred. The state constitutional convention of 1821 had been called, in part, to remedy this situation by revamping the judicial structure, but this did little good.

Among the obstacles impeding the speedy resolution of legal disputes was the highly complex form of English procedural law used by the courts.[70] The judges themselves suggested that practice needed simplification to speed their work. In a report to the legislature on the problem of delays in the law, they claimed that they had "endeavored to simplify whatever appeared most intricate, and to supercede whatever appeared unnecessary" in their practice but that it was not in their power to work the vital reform needed. Only the legislature, the judges declared, could abolish "unnecessary and useless forms" and bring "simplicity and precision" to the practice of their courts.[71]

Given the nature of the problem and the inclination toward legislative intervention, codification was a logical vehicle of reform. At least one orthodox practitioner suggested that unless some sort of moderate reform were undertaken, the "anti-common lawyers," as he referred to codifiers, "will soon begin to find in the people ready listeners to their declamations and we shall have to submit to a course of their experiments."[72]

New York laymen hardly needed lawyers to encourage them to take up the banner of law reform in the 1820s. Unassisted by the "declamations" of the law craft, laymen developed a powerful enthusiasm for law reform that eventually became focused on codification. Their complaints centered on the delays in the courts and the high costs of litigation. By mid-decade, "Examiner," in the New York *American,* remarked that "so loud have been their [laymen's] complaints of expense and delay of justice that it is probable our legislature will seriously turn their attention to it."[73]

Demands for cheap and speedy justice, so typical of lay law reformers, reflected their interests as consumers within the legal system. Their perception of certain purveyors of legal services—the pettifoggers—as purposefully obstructing the attainment of these ends, was no less representative. The New York *National Advocate,* a leading vehicle of lay criticism of the legal system, complained of "those licensed pests called Pettifoggers" who, like the litigation they handled, were "set at slow time."[74] Some lawyers who preyed on the pockets of the public, another complained, had been admitted to the bar even though they "could not stand before even a beetle headed village justice of the peace!!"[75]

Lay criticism reached judges as well as practitioners. While individual jurists such as Chancellor Kent were accorded some deference, the whole judiciary was not revered in New York in the 1820s. Popular odium for the bench was a product of its being the centerpiece of a legal system thought to be abuse-ridden. Furthermore, judges were perennial opponents to legal reform. "The lights of the law," one lay observer groused, "will have no change."[76] This was taken as evidence that the judges personally profited from the defects of the legal system.[77]

While laymen grumbled a good deal about the law craft, they also had complaints with the law itself and focused their energies on its improvement. It was, after all, the tool with which the legal fraternity exacted their heavy toll from the pockets of the laymen. To remedy this situation, one group of laymen suggested, in a petition to the New York legislature, that the overly technical and highly complex system of laws "copied from English practice" be eliminated and replaced by laws "founded on the plain and simple principles of common sense." The laws, especially those relating to procedure, as they now stood, the petitioners said, "tend to the accumulation of costs, and the discredit of law and its practitioners."[78] Once the law were bottomed in unadorned common sense, the layman would no longer have to fear for the contents of his pocketbook. As one put it, "[m]ake the law plain and the lawyer must be honest and the client safe."[79] If this were done, another declared, it "would add more to the character, dignity and affluence of the republic, than all the canals that ever flooded over the pillow of De Witt Clinton."[80] A good number of lawyers gave credence to such lay complaints, even acknowledging that lawyers used the defects of the legal system for their own profit.[81] While they probably would have disagreed with any notions that the law could be made simple enough for the average layman to understand completely, lawyers believed that its gross absurdities and artificial technicalities should be removed and the law rendered worthy of the layman's respect and esteem. Codification naturally had a great appeal to these lay reformers. One called it "the *only* reformation worth a moments regard."[82] Lawyers, who essentially determined the course of legal reform, were not deaf to lay demands.

Discontent with the legal system in New York among practitioners and laymen was translated by Sampson's *Discourse* and the resulting debate over codified law into a demand for legal reform through codification. Almost immediately after the address was given and printed, an intense discussion of reform was taken up.[83] The debate continued undiminished for the next several years. In fact, no other state experienced a more thorough public inquiry into codification and codified law.

The codifiers were keenly aware of the need to give publicity to their views in order to encourage the reform, and they pursued this work enthusiastically.[84] Not only was the *Anniversary Discourse* printed in an effort to reach the widest possible audience, but correspondence between Sampson and Cooper and other individuals on codification, as well as Cooper's essays from the Columbia *Telescope,* were reprinted in several New York papers and periodicals. Certain members of the New York bar who favored the reform induced the *New York Review and Atheneum Magazine* to reprint letters of Charles Watts, a former New York lawyer then practicing in Louisiana.[85] A zealous convert to codified law, Watts wrote letters that seemed potently persuasive, coming, as they did, from a man who had practical professional experience with both legal systems.

Perceiving codification as a danger to the legal order, orthodox common lawyers worked to resist the reform with no less enthusiasm. The fact that they did not take the reform movement lightly is an indication of its apparent strength. Their method of attack was the same as that employed by the codifiers: review articles, letters, and essays. They, however, lacked a figure like Sampson as a focus of energy. Nonetheless, the anti-codifiers benefited from having at least the passive support of a majority of the profession, including most of its leading members.

Unlike in South Carolina, the general codification of the law never came to a clear legislative test in New York in these early years. Rather, codification came to New York only obliquely, through statutory revision. The body of law that emerged from the revision process, known as the Revised Statutes, resulted in a true, if limited, codification of New York law, the first in any common law jurisdication. Moreover, the Revised Statutes were a clear consequence of the codification movement, manifesting every active element of that reform effort, including the partial codification of selected rules of the common law. It is difficult to say why the New York codifiers did not push the matter of wholesale codification to a decision. Possibly they realized that the powerful opposition within the profession might result in failure, which could do irreparable damage to the codification movement. New York was usually in the forefront of legal development in the United States, and other states frequently followed its lead. If the reform were clearly rejected there, its impact would transcend the state's boundaries. It may thus have appeared more practicable to go slowly. A successful codification of the statute law could be used as a springboard to more comprehensive reform. Ironically, however, the very success of the Revised Statutes had the effect of throttling the codification movement, at least for the time being.

The attempt to secure a new authoritative revision of New York's statutes had begun before the codification movement emerged. Initially, it promised to be little more than a repetition of the several revisions that had been accomplished earlier. Revision seemed necessary, not only to deal with the problem of an overgrown statute book, but also to effectuate a reconciliation between the statute law and the newly written state constitution. Numerous changes in the state's institutional and electoral structures had been made by the constitution of 1822. The new provisions either conflicted with existing statutes or required statutory implementation. The need for revision was widely recognized. As one law writer remarked, "eminent men throughout the state" agreed on the necessity of the project.[86] Largely because revisions had been frequently undertaken in the past, there was no real opposition in principle to the reform.

Governor Joseph C. Yates officially brought the matter to the attention of the legislature in January 1823. The lawmakers, however, took no action. The only laws of importance it passed were those "absolutely required by the new constitution." Jabez D. Hammond, an astute contemporary observer, suggested that legislative inaction resulted from the fact that the legislature "possessed little talent."[87]

A year later, Yates renewed his efforts to encourage legislative action on statutory revision. He declared that the reform had "become indispensably necessary." This was "verified by daily experience," which had shown "that many of our statutes are rendered inapplicable to the existing state of things under the constitution recently adopted." Furthermore, "principles contained in different statutes applicable to the same subject, are distributed in so many volumes as to make an investigation difficult and extremely laborious, almost without the reach of the citizen unless he is a professional character."[88] The *National Advocate,* always a consistent proponent of legal reform, voiced its strong approval, saying that a revision that would put the law "in a shape accessible to everyone... would be a public benefit."[89]

The legislature, however, continued to put off the matter of revision. This time, the problem was not a lack of ability; rather, matters purely political consumed the lawmakers' interest. Not only were the legislators themselves facing reelection, but a new governor and a new president were to be selected. Involved in all the Machiavellian machinations and reflecting all the acrimony that only the divisive political environment of New York in the 1820s could produce, the legislature, dominated by the Albany Regency, Hammond suggested, "could never find the time to attend to" law reform "until after the election in November." Then, just before their adjournment, realizing the necessity of the revision and "[n]ot wishing to leave the appointment of the revisors to their successors," the legislators appointed James Kent, Erastus Root, and Benjamin Butler as revisors.[90] Kent declined the honor and was replaced by John Duer, who had studied law in the office of Alexander Hamilton and who was one of the finest attorneys in the state. While political considerations no doubt played a role in his appointment, he was probably named more for his talent than for his politics. Butler's and Root's commissions were largely political. The former was a young professional associate of Martin Van Buren and a rising star in the Albany Regency, and the latter, a veteran party leader, had recently been defeated as Regency candidate for lieutenant governor. However, aside from this initial input, the interplay of political forces and political interference was conspicuously absent from the entire revision process.

The legislature assumed that the revision would be no different from those that had preceded it. The laws would be collected, obsolete and private acts would be expunged, and statutes relating to the same topic would be collected in their original form under separate heads. Additionally, the revisors were given special powers to reconcile the statute law with the new constitution. They were authorized to "alter the phraseology of the laws of this state, passed prior to the adoption of the present constitution, which may require such alterations *by reason of provisions of the said constitution, or by reason of any acts of the legislature* which have been passed *in consequence of the adoption of the said constitution.*"[91] These were more than ample powers to undertake the traditional mode of revision, and Root proceeded to work on the assumption that this was what would be done.

As matters turned out, however, Root's work went for naught. The appointment of the revisors came amidst growing demands for more fundamental reform of the law, with attendant speculation about the feasibility of codification as a mode for effecting the needed amelioration. De Witt Clinton, newly elected as governor and always sensitive to the public's mood, reflected this increased interest in law reform through codification in his message to the legislature in 1825. Besides suggesting several substantive changes in the rule of the common law that would free litigants from "the expense and delay, which are now subjects of complaint," he declared that "the whole system of our jurisprudence requires revisal, arrangement and correction." This could best be done, he argued, by formulating "[a] complete code founded on the salutary principles of the common law, adopted to the interests of commerce and the useful arts, the state of society and the nature of our government, and embracing those improvements which are enjoined by enlightened experience." Such a code, Clinton continued, "would be a public blessing," for "[i]t would free our laws from uncertainty, elevate a liberal and honorable profession, and utterly destroy judicial legislation, which is fundamentally at war with the genius of republican government."[92]

The legislature was not about to act precipitously on the matter of codification. If there were a growing sympathy favoring the reform, there was also a powerfully influential sentiment opposing it, both in and out of the legislature. Nonetheless, many lawmakers were convinced of the need for legal change, and the widespread attention given to legal reform in the state merely hardened their conviction that something should be done. Possibly the legislators believed that the recently authorized revision could be used as a vehicle for more thorough reform than had been originally intended, when they formally asked the revisors, soon after the session began: "What alterations, if any, may be necessary in the law [commissioning the revision] to attain more effectively the objects for which it was enacted."[93]

At least two of the revisors, Butler and Duer, were already sensitive to the need for more comprehensive legal reform. Instead of plunging ahead with their work as Root had, they believed it was necessary to give "full and deliberate" consideration to how they should best proceed. Consequently, shortly after Duer's appointment, he and Butler began a probing correspondence in which they exchanged ideas about "the mode of performing the revision."[94] They were not discussing the division of labor among the revisors, but rather how they should shape the form and content of the statute law to meet best the legal needs of the state. Their reply to the query of the legislature, which was made without Root's sanction, demonstrated that they had perceived a number of substantial defects in the legal system that they believed could be reformed and that they had not been deaf to the continuing debate in the state over codification.

Butler and Duer expressed their matured conviction to the legislature that the mandate given the revisors was insufficient to attain the best possible results. If they were to have optimum effectiveness, Butler and Duer declared, they should have the power to "make such alterations in style, in length and structure of sentences, and in arrangements of sections, as will render the statutes more concise, perspicuous, and intelligible." They continued expressing this belief that "our law should be comprised under appropriate titles; and that these titles should be classified in their natural order; and more especially... various provisions of each statute should be arranged in the clearest most scientific method, which the nature of the subject will permit."[95] In short, they wanted authorization to codify the statute law of the state, although they assiduously refrained from using the term "codification." While substantive reform was not an important part of their suggestions, it was latent in their desire to rewrite the statutes. Such reform would take on increasing importance as their work progressed.

The two revisors suggested a number of advantages that would accrue from their proposed revision. It would ease acquisition of knowledge of the law by reducing the size of the statute book by half. The law would also be rendered more intelligible and certain by eliminating "the uncertainties and obscurities arising from the long involved sentences, and from... intricate and obsolete diction." Once the law were systematically arranged, the necessity for future revisions would be superseded, as changes in the statutes could be easily inserted in their proper place by the legislature. Lastly, once completed, the proposed revision would set an example for other states to follow. To "more fully indicate the nature and advantages" of what they were suggesting, the revisors included a sample revision relating to the court of errors and the court of chancery.[96]

Realizing that the charge of "rash and unnecessary innovation" would be directed against their proposal, Butler and Duer insisted that "a close examination of our whole scheme" would show that they proposed "to do nothing more than to free our written code from the prolixities, uncertainties, and confusion incident to the style and manner in which it has hitherto been framed, and to apply... those principles of an enlarged philosophy, which now obtain in every other department of knowledge." They did not want to cause disruption in the legal order; they only hoped to make it more certain and secure. The two revisors concluded their message to the legislature by stating that the period had arrived "in which an effort of this sort is imperiously demanded, by a just regard to the interests and honor of the first State of the American Republic."[97]

New Yorkers inclined to law reform greeted the proposal with interest and enthusiasm. Soon, the *National Advocate* was calling the proposed revision a "very interesting and important subject."[98] The *Advocate,* always a bellwether of the lay reformers' position, expressed the belief that if Duer and Butler were given the "proper encouragements," they would rescue the law from "all the affected mystery and actual nonsense with which it has been shrouded by the interest of empires and the lapse of ages." Once completed, such a revision would lift the legal profession "from the imputation of craft and fraud." With grandiose expectation, the *Advocate* predicted that revision would be "followed by a complete *American Code* in which we trust the regenerated nations of the southern part of our hemisphere will join us forming indeed a sacred and holy alliance of wisdom, liberty, and virtue, the sure ground of a hearty permanent conjunction."[99] It is doubtful that the two revisors and their fellow professionals who supported their proposal anticipated a similar result.

A good number of practitioners expressed strong reservations to the plan or opposed it outright. The crux of their opposition focused on the revisors' request that they be authorized to rewrite the statutes and alter the style and phraseology as they believed necessary. If granted, it was claimed, such power would make the revisors legislators, and the result would be "an entire, complete and radical change in our laws," in which "all the ancient landmarks would be, if not permanently, at least temporarily removed."[100] The judicial construction of the statutes that the revisors were proposing to reformulate was based on the way they were originally written. Many orthodox common lawyers feared that modifying the phraseology could lead to new constructions that would threaten established property rights.[101] Of course, fear was at the heart of the orthodox critique of codification.

The *National Advocate* believed that this concern was misplaced. It had no desire to maintain the law in its present form because "legal delays and uncertainties [are] incident to the present *verbal condition* of the law." The *Advocate* wondered how anyone could believe "that a regular classification, ably and clearly condensed, of all the matter which whether various or anomalous, is now spread and scattered as if by the winds, over several volumes, would be of no benefit to the state."[102] The *Advocate* saw an ulterior motive behind professional oppositions to the proposed revision. "[O]ur professional friends," it declared, "have taken alarm...with an eye to private pickings." The newspaper added, with characteristic derision, "[w]e know that a reduction of legal phrases, or clear exposition of the principles and objects of the law, would create amongst the fraternity a sort of dead reckoning which, with their habits, they could not very readily make up."[103] The charge that the revisors would be made legislators, if their proposal were accepted, was "a miserable quibble." Not only would the revision be done "in full light of the public interest," the *Advocate* declared, but the completed revision would have to be submitted to the legislature for approval, and there the people would have the final say.[104] It seems fair to assume that many practitioners did not look upon public inspection as the proper sort of safeguard against the problems they envisioned arising out of the revision.

Debate in the legislature reflected the debate in the public press, but an act giving the revisors powers along the lines they had requested was passed by less than commanding majorities. For a time, approval was threatened by the problem of what to do with Erastus Root, who had originally been appointed as one of the revisors, but who was neither inclined to undertake extended revision nor to step down quietly. In the end, the legislature pensioned him off for the few months' work he had done, with a thousand dollars—the amount that was to be paid to each revisor for the whole project.[105] Henry Wheaton, the reporter of the United States Supreme Court, was appointed in his place. He, too, resigned a year later for personal reasons and was replaced by John C. Spencer, a young New York attorney.

The new act gave the revisors broad authority to undertake their work. They were empowered to: (1) collect and reduce into one act the different acts and parts of acts relating to the same subject that they believed proper to consolidate; (2) distribute the acts to be consolidated under titles, divisions, and sections; (3) omit all legislation that was repealed, had expired, or was repugnant to the constitution; (4) suggest to the legislature contradictions, omissions, and imperfections in the law and the mode in which they might be ameliorated; (5) designate acts or parts of acts that ought to be repealed; (6) recommend new acts or parts of acts that they believed necessary; (7) complete the revision in all other respects in a manner that they should "deem most proper, to render the statutes more plain and easy to be understood." They were also expressly instructed to make no changes "in the phraseology or distribution of the sections of any statutes, that have been the subject of judicial decision, by which the construction of the statute, as established by such decisions, should be affected or impaired."[106]

In effect, the revisors were given nearly plenary powers to redesign, reformulate, and redevelop the whole body of New York statute law, which had been a century and a half in the making, to say nothing of received British statutes of a longer lineage. The only limitations on their work were the requirements relating to judicial construction and, of course, the need for final legislative sanction.

Such a mandate was totally without precedent in Anglo-American legal history. It was well that Kent declined appointment as a revisor, or this new mode of revision would probably never have come before the legislature.

What could induce a legislature largely dominated by lawyers to approve such a sweeping scheme of legal reform? No simple answer can be given, as a variety of considerations resulted in the legislature's approval. First, New York had a tradition of law reform that stressed the need to make the law more practically accessible and, concomitantly, more certain. To be sure, the proposed revision went far beyond the bounds of that tradition, but, nevertheless, it was a helpful precondition in that it was not necessary to overcome the opposition to any sort of revision that existed in some states. More importantly, the legislators accepted much of their constitutents' sense of legal abuse. The statutes book had grown almost uncontrollably large. The statutes themselves were frequently abstruse, obscure, and unnecessarily complex. These defects were at least partly responsible for the real delays in justice of which both practitioner and layman complained. Certainly there was pressure on the legislature to do something to correct these deficiencies. Inaction could only bring demands for more radical reform. The proposed revision could be cited as evidence that the legislature was moving ahead on the matter of law reform and might tranquilize the demands for legal change. The legislature certainly used the revision for this purpose once it was under way.[107]

The codification movement in New York also had an impact on the approval of the project in a more positive way. In fact, the revision must be seen as part of that movement. The reform effort, with all its inherent iconoclasm, had encouraged a fundamental analysis of the form and content of the law that went beyond traditional premises. Time-honored assumptions were being tested, and men were looking for new solutions to legal problems. The proposed revision, breaking from the traditional mold, reflected, not only the overall goals of that movement, but also its specific methods.

For those not quite convinced of the efficacy of codification, the proposed revision may have appeared as a necessary experiment by which the practicability of a more thoroughgoing reform could be judged without the dangers inherent in the codification of the common law. Even some opposed to codification might have supported the new mode of revision. Most of their strictures against the reform concerned the codification of the common law. And there were safeguards in the revision process, as the revisors were not to tamper with statutes that might upset established judicial constructions. Furthermore, the legislature had to give its final approval.

The state's leading codifier, William Sampson, greeted the revision with something less than total enthusiasm. He considered it an "awkward expedient" because he believed it was not possible "to run any clear dividing line between the common law and statute law, so as to amend the one and leave the other untouched." He suggested that "the impossibility of this will be so apparent" that no matter how well the revision will be done, "it will have to be begun again from necessity." However, Sampson believed that "it may lead in the end to a more perfect endeavor, and to the eventual purifying of our laws."[108]

The revision was being watched outside the state with great interest. Peter S. Du Ponceau saw great potential in the revision, even though he was not a codifier. He expressed his belief that "much may be expected from it."[109] Not everyone was as enthusiastic, however. William H. Gardiner, in a thoughtful review of the revisors' first report to the legislature a year after they received their new commission, found "room for fear" in the project. He suggested

> that in the general methodizing and amending even the statute law alone, too much of substance may be sacrificed to mere method; or rather too much new law may be suddenly introduced, from the great temptation of filling out a noble outline and creating a perfect system; in short there is some reason to fear lest systematizing should degenerate into absolute codification.

To the revisors, he urged moderation and suggested they take counsel from Matthew Hale, who once declared that "the business of amendment or alteration of the law is choice and tender business" that should be undertaken "very cautiously and warily."[110]

The first report of the revisors, tendered to the legislature in March 1826, showed that they had indeed pursued their mandate zealously. Throughout the report, they expressed a concern for the totality of the statute law in the revision, focusing, not only on the need to create the best possible external arrangement for the whole, but also on what they considered to be a mandatory requirement of the revision—that it have internal integrity. Emphasis on these matters was grounded in the revisors' desire to reformulate the law in such a way as to create optimum accessibility and completeness. This stress on the aggregate of the law was closer to civilian than common law practice, which tended to treat the law as a set of nearly discrete particulars. Further evidence of the civilian proclivity of the revisors is seen in Henry Wheaton's designation for his overall organizational plan for the revision, against which Butler and Duer registered no complaint. He called it the "*Projet* or General Plan of Revision." *Projet,* the French term applied to a proposed codification, gave a good indication, in the words of one analyst of the Revised Statutes, of the "novel and far-reaching proportions" of the scheme.[111]

If the revisors' concern for organization did not reflect their training as common lawyers, the general structural outline they adopted did. The statutes were to be classified under the divisions similar to those found in Blackstone's *Commentaries*. Under the first general head would fall all laws relating to the internal administration and civil polity of the state. The second would contain the substantive laws relating to property, domestic relations, and private rights. The third would be comprised of laws relating to the state's judicial machinery and civil procedure. Criminal law would be found under the fourth title, and the last would include all public laws of a local and miscellaneous character. The revisors considered their arrangement "the most natural and at the same time the most scientific of which the subject was capable." They were probably right, for, regardless of its parentage, the plan of organization did make a good deal of sense. An added inducement to its adoption was the fact that it was naturally compatible with the "actual state of our jurisprudence."[112]

The revisors began their work with the laws that comprised the first title, and appended several chapters to their initial report. They readily admitted that in their revision, they had "carried to their full extent, the powers given us by the legislature." Indeed, the chapters they submitted, the revisors acknowledged, "can hardly be called revisions of the existing laws; many changes having been made, and many new provisions introduced."[113]

To begin with, the laws were thoroughly rewritten. This was necessary, they said, because the original statutes had "not only been drawn up carelessly and unmethodically, but in all of them, numerous propositions are crowded together in the same section, and words are multiplied without motive or necessity." They were replaced with chapters of the "most simple arrangement," consisting of sections of "short propositions," which omitted "unnecessary words" and avoided "as far as practicable, all ambiguities of expression."[114]

This "liberal application" of their powers to rewrite the law, the revisors argued, was justified. Because these statutes related to the civil administration of the state, they were frequently consulted by laymen who were civil officers and citizens "engaged in active business... under circumstances which render professional advice unattainable." Therefore, it was thought best to make them "so simple and intelligible, as to be level to the comprehension of all who are obliged to use them." Furthermore, they argued that their "plan of consolidation and amendment" could be applied to these particular laws "with greater facility and less hazard, than any other portions of the written law." For the most part, they were "independent of the common law" and had "but little connection with the general civil and criminal codes." Consequently, they lent themselves to freehanded reformulation without sending repercussions throughout the whole legal system. "As they have but rarely been made the subject of judicial decisions," the revisors pointed out, "and as no general rules of property depend on them; their phraseology may be improved, without endangering titles to property, or disturbing the rules by which private rights have been governed."[115]

The revisors, keenly aware of the threats to property some saw in their system of revision, did their best to quiet those fears lest the project be aborted. If the point were not already clear, they added that they did not expect "that the other branches of the written law, can be rendered perfectly intelligible, to any but professional men." In addition, the revisors confirmed their belief that "the difficulties to be met and the caution to be exercised" would be greatly increased in the revision of statutes relating to property. Not only were property rights involved, but "almost every line of them has been subject to judicial interpretation," making their reformulation especially ticklish. They stated that they were "fully sensible" to the concerns of "our professional brethren" that "the least alteration in phraseology or arrangement" could alter the rules of property and overturn long-standing decisions. Any changes, they promised, would be "weighted with great deliberation."[116]

As to the content of the law under the first general head, the revisors, pursuant to their power to suggest defects and to propose remedies, declared that they had made or were planning to make numerous changes. Instead of merely making suggestions, the revisors concluded that it was "expedient to prepare draughts of the statutes" reflecting the recommended changes. Undoubtedly, they believed that if the task of actually implementing the suggested changes were left to the legislature, lethargy and poor draftsmanship would prevent optimal action.[117]

The extent to which they proposed to alter the law was apparent in the chapters that accompanied the report. One concerned elections. Not only did they incorporate a host of minor changes suggested by experience as well as by court decisions, but they also created a whole new body of law to cover special elections, a subject theretofore uprovided for. All this was done, they claimed, to "render the whole subject more simple and consistent—and to secure the regularity, order and solemnity of proceedings at the poll."[118]

Contending that their work to date had proved an "entire success," they predicted that the same happy result would be achieved with the laws relating to courts and civil procedure and criminal matters. They even suggested that given legislative sanction, they "would not shrink from the labors and difficulties" of forming "a new and complete code of penal law adapted to the genius of our government, and enlightend policy of the age." Indicating what they had in mind, they cited "the great experiment now making in Louisiana [Livingston's criminal code] under the auspices of an accomplished jurist, a native of this state."[119]

Care in presenting their project worked well. The report was greeted in the legislature and by the legal profession with a more enthusiastic response than they had expected. A typical reaction was that of Peter W. Radcliff, a veteran New York practitioner, who approved the project "in strong terms." Duer remarked that Radcliff's approval was "unexpected and gratifying" as he "thought him a stickler for the black letter school."[120]

The legislature warmly endorsed the work of the revisors and did not waver in its support during the three years it took to complete the project. Of course, the lawmakers did not enact the proposals of the revisors uncritically. Frequently, they preserved things that the revisors would have eliminated, or added clauses they deemed necessary.And, on at least one occasion, they directed the revisors to deal more boldly with the law than they had ventured to do. However, if objections were raised or changes made, they were directed at matters of content, not at the format or the general mode of revision.[121]

The popularity of the project in the legislature no doubt reflected a continued enthusiasm for the revision in the state as a whole. Governor De Witt Clinton echoed this sentiment directly when, in his annual message to the legislature in 1828, he lauded the revision as creating "a system of statutory judisprudence in laconic and perspicuous style, and lucid, methodical, extensive and comprehensive in contents and details."[122] One measure of the widespread favorable opinion of the revisors' work was a significant decrease in the demands for law reform both in number and in vociferousness after 1826. If the legislature's purpose in instituting the revision was to quiet agitation for radical reform, the lawmakers would seem to have succeeded in their goal. Concomitantly, the enthusiasms for general codification waned.[123]

Not everyone found the revision gratifying. Some practitioners raised their voices in objection along orthodox lines to the more sweeping reforms proposed by the revisors.[124] But the force of their criticisms was neither strong enough to effect a rejection of specific proposed improvements in the law nor collectively potent enough to abort the whole project.

While the Revised Statutes did not result in a revolution in the Anglo-American legal tradition, as would have been consummated by the codification of all the law of the state, they did make a distinct break with the past. This is nowhere more apparent than in the changes made by the revision in the objective body of the law. In other states, the law relating to a given subject could only be found in a variety of books and in a patchwork of statutes that frequently contained extraneous matter that confused the issue. The New Yorker in possession of the Revised Statutes could find the statute law on a given matter in a relatively short section classified with other related topics in one of three volumes. However, as the revisors pointed out, the individual consulting the revised statutes was not to expect to find all the law on the subjects that they treated. Because statutes comprised "but a small portion" of the law of the state, the common law would have to be consulted for comprehensive understanding. But who could deny that a striking improvement had been made?

The disparity between the ill-ordered mass of state law that was replaced by the scientific arrangement of the Revised Statutes was made more striking by the fact that the law was laid down in simple and concise declaratory statements. Indeed, as the revisors admitted, in fulfilling their purpose of simplifying the language of the law, the "original form" of the statutes had "seldom been preserved."[125]

The content of the Revised Statutes manifested a no less fundamental break with the past. As James Kent correctly observed, the Revised Statutes "made great alterations in the law," which, in their aggregate, constituted "the most extensive innovations, which have hitherto been the consequence of any single legislative effort."[126] The revisors themselves remarked that statutes that underwent the revision process "have been materially modified. Their details have been perfected; they have been conformed in express terms, to the constructions given them by the decisions of our courts; and in many cases new provisions have been introduced, essentially changing their principles." Moreover, "[i]n numerous instances... rules of the common law have been reduced to a written text... whilst in other instances those rules have been enlarged, modified, or varied, the more fully to conform them to the nature of our government, and to the habits and exigencies of the people."[127] Signfiicant innovations had been made in the content of the law before. Efforts had even been made on occasion to give some systematic order to portions of the law. But never before had an attempt been made to deal so comprehensively with some of the most difficult problems of the legal structure, both in form and in content.

The revisors' critique of existing property law was much the same, though necessarily more elaborate and concrete, as that of the leading radical codifiers, and they espoused the same purposes in reforming it. Real property law, the revisors declared, was "not an uniform and consistent system, complex only from a multitude of rules, and variety of details; but it embraces two sets of distinct and opposite maxims, different in origin and hostile in principle." On the one hand, there were the rules of the common law, "connected throughout with the doctrine of tenures, and meant and adapted to maintain the feudal system." But, on the other hand, "an elaborate system of expedients" existed that were "devised in the course of ages... for the express purpose of evading the rules of the common law." The conflict between the two "hostile systems" was the creation of "that infinity of subtleties and refinements, with which this branch of our jurisprudence is overloaded." The result was "inextricable doubt" and the triumph of "technical and arbitrary constructions... over reason and common sense." Its reform was necessary, they declared, if the "nation was to advance at all in civilization and freedom."[128]

The revisors admitted that the full force of artificiality, scholastic sublety, and uncertainty found in English property law did not exist in New York. However, they feared that these problems "will not fail to display themselves" as the state developed and as society became more complex.[129] It was considerd best to solve any potential problems legislatively, as it was an established maxim that rules of the English common law, wherein most of the complexities were found, were presumed to exist in the state until it was authoritatively demonstrated otherwise.[130]

What the reformers desired to do was, in effect, to modernize property law by abolishing "all technical rules and distinctions, having no relationship to the essential nature of property and the means of its beneficial enjoyment, but which are derived from the feudal system." This did not mean that the law would take on a whole new content. The terms they employed and the concept they used were taken from the existing law, and the key to their construction would be the decisions of common -law judges. The revisors clearly laid down the principles they used in reforming property law: "If a rule of law is just and wise in itself, apply it universally, as far as the reasons upon which it was founded extend, and in no instance permit it to be evaded; if it is irrational and fanciful, or the reasons upon which it is rested have become obsolete, abolish it at once."[131]

On this issue, the revisors largely ignored their instructions not to upset the phraseology of the acts relating to property that had been subject to construction by the courts. While they claimed that they approached the revision of this part of the law with "caution and circumspection," the revisors saw the goals of systematic arrangement and lucidity as so important that they largely disregarded the command not to render changes in the phraseology or order of the law. Where it was "practical and consistent with the general plan of the revision," the revisors stated, they "preferred to retain the important words of the present statutes" and made every effort to do so. However, where the law had "received a settled construction which would not at once occur to an attentive reader...the language of the courts has been substituted, whenever it appeared 'more plain and easy to be understood.'" By this method, they believed that the "utility" or the accessibility of the decisional law, and thus the meaning of the statutes, would be greatly improved. The revisors pointed out that these statutes had been subject to "judicial exposition" and "professional criticism" for a half century in the state and in many cases for centuries in England. "If by this time," the revisors declared, sounding like the codifiers that they were, "a knowledge of their meaning, and of their defects, has not been attained, it probably can never be acquired. But it is believed, that a meaning has been affixed to them...and that industry and care only, are necessary to comprehend their meaning" and reduce it to a written form.[132]

Keynoting the sort of reformation of real property law undertaken in the Revised Statutes was the change they effected in tenures. The whole mass of English and New York statutes, as well as case law, directly relating to feudal tenures was brushed aside with the declaration that "[a]ll lands within this state are declared allodial, so that, subject only to the liability of escheat, the entire and absolute property is vested in the owners, according to the nature of their respective estates; and all feudal tenures, of every description, with all their incidents are hereby abolished."[133]

The change was largely technical, with little meaning in substance, but it had great impact.[134] Even in England since the reign of Charles II, most lands were held by the tenure of free and common socage, with the only incident being fealty.[135] In New York, some lands, chiefly the older valuable estates, were held under this tenure, which made them, in substance, allodial. Others, including those that had changed hands since the Revolution, were allodial. The revisors believed that the abolition of feudal tenures would be "useful...for purposes of general information, and to remove a singular diversity which now exists in that part of our law," which might lead to "inconvenient and perplexing consequences." Furthermore, their elimination was mandated by the logic of the revisors' objective of modernizing real property law. The whole concept of tenures is feudal, denoting a relationship between lord and vassal, whereas allodial lands carry no such notion. Also, because the whole of the inherited real property law was grounded in these feudal tenures and in the feudal relationship, their destruction, while practically inconsequential, in itself was the first step in reworking the law of real property on a model more fitted to contemporary realities and needs.[136]

When the revisors tackled the problem of expectant estates, they went beyond changes of mere form to undertake substantive reforms. These reforms, carefully designed not to upset existing property rights, struck at the very roots of the common law. Such reform was typical of the work of the revisors. There were three classes of expectant estates: remainders, springing and secondary uses, and executory devises. Each was regulated by a different set of frequently inconsistent, arbitrary, and technical rules riddled with fictions. However, each had the same sort of function of creating an estate *in futuro*. The validity of an expectant estate, under these rules, was generally not dependent on such substantive considerations as the intent of the creating party or, in the words of the revisors, "by any consideration of the nature and policy of the limitation itself," an important matter in their eyes. Rather, it was determined by "the formal character of the instrument in which the limitation is contained, or the technical force of the language it expressed."[137]

These varying modes of estate in expectancy were originally created—some as early as the twelfth century—to escape the structures designed to protect the feudal land system by allowing a family to maintain ownership of lands regardless of whether or not they could fulfill the feudal obligations that went with ownership. While some limitations served legitimate ends in modern society, which the revisors recognized, these complex and artificially technical means of fulfilling those ends had no real relevancy to the actual character of the property involved.[138] Furthermore, they unnecessarily added intricacy to what should have been a relatively simple matter. This was productive of litigation and expense and frequently defeated the purpose of the limitation.

Typical of the sort of artificial distinction found in this class of property law was the rule that, where a future limitation took the form of an executory devise, it received the full protection of the law against destruction by fraud or other patently illegal means. However, other types of future limitations were technically denied that protection. The distinctions had nothing to do with the intention of the party creating the estate. As the revisors observed, "the ingenuity of lawyers had long since invented an effectual mode of evading" the rule. Consequently, they continued, "it answers no other purpose, at the present day, but to render titles more complicated, and to increase the expense and difficulty of alienation."[139]

To reform the law of expectant estates, the revisors abolished all purely feudal, technical, and arbitrary rules and removed all ambiguities and inconsistencies applying to this class of property. Possibly the most striking detail in this overall reform was the abolition of the rule in Shelley's case because they considered it "purely arbitrary and technical." The rule dated from 1579 and was a well-known landmark in the common law around which a good deal of subtle thinking and vexatious litigation had developed. The revisors saw no "other motive for preserving it...except that it may remain as one of the subjects on which the ingenuity of the bar is to be exercised at the expense of suitors."[140] In place of the varied mass of law applying to the three types of expectant estates, the revisors created a single set of rules that would apply to all classes of this sort of property. They created no new rules, but rather extended and gave a single precise definition to valuable existing rules that had only a partial application to all expectant estates. James Kent, while he had many reservations about other portions of the Revised Statutes, was generally pleased with the changes wrought by the revisors in the law of expectant estates. Surveying the reforms, he declared that they caused him "some relief" when he considered "the endless discussions, and painful learning, and still more painful collision of opinion" on many aspects of this part of the law. On the whole, he considered these reforms "judicious and beneficial."[141]

The revision, by careful definition, severely confined within precise limits the power of property owners to circumscribe the ability of future generations to alienate lands. Before the Revised Statutes were enacted, it was actually possible to render lands more effectively unalienable through the creation of an expectant estate than through the creation of an entail, that celebrated mechanism designed to perpetuate the power of an artistocracy that had been destroyed by an earlier American generation as contrary to the spirit of the Revolution. The revisors also keenly felt the need to limit the ability to create perpetuities because of the limits they placed on alienation, which they deemed contrary to the genius of republican government and the nature of American society.

The revisors' desire to free land from any unreasonable restraints on alienation can be seen still more clearly in their reform of the law of powers as it related to real property. Powers were an important part of contemporary English property law, "found in almost every conveyance or settlement." They were "of admirable use in perpetuating estates in families, and securing the possessions and power of a landed artistocracy." Their use for this purpose, the revisors observed, was "hardly consistent with our habits of society and general modes of alienation." Even though the use of powers for this purpose was largely unknown in the state, the revisors proposed that they be modified to obviate their future use. "[I]t should never be forgotten," they remarked, expressing the logic behind their recommendation, "that it is the partability, the frequent division, and unchecked alienation of property, that are essential to the health and vigor of our republican institutions."[142]

Among the other important reforms effected in real property law were the abolition of uses and trusts, except in certain clearly specified cases, and redesigning the action of ejectment, relieving it of its fictional characters and making it a simple mode of adjudicating titles to land. While other portions of the law did not exhibit the striking changes found in real property law, every area of the law that had a foundation in statutes was at least reorganized and simplified as to language. The result was a code of statute law so lucid and progressive that it was not found necessary to undertake a revision of New York statute law again until the end of the century.

One might well ask, what could induce the New York legislature to approve of the Revised Statutes, considering the sweeping changes in the forms and content of the law? The query seems especially important when one considers the resemblance of the revision to the goals of the codification movement. Major portions of the law were reduced to a systematic arrangement of clear and concise statements. Rules theretofore found only in the common law were reduced to a statutory form, and significant reforms were worked in the content of the law. The similarity between the Revised Statutes and the espoused ambitions of the codifiers was not lost on contemporaries, many of whom saw the revision as a codification or at least a necessary first step toward the codification of all the law.[143] Others criticized the revision because it smacked of codification.[144] A majority of the legal profession, by the revisors' own count, opposed codification. The legal profession had a commanding voice in matters of law reform, yet the revisors received legislative sanction.

Many of the same considerations that had prompted the legislature in 1825 to permit Duer and Butler to undertake their unusual proposed reform figured in their approval of the completed revision. The law, most agreed, was in need of reform, and the work of the revisors only confirmed this belief by pointing out existing defects. The revisors eliminated these defects and brought clarity and simplicity to what had been complex and elusively abstruse. Much of this sort of reform must have appealed to the thoughtful members of the profession. James Kent, representative of the conservative element of the legal fraternity, for example, found a good deal in the revision that met with his hearty approval and went so far as to suggest that the Revised Statutes "will deserve and receive the attention of lawyers and statesmen throughout the union."[145] To be sure, Kent and others found some of the bold changes in the revision not to their liking. However, their objections focused largely on individual substantive reforms, not the whole revision, and once the revision process gained momentum, it was difficult to restrain selectively.

The reforms undertaken by the revisors were, on the whole, judicious. As one later commentator put it, the revisors "had the spirit of reformers without the rage of iconoclasts."[146] They did not attempt to overthrow the established legal order and build a new structure based on theoretical considerations. The final product, while it contained some startling changes, was created out of the familiar and well known. If it seems incongruous that the orthodox common lawyers who declared their strong opposition to the improvements espoused by the codifiers could find merit in the reforms of the Revised Statutes, the contradiction is explained by the fact that their opposition to the codifiers' demands were, of necessity, rather abstraact, as they were not reacting to concrete proposals. They only heard the codifiers overstating their case against the common law as an unnecessarily complex and barbaric legal system, and demanding sweeping change. The orthodox lawyers naturally registered their strong opposition. However, the Revised Statutes appeared not to be the work of visionary innovators but to embody many beneficial and largely prudent reforms, suggested only after careful introspection.

The revolutionary format of the revised statutes was probably easier to accept than were the substantive reforms. The idea of the law being clearly stated in a systematic order appealed to all but the rascals in the profession.[147] Even with the substantive changes, moreover, the common law continued to exist as a major tool of statutory interpretation. The revisors were occasionally accused of being unwarrantably zealous in their attempt to compress the law, but, again, appeal could be had to the common law for understanding and elaboration.[148] In short, the common law was left largely undisturbed.

It appears, then, that while the revisors incorporated into the revised statutes the methodology of codification, they were largely free from those elements on which the orthodox common lawyers based their opposition to the reform. Their use of the techniques of codification brought brevity and clarity to the statutes of New York that the legal profession found attractive, and therein lay the key to the approval of the revised statutes by the legislature. All this is not to say that the legal profession was free of misgiving concerning the project. James Kent's son, William, himself a lawyer and judge, commented some years after the revised statutes were implemented on "the reluctance and apprehension with which those laws were received."[149] As we have seen, the legal profession had a strong fear of legal reform. In many ways, the New York revised statutes tested the limits of that anxiety and, consequently, tested the limits of legal reform through codification in the United States. In retrospect, it seems unlikely that legal reform through codification could have gone much further than the frontiers marked by the revised statutes. The history of the codification movement in the next two decades bears out this observation.

However, the revision also pointed up the utility of codification in the American legal system by suggesting the beneficial use to which its methods could be put without jeopardizing the traditional framework of the legal system. Classifications of the law could be reformed and reduced with good effect under systematically arranged titles. While sort of code would not contain the whole of the relevant law, and would not be expounded any differently than any other statute in a common-law legal system, it diminished the need to consult the old law by consolidating past legal growth and offering a relatively clear integrated statement of the law as a fresh starting point for legal development. Furthermore, such a code offered a model for statutory draftsmanship that, while not always adhered to, concretely illustrated what could be done.

If the revised statutes demonstrated the utility of codification, they also manifested the limited potential of the reform to achieve the advantages the codifiers claimed would accrue from its implementation. While the revisors removed much of the scholastic refinement and unnecessary subtlety from the law and endeavored to state the law as clearly as possible, the law remained intricate, on many points, even for the practitioner; meanwhile, the layman was hardly provided with the sort of tool that lay codifiers were demanding. In spite of all the revisors' efforts, ambiguities still lurked in their work, and defects showed themselves immediately upon its implementation. Orthodox common lawyers had suggested that the sort of changes involved in codification and thus in the revised statutes would be productive of uncertainty and litigation. This, indeed, was one of the fruits of the revision, although it was not as disruptive as they claimed it would be. Nonetheless, the courts had, of necessity, to expound and apply newly rewritten law, no matter how carefully drawn. If the pre-code case law did not have to be consulted as frequently as before, the number of reported cases continued to grow undiminished. As a result, the revised statutes fostered the growth of a whole new set of law books designed to explain them.[150]

NOTES

1. Quoted in William Sampson, *Sampson's Discourse, and Correspondence with Various Learned Jurists Upon the History of the Law,* Pishey Thompson, comp. (Washington, D.C.: Gales & Seaton, 1826), p. 101.

2. Benjamin James, *A Digest of the Laws of South Carolina*...(Columbia, S.C.: Telescope Press, 1822), p. x.

3. John Faucheroud Grimke, ed., *The Public Laws of the State of South Carolina* ...(Philadelphia: R. Aitken and Son, 1790), p. iii.

4. Thomas S. Grimke, *An Oration of the Practicability and Expediency of Reducing the Whole Body of the Law to the Simplicity and Good Order of a Code* (Charleston, S.C., 1827).

5. Joseph Brevard, *An Alphabetical Digest of the Public Statute Law of South Carolina,* 3 vols. (Charleston: John Huff, 1814).

6. James, *A Digest.*

7. Meira G. Pimsleur, ed., *Checklist of Basic American Legal Publications* (S. Hackensack, N.J.: Fred B. Rothman and Co., 1962), "Pennsylvania," pp. 1-2; "South Carolina," p. 1; "Virginia," pp. 1-3.

8. Frederick C. Hicks, *Materials and Methods of Legal Research,* 2d ed. (Rochester, N.Y.: The Lawyers Co-Operative Publishing Co., 1933), p. 429.

9. Charleston *Courier,* 26 Nov. 1823. On the problem of courts in South Carolina, see Donald Senese, "Building the Pyramid: The Growth and Development of the State Courts System of Antebellum South Carolina, 1800-1860," *South Carolina Law Review* 24 (1972): 357-89.

10. Ibid.

11. Sampson, *Discourse,* pp. 95-96, 97.

12. James, *A Digest,* p. x.

13. Grimke, *Oration,* p. 7.

14. See Charleston *Courier,* 12 Nov. 1822, 25 April, 9 and 14 Sept. 1825.

15. Republished in New York *American,* 18 Oct. 1824.

16. Ibid., 8 Oct. 1824.

17. Sampson, *Discourse,* p. 97.

18. Quoted in Donald Senese, "Legal Thought in South Carolina, 1800-1860," unpublished Ph.D. dissertation, University of South Carolina, 1970, p. 170.

19. Ibid.

20. Charleston *Courier,* 30 Nov. 1822.

21. Ibid., 23 Dec. 1822.

22. Ibid., 26 Nov. 1823.

23. Ibid., 13 Dec. 1823.

24. Sampson, *Discourse,* p. 124.

25. Ibid., pp. 52-58, 60-75.

26. See, for example, Charleston *Courier,* 29 Aug. 1824.

27. New York *American,* 18 Oct. 1824.

28. Sampson, *Discourse,* pp. 95-97.

29. Ibid.

30. John L. Wilson to William Sampson, 24 Aug. 1825, ibid., p. 103.

31. William Sampson to John L. Wilson, n.d., ibid.

32. See, for example, Charleston *Courier,* 15 and 27 April, 9 and 14 Sept. 1825; Charleston *Mercury,* 28 July 1825.

33. See Charleston *Courier,* 2 Dec. 1825.

34. Ibid., 20 Dec. 1826.

35. Ibid., 1 Dec. 1826.

36. Ibid.

37. Ibid., 6 Dec. 1826.

38. Ibid., 13 Dec. 1826.

39. Ibid.

40. For one contemporary's reaction, see ibid., 18 Dec. 1826.

41. Quoted in Senese, "Legal Thought," p. 207.

42. Charleston *Courier,* 18 Dec. 1826.

43. Ibid., 19 Dec. 1826.

44. Ibid., 25 Dec. 1826.

45. ibid., 20 Dec. 1826.

46. Grimke, *Oration.*

47. John L. Wilson, *Codification* (New York: Gray and Bunce, 1827).

48. The Committee Appointed 20th December. Last, to Report on the Practicability of a Code of Statute and Common Law of the State... Beg Leave to Report as Follows. Columbia, S.C. 1827.

49. See Cooper's "Bentham's Rationale," *Southern Review* 5 (1830): 381-426 and Legare's "Codification," *Southern Review* 7 (1831): 391-412.

50. John L. Wilson to William Sampson, 24 Aug. 1825, Sampson, *Discourse,* p. 101.

51. William W. Freehling, *Prelude to Civil War* (New York: Harper and Row, 1966), pp. 180-81, 216, 295, 310-12; Gerda Lerner, *The Grimke Sisters from South Carolina* (New York: Schocken Books, 1967), pp. 92-93.

52. Senese, "Legal Thought," p. 412.

53. Charleston *Courier,* 1 Dec. 1826.

54. Quoted in Senese, "Legal Thought," p. 226.

55. U.S. Bureau of the Census, *Historical Statistics of the United States, Colonial Times to 1957* (Washington, D.C.: Government Printing office, 1960), p. 13.

56. David M. Ellis et al., *A History of New York State* (Ithaca, N.Y.: Cornell University Press, 1957), pp. 163, 174, 177.

57. Grace E. MacDonald, comp., *Check-List of Session Laws* (New York: H.W. Wilson Co., 1936), pp. 159-60.

58. New York *American,* 24 April 1828.

59. MacDonald, *Check-List,* pp. 224-25.

60. Revisions were completed in 1789, 1801, and 1813. This was a continuation of provincial practice. The colonial government revised its laws in 1752, 1762, and 1774.

61. Pimsleur, *Checklist,* "New York," pp. 1-2.

62. Hicks, *Materials and Methods,* pp. 423-24.

63. New York *American,* 25 Sept. 1828.

64. James Kent, *Commentaries on American Law,* 4 vols. (New York: O. Halsted, 1826-30), I: 443.

65. Ibid., p. 44.

66. Donald M. Roper, "An Atmosphere of Flux—An Objective of Certainty: The New York Supreme Court in the Early Nineteenth Century," a paper delivered to the American Society for Legal History, 10 November 1973, p. 12.

67. [Theron Metcalf], "Wheaton's Reports," *North American Review* 17 (1823): 119.

68. [Henry Dwight Sedgwick], *The English Practice* (New York: J. Seymour, 1822).

69. See his argument in *Trial of the Journeymen Cordwainers of the City of New York*...(New York: I. Riley, 1810), esp. pp. 116-25.

70. *National Advocate* (New York), 16 Sept. 1825.

71. New York *American,* 26 Jan. 1826.

72. "Judiciary in New York," *United States Law Journal* 2 (1826): 141.

73. New York *American,* 24 Jan. 1826.

74. *National Advocate* (New York), 5 April 1825.

75. Ibid., 15 Sept. 1825.

76. Ibid., 5 April 1825.

77. On this point, see ibid., 24 Jan. 1826.

78. New York *American* 27 March 1826.

79. *National Advocate* (New York), 31 March 1825.

80. Ibid., 9 April 1825.

81. See [Sedgwick], *The English Practice;* New York *American,* 26 Jan., 8 July 1825, 11 Feb. 1826; *National Advocate* (New York), 16 Sept. 1826.

82. *National Advocate* (New York), 21 April 1825.

83. See review of Sampson's *Discourse* by "Jay," and the reply of "Philo-Jay," New York *American,* 16 and 20 Jan. 1824.

84. See, for example, New York *American,* 8 and 18 Oct. 1824; Sampson, *Discourse,* pp. 53-75.

85. Charles Watts to William Sampson, n.d., *New York Review and Atheneum Magazine* 1 (1825): 400-405, 473-85.

86. "Revision of the Laws," *Atlantic Magazine,* 2 (1825): 459.

87. Jabez D. Hammond, *The History of the Political Parties in the State of New York from the Ratification of the Federal Constitution to December 1840,* 2 vols. (Albany: C. Van Benthuysen, 1842), I: 107-108.

88. *National Advocate* (New York), 10 Jan. 1824.

89. Ibid., 9 Jan. 1824.

90. Hammond, *History of the Political Parties,* pp. 181-82.

91. "Revision of the Laws," p. 460.

92. Charles Z., Lincoln, ed. *Message from the Governors, Comprising Executive Communications to the Legislature*...11 vols. (Albany: *J. B. Lyon, 1909),* II:90.

93. New York *American,* 24 March 1825.

94. Ibid.

95. Ibid.

96. Ibid.

97. Ibid.

98. *National Advocate* (New York), 8 April 1825.

99. Ibid., 13 March 1825.

100. "Revision of the Laws."

101. See New York *Evening Post,* 8 April 1825; New York *Daily Advertiser,* 20 March 1825.

102. *National Advocate* (New York), 21 March 1825.

103. Ibid., 31 March 1825.

104. Ibid., 21 April 1825.

105. See William A. Butler, *The Revision of the Statutes of New York and the Revisors* (New York: Banks & Bros., 1889), pp. 12-13; New York *Statesman,* 27 April 1825.

106. Report from the Commissioners Appointed to Revise the Laws of the State of New York...Communicated March 15, 1826; (*Albany: 1826),* pp. 5-6.

107. Sampson, *Discourse,* p. 62.

108. Ibid., pp. 62, 65.

109. Ibid., p. 65.

110. [William H.Gardiner], "Revision of the Laws of New York," *North American Review* 24 (1827): 206-207, 209.

111. Butler, *Revision of the Statutes,* p. 19.

112. Report from the Commissioners...Communicated March 15, 1826, p. 8.

113. Ibid., p. 19.

114. Ibid., p. 18.

115. Ibid., pp. 8-9.

116. Ibid., pp. 17-18.

117. Ibid., p. 19.

118. Ibid., p. 20.

119. Ibid., pp. 16, 21.

120. Butler, *Revision of the Statutes,* p. 25.

121. See New York *Enquirer,* 18 Sept. 1828.

122. Lincoln, *Messages,* II: 210.

123. Occasional interest was expressed in the need to go beyond the Revised Statutes to effect a more thoroughgoing reform, but these were few in number and generated no enthusiasm. See *National Advocate* (New York), 28 Feb. 1828 and New York *American,* 17 Dec. 1828.

124. Butler, *Revision of the Statutes,* pp. 29-30.

125. The Revised Statutes of the State of New York, Passed in the Years 1827-1828 (1830), I: iii.

126. Kent, *Commentaries,* IV: 345.

127. Revised Statutes, pp. iii-iv.

128. Chapter 1 of the Second Part of the Proposed Revision of the Statute Law of the State of New York, p. 37.

129. Ibid., p. 21.

130. See *Canal Appraisers v. People,* 17 Wendell (N.Y.), 571, 617.

131. Chapter 1 of the Second Part, pp. 21, 26.

132. Ibid., pp. 6-7.

133. Revised Statutes, p. 718.

134. Because it was merely a technical change, James Kent thought it unnecessary and lacking in wisdom. See Kent, *Commentaries,* IV: 3. Any substantive rights involved in the old tenures in the form of rents or services to the present landowners were carefully preserved in the revision. The revisors were always heedful of the need to preserve existing property rights when making any sort of reform in style or substance.

135. For the state of English law on the matter, see J. H. Baker, *An Introduction to English Legal History,* (London: Butterworths, 1971), p. 136.

136. Chapter 1 of the Second Part, pp. 5-6.

137. Ibid.

138. Ibid., p. 27.

139. Ibid.

140. Ibid., p. 26.

141. Kent, *Commentaries,* IV: 266, 274.

142. Chapter 1 of the Second Part, p. 61.

143. See "Judiciary System of New York," *American Jurist and Law Magazine* 26 (1841): 38; "American Law—Kent's Commentaries," *United States Law Intelligencer and Review* 2 (1830): 239.

144. See Kent, *Commentaries,* IV; 345-47.

145. Ibid.

146. Butler, *Revision of the Statutes,* p. 22.

147. See "Legal Reform," *American Jurist and Law Magazine* 9 (1833): 289.

148. See Kent, *Commentaries,* IV: 346.

149. Butler, *Revision of the Statutes,* p. 51.

150. "Judiciary System," p. 38; "American Law—Kent's Commentaries," pp. 238-39; "Difficulties Under the Revised Statutes of New York," *United States Law Intelligencer and Review* 2 (1830): 147-48; "Codification," *United States Law Intelligencer and Review* 3 (1831): 101-102; "The Revision of 1830—The Innovations of 1847 and 1848," *New York Legal Observer* 6 (1848): 49-53.

7

WORKING FOR CODIFIED LAW: DEVELOPING NATIONAL PATTERNS, 1830-1850

After 1830, the American codification movement began its second, and final, phase. One of the elements that distinguishes the 1830s and 1840s from the preceding years was the impact of Jacksonianism on attitudes toward the legal environment, which became manifest in demands for greater democracy in the American legal structure. This impulse was most visible among the lay law reformers. With certain exceptions, it seems to have had little impact among reformers within the legal fraternity, though many continued to be sensitive to popular demands.

Before the 1830s, lay criticism of the legal order was largely nonideological in nature and focused on the practical desire of lay consumers for quick and speedy justice. Democratic notions were occasionally discernible in their statements. Thereafter, while their essential concerns remained the same, democratic theory figured ever more prominently in their discussions of the legal system. Lay reformers now alleged, for example, that practitioners kept the law a "dark chaos" in order to maintain a monopolistic and undemocratic control over legal practice.[1] A writer in Gilbert Vale's reform-oriented journal, *The Diamond,* announced, the "Democratic Creed recognizes no exclusive privileges, no selfish monopolies."[2] Frederick Robinson, a radical Massachusetts labor leader, claimed that greed was the motiviation for denying laymen knowledge of the law. "You know," he declared in an angry open letter to a practitioner, "that no one will pay you for advice on laws which he himself can understand." The monopolistic bar, he claimed, was a decidedly undemocratic "privileged order" that "saps the liberties of the people" and looks "upon the rest of the world as inferior, plebian laborers, educated only for menial employment."[3] The law was kept profitably enshrouded in an impenetrable veil of mystery, Robinson and others claimed, by an essentially conspiratorial and secret bar, which regulated its own membership. Thus, the law craft was analogized to the Masons, Mormons, and Catholics, other objects of contemporary criticism because of their alleged mysterious and conspiratorial designs for wrecking the American democratic experiment.[4]

The profession, Robinson asserted, manifesting another strain of democratic thought, "ought to be left open to universal competition." After all, it was nothing more than "a trade or calling" by which men "get a living." He asked the legal fraternity, "[w]hat right have you to form associations for the purpose of preventing others from competing with you, more than the followers of any other trade? What can be more anti-republican than associations of this kind?... The spirit of democracy demands the total annihilation of the secret brotherhood of the bar." It was, Robinson declared, "an encroachment on the natural rights of man" to deny a person the right to practice law, because all people shared "every right and every privilege, in our country, which any other can enjoy." However, something more was at stake than the right of individual development in a freely competitive society. The denial of knowledge of the law and the inability to pursue justice in the courts without hired counsel was said to threaten basic liberties that the law was supposed to protect. "Without a knowledge of the laws under which we live," asked Robinson with a sense of anxiety, "are we not deceiving ourselves, if we suppose ourselves freemen?" He considered it "incredible in our country, where we boast so much of freedom and equality," that the citizen was restricted from using "those institutions formed for securing our freedom and equality."[5]

Democratic reformers charged that the bar established and maintained its monopoly over the legal system by utilizing the common law, which was "contained in ten thousand different books." Not only was the common law incomprehensibly voluminous, Robinson asserted, but it was also "so intricate, so ambiguous [and] so contradictory, that no man ever understood" it. Furthermore, its very intricacy and obscurity, in effect, gave the legal profession license to become involved in all sorts of chicanery that subverted justice and hurt the honest suitor.[6]

The dimensions of received English law together with its American additions, covering a myriad of human affairs, were considered contrary to democratic precepts. The *Democratic Review,* defining the elements of "that high holy DEMOCRATIC PRINCIPLE" on which the "American experiment" was based, declared unequivocally that "[t]he best government is that which governs least."[7] Pursuing this same theme, a writer in a later issue of the *Review* in an article entitled "The Duties of the State to Its Citizens," observed that a "[g]reat multiplicity of laws disgraces a nation; it implies that they are unskilled in the principles of government, or that the people have thrown off their allegiance to themselves." Even as the "interests and pursuits" of a nation "become intricate and multiplied... heaping laws upon laws" was actually counterproductive in meeting legal needs. Laws, he believed, should be accessible and simple.[8] Another writer expressed the same idea somewhat differently. "It is with law as with physic," he said, "the less we have to do with it the better, both commodities being but a negative good, if not a positive evil."[9]

If these law reformers of a democratic bent found the size and content of the common law objectionable, they also looked with a no less jaundiced eye on the methodology and technique of the common law as a legal system. It was judge-made law, and, as such, it was undemocratic. The common law, observed one commentator, was "deposited only in the head of the judge, so that whatever he says is common law, *must be* common law."[10] In this situation, declared a writer in the Boston *Statesman* in 1835, personal rights could become "mere nullities depending on the caprice of some weak or wicked judge."[11] Because it was impossible to know what the common law was before it was expounded by a judge, it was also claimed that the common law was *ex post facto* law and, as such, contrary to the constitution of every state.[12]

The common law was considered constitutionally repugnant on yet another count. The decisions of the courts carried the force of law, but only the legislature had the power to make law.[13] This usurpation of legislative power was made doubly evil by the fact that judges, being appointed and holding their offices during good behavior, were politically irresponsible. The American judicial system, one writer declared, was "based on false principles," because of "[t]he entire omission, in its organization, of the element of responsibility to public opinion—that great conservative principle on which the health and vitality of every other department of our system depend."[14] Another angry writer declared that the judiciary was "the only *arbitrary* power in the country." Being beyond public control, it had become "the natural and dangerous refuge of the foes of democracy."[15] In contrast to the common law, Robert Rantoul, a radical Massachusetts lawyer and a Democrat, declared, "[s]tatutes, enacted by the legislature, speak the public voice." The legislators are chosen because they have the people's confidence and, once elected, remain amenable to their will. "They must sympathize with the public, and express its will," Rantoul continued, "should they fail to do so, the next year witnesses their removal from office, and others are selected to be the organs of popular sentiment."[16] "Judicial despotism," urged another critic, was "the worst of tyranny. It has been borne long enough, and must now be put down."[17]

The democratically oriented law reformers saw codification as a remedy for the ills they perceived in the legal system. Their conception of codified law was shared by the radical codifiers within the legal profession who had a particularly strong ideological bent. A code, according to Rantoul, would be "a positive and unbending text" that would be mechanistically applied by the courts.[18] One writer for the *Democratic Review* claimed that a judge with a code in his hand "in a moment" could "ascertain his own powers... detect what is an offence ... discover how it is to be proved... [and] administer the punishment."[19] As a result, the bench would no longer make law and would, as another commentator put it, be brought "back to the administration of the *law*" so that "judicial despotism" would be "put down."[20]

A properly drawn code, Frederick Robinson agreed, would eliminate all the intricacies of English legal science and state the laws that governed human affairs with "the greatest simplicity and conciseness, [and] arrange the law in a single book, so that every one could read and understand them."[21] Another reformer noted that a code would permit the individual to be informed of the law "with... ease, when his rights have been infringed or when his interests have been protected."[22] In effect, codification of the law would obviate the need for the law craft by making the law simple enough for every man to be his own lawyer.[23] Such ideas reflected the radicalism of the democratic approach to law reform through codification.

However, the law reform agenda of some laymen went beyond the codification formula because they believed it would not effectively check the judiciary or do away with professional lawyers. The existing system of courts, ostensibly the one that would apply any code, was, as one severe critic observed, "a withered sepulcher filled with the rotteness of dead men's bones." The judges' minds were married to the old legal order and could not possibly use a code in the manner that was intended. "Rather than attempt to codify the law," he suggested, "it will be the shorter and better course [to] haul up your judges to the letter and spirit of the constitution" by impeaching them for usurping legislative powers. Then they should be replaced by an elective judiciary. Being elected for "limited and short terms," they would be made representative to the people and sensititve to their needs, and, as a result, the judiciary would be "harmonized with the genius of our institutions."[24] Increasingly, the idea of an elective judiciary gained weight as a feasible means of injecting more democracy into the legal structure.

Others suggested even more fundamental applications of democratic principles to the legal order. One individual writing in the *Democratic Review* proposed that the legal system be revolutionized by the elimination of "the whole mass of English law," including "all the judicial opinions and precedents." Instead of allowing existing institutions to redevelop the law, he further recommended that "trial by jury [be] restored to its primitive simplicity and jurisdiction, as it originally existed amongst the Anglo-Saxons." This institution, he said, "was the natural progenitor of democratic government." It was popularly elected and "in no way subordinate" to anyone. The jurors were "in fact the elected representatives of the people," who, being guided only by "the dictates of reason and of conscience," tried all questions of law and fact. Such an institution would be "economical and... consistent with democratic republican principles, as well as... conducive to adjudication of exact and conscious justice." With the elimination of professional judges and practitioners, all branches of American government would "exhibit in theory, in practice, and virtue, the great principle of democratic representation." Its adoption, he submitted, "would be the greatest achievement of the age, the best improvement of jurisprudence, and... most beneficial to our social conditions."[25]

Still others desired to lessen dependence on all existing institutions as much as possible, suggesting what were essentially anarchistic solutions to the defects they observed in the legal system. Stressing the principle that "[t]he best government is that which governs least," the *Democratic Review* suggested that "[g]overnment should have as little as possible to do with the general business and interests of the people." The only proper sphere of intervention by the state into the society was "the administration of justice, for the protection of equal rights of the citizen, and the preservation of social order," an admittedly small scope of action. "In all other respects, the VOLUNTARY PRINCIPLE, the principle of FREEDOM... is alone abundantly competent to work out the best possible general result of order and happiness from that chaos of characters, ideas, notions and interests—human society." This notion seemed to call for the application of natural law, the golden rule, and mutual trust to interpersonal affairs. The *Review* asserted that the "spontaneous action and self-regulation" that were implied in the function of the voluntary principle would produce order and regulate the society better than any government could.[26] Perhaps the most radical of all critiques came from P.W. Grayson, in his vitriolic attack on the legal system and the law craft in *Vice Unmasked,* written in 1830. Grayson viewed the existing law as a system of unjust and artificial restraints characterized by ruthlessness, inflexibility , and gross absurdity. Its chief function was to make lawyers rich. Justice, he believed, lay in the direction of radical simplification. His solution was to *"repeal all law*... as a matter of evil." In a society unrestrained by law, only "the dishonest and crafty" would suffer.[27]

To knowledgeable contemporaries, it must have seemed unlikely that any of these democratic reform proposals would be implemented, at least as they understood them. Some, like the reinstitution of the Anglo-Saxon jury, were too absurd to consider seriously. Others, such as the idea of an elective judiciary, ran directly counter to an important Anglo-American political and legal tradition, though it would soon be changed. Even if the law were to be codified, certainly the Benthamite concept of codification expressed by some of these reformers would not be the model used by any prospective jurisconsults. The legal profession remained in command in matters of law reform, and the legal fraternity, by and large, had little liking for the type of reform suggested by these laymen.

Some professionals continued to believe that there was little cause for complaint concerning the legal order. John Pickering, a well-known Massachusetts attorney, considered accusations leveled by laymen against the law and the legal profession as "unfounded as a thousand other charges which are daily reiterated against every institution and profession in our country." Their critique, he charged, was a typical "flippant aversion" made by men who "deprecate and find fault with what they least understand." Pickering and others of a similar mind found "abundant reason...to be satisfied" with the condition of the American legal order. If defects existed, they were not intolerable compared to the dangers inherent in reform. "In projecting improvements," Pickering warned a Massachusetts audience, "we must not be too impatient of existing laws, nor too eager to adopt new ones." Laws, he suggested, must be proven to "operate injuriously" before any change should be attempted. To drive home the point, Pickering further remarked that "[i]f our jurisprudence as a *whole,* has a salutary operation," and he believed it had, "we need not be over zealous to provide for points of inferior importance."[28]

Not all practitioners viewed the legal environment with as much satisfaction as did Pickering, nor did they exhibit his reluctance to take up reform. If anything, the legal profession manifested an increased willingness to improve the legal system after 1830, often through codification. The same sources of complaint that had originally encouraged the codification movement persisted, often in an intensified form. Instead of seeing only minor substantive defects, many practitioners voiced their belief in the need for thoroughgoing improvements in the content of the law. A writer in the *American Jurist* commenting in 1831 on "the bitter fruits of legislative imbecility," declared that "[h]alf our laws exist only because they have never been examined. Established as they were in days of ignorance and superstition, they derived their support from prescription and ancient usage, rather than intrinsic worth." Statutes, he continued, frequently exhibited "mis-placed standards...treating as criminal what is beneficial, and as praiseworthy what is injurious. Such laws exist only because they have heretofore existed, not because they ought to continue."[29] Another, speaking to the need for reform of the content of the common law, claimed that "[t]he observation and experience of every lawyer, who has studied his profession with care, must bring him to the conclusion that many cases now exist in which the rule of law and the rule of reason are widely apart." He assured his fellow practitioners that it was not disrespectful of the law or tradition, nor was it unadorned radicalism, to desire to change common law doctrines that were "in some particulars wholly unsuited to the conditions of things at the present day." If the reform effort were "judicious and well directed," the profession should be pleased to see the legal system improved by the elimination of "rules productive of hardship and injustice."[30] Another writer, commenting on the rules of evidence in the common law, was more specifically emphatic on the need for reform. While the common law of evidence was "the result of the most enlightened intelligence," its operation was "so bad, that society can hardly exist under their influence." He observed that "at common law they do not discover the truth...they decide without such discovery." Equity jurisdiction was originally designed to circumvent the injurious rules of common law so that justice might be done. However, the writer continued, while it fulfilled this purpose in part, it also created problems. The jurisdictional lines between the two systems of courts were "so involved in doubt and uncertainty, that neither judges nor chancellors can agree, and whether each or either will afford redress can only be known with certainty after trying the experiment."[31]

These were the not ravings of Benthamite radicals, or even overcharged denunciations of the sort that William Sampson displayed, but rather they were studied concerns of temperate, reform-minded professionals. Their criticism was, on the whole, balanced and judicious and pointed up the need for change if the legal system were to meet the needs of a developing society. As such, they reflected a growing sense of urgency within the legal profession after 1830 with the necessity of legal reform, especially in matters of procedure and practice—not that substantive areas of the law were considered to be free from defects. Reflective of this concern, the *American Jurist,* the highly respected and leading law journal of the day, was replete with articles suggesting the need for reform in all branches of the law. At the end of its first decade of publication in 1839, its editors, Charles Sumner, Luther Cushing, and George Hilliard, reaffirmed their purpose of including law reform as one of the important subjects "embraced in the general plan of the *American Jurist.*" They declared that they would continue to afford "free scope for discussion of proposed alterations in the laws."[32] In keeping with this declaration of intent, S.F. Dixon, one of its later editors, wrote a series of essays, over a number of years, for the journal entitled "Codification and the Reform of the Common Law," in which he discussed at length those subjects of the law that he believed required improvement as part of a codification process.[33]

To be sure, the law was not standing still. Reform was taking place as an ongoing process. To a certain extent, the orthodox common lawyers' assertions that the common law had an inherent self-improving function was correct. In the area of real property law, for example, a reviewer of Francis Hilliard's digest of American property law noted in 1838 that the United States was "gradually departing...from the principles on which the English law of real property is founded." This, he said, could be observed "in the decisions of our numerous state and federal courts." He suggested that "a distinct and independent American real property law" was emerging. Howver, the transition to a truly indigenous legal product was not always smooth or uniform. This fact pointed up a source of enduring complaint within the profession. The reviewer remarked that "in some of the states, the departure from the common type has been greater than in others...in all it has been sufficient, we imagine, to perplex and embarrass the practicing lawyer, and to tax the highest power of the judge."[34] This statement manifested a continuing and pressing concern with doctrinal diversity as well as with the size of the objective body of American law. Something over a decade before, Nathan Dane had complained that it was impossible for anyone to keep pace with the growth of American law. The situation had not improved.

In 1836, David Hoffman counted four hundred and fifty volumes of American reports that "now load our shelves!"[35] In addition, there were at least an equal number of English reports, imported or republished in the United States with notes or other native additions, numerous translations, treatises, and law journals—all continually adding to the aggregate body of materials with which the practitioner had to contend. A year later, Timothy Walker, an aspiring law teacher in Cincinnati, in the preface of his *Introduction to American Law,* felt constrained to offer "an apology for adding to the multitude of books" that dealt with the law.[36] And another writer commenting on "the present multiplicity of law books" that "seem to stretch to the crack of doom," expressed a longing "for the good old days, even after Sir Edward Coke was cold in his grave, when it could be said that all books of the common law might be carried in a wheelbarrow."[37]

The nature of the federal system itself continued to provoke doctrinal diversity and uncertainty. As S.F. Dixon observed: "Every question of doubt must be argued *de novo* in each State; as the exigency occurs, and the vast mass of English and American authorities passed on." Consequently, there were as many "versions of the common law" as there were states, and "each was essentially variant" from the others.[38]

However, Dixon and other commentators also pointed to more fundamental causes for the continuing doctrinal diversity found in the common law. Judges themselves, within some jurisdictions, often disagreed as to what was the law, "often to such a degree that it is impossible to decide the case in question without weighing the mass of precedents against each other, or recurring to first principles without regard to authority." As a result, the common law was anything but a perfect science. While volumes of reports might "embody displays of talent and learning, they transmitted an inadequate and often contradictory system."[39] Many contemporaries cited as proof of this situation the second edition of Simon Greenleaf's *Cases Overruled,* published in 1838. Greenleaf listed nearly twenty-seven hundred cases once taken as authority that were subsequently limited or overruled. Because of the confused picture the reports presented, Greenleaf himself called them "terra incognita."[40]

Codification remained an actively proposed reform formula for the defects perceived in the legal environment. In fact, it had gained a good deal of respectability within the legal profession. Orthodox common lawyers, to be sure, still leveled charges against it, claiming that its implementation would wreck the salutary and superior workings of the common law by replacing its flexibility with in inflexible and static text.[41] However, for many , the codification movement had lost its association with Benthamism. They accepted the idea that the law could be codified in such a way as to avoid radical and injurious innovation. In 1835, a writer in the *American Jurist* declared that

> [a] few years ago, *codification* had a direful import to the conservative party of jurisprudence; and not wholly without reason; since some of its early champions were sturdy radicals in legal reform.... The most fearless promoters of codification were ready to

frame codes, according to certain leading doctrines, for any people whatsoever, without any knowledge of their existing institutions, laws and customs. In their view codification was another name for juridical revolution, and as such was accordingly regarded with some consternation. But the alarm has subsided.[42]

Representative of the increased acceptance of codification as a viable and reasonable means to improve the legal system was the conversion of Theron Metcalf, a prominent Massachusetts practitioner who had earlier opposed codification.[43] Metcalf, while he had a brief connection with radicalism in his early years, was known for his conservatism in politics and law. Indeed, one legal historian described him as being "so steeped in the common law that he detested statutes."[44] Yet, Joseph Story convinced him that the law could be beneficially reduced to a code without a deleterious effect on the legal system.[45] Possibly the *American Jurist* had Metcalf in mind when it declared in 1838 that there was "abundant evidence" to demonstrate that "[a] codifier is not necessarily a radical."[46]

Unfortunately for the cause of codified law, some of its new disciples did not exhibit the zeal that frequently characterized converts. They were still common lawyers at heart, who accepted the logic of codification, but they were only grudgingly enthusiastic about the reform and believed that it should be implemented only on a limited basis.

Men like Metcalf, as one might expect, did not agree with the radicals' idea of the means and ends of codified law. Rather, it was the moderates' conception of codification that they embraced. Indeed, as in the 1830s, radical notions of codification were heard only infrequently from the profession. In accepting the viability of codified law in the American legal order, practitioners concluded that the horrors they had previously anticipated from the reform would not necessarily occur. The content of the legal system would be preserved in a reformed condition, and the techniques of the legal system would remain essentially unchanged.

Statements by codifiers in the 1820s, such as William Sampson's *Discourse,* had led many practitioners to fear that codification would result in a wholly new body of doctrine to replace the rules of the common law in which the social order was grounded. Such a change, it was claimed, would produce "endless confusion" that would threaten the economic and social status quo.[47] Codification, Willard Phillips observed in 1840, had been "considered to be some terrific innovation" because it was suggested by "speculative philosophers" who "were fiercely bent upon up turning the whole mass of laws and introducing many new ones, as foreign to the habits and business and wants of the time." In this situation, men thought it was better to "bear the ills they had, than fly to others they knew not of." Phillips remarked that "that horror has subsided," and codification was considered to be "nothing more than a systematic arrangement of the law," which men were "not afraid" to undertake.[48] Another writer made the same observation somewhat differently. "The idea," he said, "of opening a philosophical laboratory of constitutions and codes for all kinds of communities in any latitude, or for any period is abandoned; and the doctrine now seems to be acquiesced in, by general consent, that a code must be a digest and arrangement of existing laws, than a body of enactments made *per saltum.*" Consequently, he declared, "reckless experiments" need no longer be feared.[49]

The increased attraction of the moderates' argument for other professionals derived in good measure from its development and elaboration. Whereas in the early days of the codification movement, the points of view expressed by both the radicals and the moderates were frequently sketchy and easily confused, as the movement progressed, the moderates' notions matured into a clearer statement of their techniques and objectives of codification.[50] Consequently, it was easy to conclude that codification could be something besides radicalism.

Equally important was the successful application of the principles of codification in the New York Revised Statutes. Until then, codification remained, for many practitioners, visionary speculation. If practical examples such as the Code Napoléon had been cited earlier, they were viewed by the anti-codifiers as either inapplicable to American circumstances or as proof that codification would not have the beneficial results that its proponents claimed. It was impossible to disregard the New York experiment. New York was one of the leading states in the Union, and its legal experience was frequently a source of guidance for others. Furthermore, the Revised Statutes, while not free of defects were generally believed to have had a salutary effect on the legal system of the Empire State. For the practitioner wearied by the artificially long and maze-like statutes of his own state, the New York code of statute law was an appealing sight, indeed.

Taking the Revised Statutes as evidence of the practicability of codification as well as its desirability, one enthusiastic law writer declared that codification was "destined to be done in this country. New York has honorably led the way and shown what may be done." He called upon the other states to "follow her in her track."[51] In a similar vein, another commentator suggested that "[t]he substitution of the terms *revision* and *consolidation* of statutes for that of *codification* has contributed, in no small degree, to the change of thinking on this subject, though they are the same." The "general revision of the whole body of statute law,"he continued, "as in the case of New York, is, in fact, the formation of a code upon the model, or at least, upon the principles of the codes of Justinian and of France."[52]

For others, however, the New York experience had a more restricted relevance. To them, the Revised Statutes pointed up the limited use of the codification concept in improving the workings of the legal system without swallowing the reform whole. These were codifiers of the most moderate sort, who did not favor any plan of general codification. In their view, only selected portions of the law, usually those thought to be most in need of greater precision and clarity or those believed most in need of substantive reform, should be codified into a single authoritative statement.[53]

After 1830, statute law became a frequent object of partial codification. Being already written law, the objections that were directed against codification of the common law did not apply. As in New York, aside from the obvious advantage of making the law more accessible, the codification of statutes was also found appealing for other, and not always complementary, reasons. For law reformers bent on general codification, it was an important step toward their ultimate goal. For others, unconvinced of the practicability or safety of general codification, it was a means of curbing the demands, especially those made by radical reformers, that all the law be reduced to a code. Revision through codification, "Alex" suggested in the Boston *Courier,* would leave a portion of the law reformed and simplified, and this might check the plea of laymen for more revolutionary changes in the legal system. "Revision" of the law, he said, was "the neutral ground on which the lawyers and the people at large may meet."[54]

The Revised Statutes gave added impetus to this sort of partial codification because they could easily be drawn upon without seriously taxing local industry or creativity. Furthermore, borrowing from the Revised Statutes was compatible with the widely held belief among practitioners that experiments in the law should be implemented only if they had been tried somewhere else. In fact, Mississippi enacted most of the important portions of the New York statute code verbatim shortly after it was promulgated in the Empire State.[55]

Because of the widespread borrowing of legal doctrines and techniques that went on among the states, one writer complained in the *American Jurist* that "the states are mere copyists of each other. And like rival mechanics they seem more ready to appropriate each other's innovations, than to be at the expense of making improvements for themselves."[56] However, others believed that basing a revision on the New York model was a means of making American law more uniform. The commissioners of the Massachusetts revision had this in mind when they adopted the format of the Revised Statutes.[57] A writer in the *American Quarterly Review* suggested that "the practice of revising the law throughout the United States, will... bring the discordant enactments of the different legislatures nearer to the same standard, since the fundamental principles of truth, justice and real expediency, are everywhere the same."[58]

In states that codified their statutes, there seems to have been little significant debate over the feasibility or appropriateness of the reform, as far as modifying and systematizing the form of the law was concerned. Whether or not it would be done in a given jurisdiction depended on local circumstances, which did not include resistance to the idea itself. Indeed, by 1840, opposition to consolidating statute law into a code had largely evaporated. Anxiety that modifications of the form of the statute law would have an unsettling effect on the legal system was replaced by gratification with the new legal precision and clarity found in the law. One commentator happily observed of the Pennsylvania revision that "[t]he verbosity and tautology of the old statutes are gone, but all the rest remains."[59] Another, complaining that "new laws are generated like noxious humors in the natural body" and "every son of earth is an L.L.D. by instinct," saw codification of the statutes as a "positive antidote."[60]

Some states pursued the logic of codification more enthusiastically than did others. The New York Revised Statutes probably represented the most thoroughgoing codification of statute law undertaken in the antebellum period. Pennsylvania, on the other hand, was more cautious. Instead of the freewheeling restatement of the law that marked the work of Butler and Duer in New York, the commissioners in Pennsylvania undertook to retain existing phraseology wherever possible, especially, in their words, those "forms of expression which have received judicial construction." The existing statutory text was altered only where it was found essential to "divest it of redundant phrases and useless verbiage."[61] Furthermore, the state did not complete a comprehensive revision of its statutes. Only those subjects whose revision was of immediate and practical importance were improved upon.

In codifying their statutes, each state followed an already well-established practice of appointing special commissioners to formulate the codes. Committees of the legislature were rarely named to draft any important legislation. Given the poor record of legislative draftsmanship that lawmakers themselves acknowledged, it is not surprising that they would resort to such an extraordinary body. It was believed that commissioners had more time and skill than did the average lawmaker. Consequently, the possibility of "superficial, confused, or inadequate legislation" was diminished.[62]

Leading members of the bar were usually appointed as commissioners. For example, Asahel Stearns and Charles Jackson were among the Massachusetts revisors. Pennsylvania named William Rawle, T. I. Wharton, and Joel Jones. James Iredell and William Battle were commissioners in North Carolina. By naming such men, the legislatures, not only guaranteed a suitably drawn code, but they also lent respectability to the project and increased the likelihood that the codified statutes would be approved. Each of the commissioners was closely associated with the existing legal order and had extensive practical experience. Visionary innovation, an anathema to the legal profession, was the last thing one would expect from them. Charles Jackson's appointment as one of the Massachusetts commissioners was typical in this regard. He had read law under Theophilus Parsons, the foremost member of the Massachusetts bar at the time, and had practiced successfully for a decade and a half before his appointment to the highest court in the state. Highly skilled in the black-letter art, he authored a treatise on pleadings and practice in real actions. While never active in political affairs, his preferences were always well known. He began his career as a conservative Federalist and ended it as a conservative Whig. The *American Jurist* observed that when such men as Jackson, "able and enlightened jurists," were appointed to codify statute law, the code would contain no charlatanry; no visionary attempts... no erecting of the statutes in a bed of Procrustus; no violations of the natural progress of society, and order of human affairs; no retrogradation, nor anticipations: all would be adopted to the people and the time, and would be a true development of the spirit of the nation.[63]

Aside from the obvious improvement in the body of the statute law that resulted from its consolidation on the basis of a systematic scheme, each state that codified its statutes reformed the content of the law in varying degrees. Some of the revisions contained surprisingly liberal and creative reforms. However, substantive rights were never threatened in the reform process; if anything, they were strengthened through restatement. In undertaking substantive reforms, the purpose of the commissioners was to improve the workings of the legal system by making the law more functionally adapted to contemporary legal needs. Few states, however, were as energetic in the business of reform as New York had been in its Revised Statutes. This caused disappointment in some quarters. One writer, viewing the revisions accomplished in the United States by 1844, declared that most exhibited only "partial and merely superficial reforms" instead of the "systematic and fundamental revisions" he believed necessary. This record, he observed, had taught him not to be "very sanguine of improvement" in future revisions.[64] Despite the limited nature of the reforms undertaken, conservative practitioners feared that matters had already gone too far. One critic claimed that "[i]n this present era of reform (so called) nothing can be regarded as entirely safe from the pruning knife wielded by innovating hands."[65] Another condemned "those vandals of the present day who would attempt to destroy the very rememberance of the origin of our laws."[66]

Typical of the kind of changes made were the improvements in property law that accompanied a revision of Massachusetts' statutes in 1836. Besides confirming changes in the inherited legal doctrines that were already sanctioned by custom, transfers and conveyances were simplified. The state's revisors also modified the law of expectant estates to permit easier alienation. They eliminated Shelley's Rule as it applied to conveyances by deed as well as in devises and noncupative wills were abolished.[67] Such changes hardly wrought a revolution in property rights in Massachusetts. Rather, they removed anomalies and doubts in the law and thus causes of litigation, abuse, and fraud, as well as anachronisms that had no place in American society. A similarly limited reform was achieved by the Pennsylvania revisions in the law relating to trustees. The revision strengthened the restraints placed on trustees by more clearly defining their duties and the remedies available against them.[68]

The reforms made by some states in their procedural law were occasionally more creative and momentous. "No portion of the law," one commisisoner of revision observed, "has been the subject of more frequent reproach than the system of pleadings of the common law courts, and none has been more encumbered or disfigured by refinements foreign to its object."[69] Being not directly related to property rights, practice was more susceptible to innovative reform. Furthermore, archaic rules of pleading had long been a source of professional complaint. The goal of progressive legal reformers was to streamline and simplify procedure so as to insure the speedy resolution of litigation on the basis of all pertinent facts, not through artifice and technicalities. Aiming for this objective, the Massachusetts commissioners abolished all forms of actions relating to real property except the writ of entry, which was simplified and made generally applicable. And to prevent vexatious litigation, a right of action for the recovery of real property was limited to twenty years. "By these changes," the *American Jurist* remarked, "the law of real actions is very much simplified, and a great deal of learning in the books becomes merely a matter of curiosity."[70] The observation had greater meaning than one might perceive at first glance. Both of the Massachusetts commissioners, Jackson and Stearns, had written texts on the system of real actions that they had abolished. Their reform considerably lessened the value of their publications.[71] These changes in procedural law did not result in the creation of codes of civil procedure or systems of code pleading. Much of the old common law practice remained. However, they were important steps in the direction of our modern system of pleadings.

None of these revisions attempted to codify the common law beyond what was required in revising the statutes. Only those portions of the common law closely related to the statutes and thought to be demonstrably in need of reform were placed in the text. Some revisors, while they quite obviously saw the utility of statutory codification, were skeptical of the idea of reducing all the common law to a code. The Massachusetts revisors, for example, in their initial report to the legislature, remarked that they "have not attempted to embody in the present revision the principles of the common law, any further than has heretofore been gradually done at different periods of our legislation." This was not "the result of unintention or accident," however, as they considered it of "questionable utility" to put "into the form of a positive unbending text, numerous principles of the common law, which are definitely settled and well known."[72] This declaration was not taken as the final word in the matter. A significant movement to reduce the common law to a code still existed, and it was nowhere more visible than in Massachusetts after its statutory revision was completed.

If anything, the codification of the state's statute law whetted the appetite of Massachusetts law reformers to codify all the law. This was especially true among reformers like Frederick Robinson and radical lawyers like Robert Rantoul. From early in the decade, their critique of the law and the legal system was heard in the state. The democratization of the whole legal structure, including the simplification of the law, curbs on judicial discretion, and the deprofessionalization of the legal practice, was their goal, and codification figured prominently as a means by which this could be accomplished.

Special conditions in Massachusetts intensified the desire for law reform along democratic lines. Occurring simultaneously with the statutory revision and continuing after that law reform effort was completed was the trial of Abner Kneeland. A born radical and a sort of latter-day Thomas Paine, Kneeland was accused of blasphemy for directly questioning the divine nature of Christ's conception and for denying the existence of God. Freedom of conscience was, of course, the central issue of the case, which rapidly became a cause célèbre among democrats. However, Kneeland's plight before the courts of Massachusetts, including its highest appellate bench, also appeared to manifest the abuses that the democratic law reformers had complained of and, consequently, resulted in increased demands for change.[73]

Kneeland claimed before the Supreme Judicial Court, as he had before the lower courts of the state, that the statute under which he was accused and had been convicted was contrary to the state constitution, which provided for religious freedom. Blasphemy, the court replied, citing one of James Kent's decisions, was a crime at common law, and the common law was not abrogated by the constitution. The worst fears of the reformer seemed to have been realized. Judges, by appeal to a faceless common law, threw a cloud over constitutional government. Furthermore, the fair conduct of Kneeland's trials (he had several) appeared to have been tainted. Grounding their actions in common law doctrines, the judges had questionably, according to the reformers, excluded relevant witnesses and had allowed the selection of biased jurors who ultimately found Kneeland guilty.

The power of the judiciary in the common law system and the common law itself became the focus of the charges by democratic law reformers. The leader of the Democratic party in the state penned a pamphlet, *Review of the Prosecution of Abner Kneeland,* in which he attacked judicial decisions based on the common law rather than on statutes and urged the popular election of the judiciary.[74] Other critics focused solely on the content of the common law, especially in criminal matters, and the need to replace it with reformed statutes. "B," rehashing old arguments, suggested in the Boston *Courier* that the Kneeland trial was evidence that the common law was "pregnant with false principles and foul practices, with absurdities and errors." He added that "it is chiefly there that mischiefs exist and chiefly there that legal plagues come forth." Furthermore, he asserted that the common law was a "great unexplored ark." "Let the dark be made light," he declared, "let the unclean be purified; and let the unknown be clearly revealed by a full and lucid written code."[75]

Democratic criticism of the legal system was also heard in the legislature, where the reform-minded attempted to translate their disapproval of the existing legal system into public policy. They lent their support to some broadly acceptable reforms, such as the revised statutes and the partial abolishment of special pleading in 1836. However, the democratic reformers also demanded more radical changes in the legal system. In 1835, Frederick Robinson, then a member of the lower house of the General Court, spoke out against the monopoly of the law craft and proposed its abolition through the destruction of rules and regulations that, he said, permitted the existence of the profession and allowed all sorts of chicanery. The recommendation was taken seriously enough that the assembly appointed a special committee to examine the matter, though nothing came of it.[76] In the debates over the revised statutes, it was similarly proposed that the legal profession be opened "to free competition, without regard to preparation."[77] Later, antiprofessional feeling ran strongly enough so that a majority of the lower house instructed the speaker not to appoint a majority of lawyers to the committees on the judiciary and on matters of probate and chancery.[78]

Codification was a natural concomitant to these demands. What would be the point of abolishing the profession, or at least opening it up to laymen, if the law remained inaccessible and complex? Demands for legal simplification among laymen were so widespread that the *Boston Courier* complained that the "[p]eople have been told, until they begin to believe it, that all necessary law could be put into a book and carried in their pocket."[79] "Alex," in the *Courier,* deprecating the "radical spirit" he saw in the state, claimed that "[p]olitical fanatics are attempting to get rid of the 'learned professions.' " Especially concerned with attempts to abolish the legal profession, he suggested it was "just as ridiculous for every man to attempt to be his own watchmaker, as his own lawyer." He added that "[t]he principles of law...are sharp-edged tools; the inexperienced workman will be sure to cut his fingers."[80]

The general enthusiasm in the state for law reform through codification led Joseph Story to remark that "the present state of popular opinion here makes it necessary to do something on the subject." Of course, Story and other moderate codifiers did not agree with the nature or intent of codification as it was proposed by men like Frederick Robinson. In Story's words, "[w]e have not yet become votaries of the notions of Jeremy Bentham."[81] The moderates hoped to channel popular support for radical codification toward the safe and productive goals they believed could be reached through codification—greater accessibility and certainty in the existing law and a limited degree of substantive reform.

Edward Everett, the Whig governor of the state and a long-time advocate of codification, recognizing the interest in the reform, called upon the legislature in his first annual message in January 1836 to take up the codification of the common law. He lauded the recently completed revision of statute law that, he said, promised to make the law more generally accessible and lessen ligitation. "The opinion is perhaps gaining prevalence, and on good grounds," he continued, "that it would be expedient to incorporate into a uniform code, with the Statute legislation of the State, those numerous principles of the Common Law which are definitely settled and well known." He believed that some improvements might be made in the content of the law. "[T]he ark of reform," he suggested, might be "carried farther" toward the removal of "perplexed and unprofitable technicalities" inherited from the English legal science. These changes, however, would be quite limited in nature. Everett had little liking for the sort of reform that radicals like Robinson proposed, with its root-and-branch improvement of English law and its emphasis on textural rigidity as a means to obviate the need for judicial discretion. A code, Everett said, should not be "reduced to the form of a positive and literal text." Rather, it should be comprised of established common law rules that would be "applied by the courts, as principles of the Common Law, when the occurrences of cases requires it." Once the laws were codified, he believed that not only would legal practice be rid of antiquated forms, but that the law would be more certain and more intelligible "to persons of good standing not of the profession," and, in consequence, it would create a better public attitude toward the law and the profession.[82]

The response of the lower house was immediate and enthusiastic. The house showed evidence of being quite reform minded, having also seriously taken up the question of the abolishment of capital punishment. On the question of codification, the lawmakers appointed a special committee of its members to take up and examine the matter and to inform the whole of their findings. Within a week, they submitted a report that strongly recommended implementing the reform.

The report manifested democratic impulses that were then strong in the lower house. In its analysis of the existing legal system, the special committee, not only found the content of the common law to be filled with injustices, abuses, and cruelties, but it also denounced it as contradictory, confused, and heavily laden with inscrutable jargon. The fact that it was unwritten only added to its essentially mysterious character. As a result, the committee submitted, power was concentrated in the hands of judges, who, contrary to the constitution, were permitted in fact to make law in a most capricious manner. Furthermore, laymen, confused by the legal morass of the common law, had to depend on hired pleaders, who were by their nature greedy masters of the art of chicanery. However, once the law were codified, the committee declared, "no laws" would "exist among us, but such as have been reduced to writing, and received the sanction of the people in legislative enactments." They declared that "our governments resting on written constitutions, require a system of public statutes." Because only statutes would have the force of law, judges could no longer make or follow precedents at their pleasure. These radical advocates of codification, unlike their moderate counterparts, did not desire to see the existing common law simply reduced to a code. Rather, the content of the law should be greatly reformed, with the purpose of simplifying it so that "the mass of the community" could understand it and pursue litigation without the necessity of hiring an attorney. Along these lines, they specifically called for the abolition of special pleading. The committee's report concluded by calling upon the house to appoint three Commissioners to begin codifying the law at once.[83]

The whole house was reluctant, however, to set about codifying the common law immediately. Instead of naming the three codifiers, it voted to call upon the governor to appoint a commission of respected jurists to examine the question of codification closely and report to the legislature.[84]

The disinclination of the house to approve the report of the special committee arose from the knowledge that the legal profession would never give its all-important assent to the sort of codification proposed, even though its members might support the more limited application of the reform idea. Typical of the response of many practitioners was that of Luther Cushing, an editor of the *American Jurist* and a noted Massachusetts lawyer. He suggested that the conclusion of the committee, that the law should be codified, was correct. However, the reasons that the committee gave to undertake the reform, he believed, were wrong. If they were the best that could give given, Cushing remarked pointedly, "that great improvement would not... be very likely to take place." The objectives of the special committee, he continued, were "clearly visionary." Speaking as a moderate codifier and as a common lawyer, he asserted that it was impossible to reduce all the law to a written form. Nor was it possible for every man to be his own lawyer, though he did agree with the idea that a citizen of the republic should be, "if he pleases," able to "inform himself of his legal rights and duties."[85]

Men like Cushing would have to give their assent to the codification of the common law and approve the final draft of any prospective code. The reform would never be implemented if the stigma of radicalism or Benthamism remained. It was necessary to legitimize the project in a consensus of the legal profession, and this could only be done if respected leaders of the bar publicly gave codification their blessing, demonstrating that there was nothing to fear in the reform. Furthermore, it was also necessary to insure that the work of codification was aimed in the right direction—that is, merely reducing the size of the law and giving it a systematic order. With these ends in mind, a special commission was appointed by Governor Everett to examine the expediency and practicability of codifying the common law.

Everett took great care in the selection process. It was necessary to name a commission that would not be likely to submit a report advocating any radical reform that would preclude the support of the legal profession. It was also imperative to appoint individuals who favored codification. As Everett wrote to George Grinnell, "I believe it [codification] a great and practicable and useful work." Consequently, he wanted to name men "who entertain the same opinion." Since "a kind of party feeling on the subject" existed, it was also necessary to make the commission as "representative as possible."[86]

Joseph Story agreed with Everett that someone from the "Jackson party" should be appointed "to avoid the possible suggestion of the scheme being a mere party measure." Story suggested that Robert Rantoul would be a "useful and satisfactory" member in this regard.[87] Rantoul's appointment would be helpful in developing "public favor and confidence" in the project, although some practitioners had suggested that "the radical character of his opinions might embarrass the prudent character of the commission."[88] In the end, Story's advice was disregarded, and neither Rantoul nor any other Democrat was appointed by Everett. The five members of the commission were Whigs to a man, and all were prominent members of the bar. Story agreed, somewhat reluctantly, to serve as chairman. The other commissioners were Theron Metcalf, Simon Greenleaf, Charles Forbes, and Luther Cushing.

In keeping with the favorable mood toward law reform in the state, the legislature undertook specific improvements in the law while waiting for the commission to report. The most significant was the partial abolishment of special pleading, a change widely applauded in the state. The black letter art, with its verbosity, mysterious jargon, technicalities, and labyrinthian character, had long been an object of criticism by both lawyers and laymen.

The general codification of the common law, however, was a far more weighty issue, which many practitioners opposed. The radicalism of the Jacksonians in matters of law reform had done little to assuage their fears. Nonetheless, many lawyer-codifiers anxiously awaited the report of the special commission, confident that it would effectively lay the issue to rest and that the work of codification could begin. Charles Sumner was typically hopeful, expressing the expectation that the report "will make an era, perhaps, in the history of the law in our country, for coming with the authority of Judge Story's name and with the cogence of his learning and reason, it will be calculated to have a very great influence throughout the country."[89]

In one sense, Sumner was not disappointed. The report, authored solely by Story, did indeed present a thoughtful and forceful argument in favor of moderate codification. In fact, in all the debates over codification in the United States, none argued as logically, comprehensively, and trenchantly for codes as Story did in this special report. In many ways, it was a summation of the decade and a half of argument over the reform that had preceded it. Once the report was submitted to Governor Everett, little was left to be said.

The report was designed to fulfill a twofold purpose. On the one hand, Story desired to dispel "some erroneous notions" concerning the potential of codification as a reform formula.[90] Specifically, he wished to lay to rest the idea that all the law could be put into a code that would obviate the need for the sort of judicial discretion that was inherent in the common law system. On the other hand, he endeavored to establish a no less important idea: that it was, not only practicable, but expedient to reduce significant portions of the common law to a code.

Story's argument against radical codification did not vary from the position of the orthodox common lawyers on the matter. In what had become a familiar analysis, he suggested that the legal system had to be flexible if legal needs that could not possibly be foreseen were to be satisfactorily met. If an attempt were made to reduce all law to a single text, "leaving nothing to the judgement of courts and of justice, beyond the direct application of the text," Story remarked, numerous unforeseen cases would arise that would be "wholly remedyless" and produce injustice. The legislature could not possibly keep up with these "perpetually accumulating" legal questions through positive legislation. Furthermore, "if any code could be framed which should aspire to provide in detail for the common run of circumstance, it would be found...so voluminous in its precepts, that a whole life would be required to master all its provisions, and more than a whole life to accumulate the materials fit for its composition." He concluded "that private convenience as well as public policy requires, that the common law should be left in its prospective operation in future...to be improved, and expanded, and modified to meet the exigencies of society, by the gradual application of its principles in courts of justice to new cases."[91]

If it were impossible to replace the common law with a code, the partial codification of the common law, leaving intact the inherent discretionary powers of its judges, was a different matter. It was "expedient," Story declared, parting company with his orthodox brethren, "to reduce to a code principles and details of the common law of Massachusetts in civil cases, which are of daily use and familiar application to the common business of life and the present state of property and personal rights and contracts." These rules had, he said, "from long examinations and critical trials, acquired a precision and exactness, which approach very near scientific accuracy" and "are sufficiently clear in their interpretations and qualifications." Criminal law and procedural law, he added, should also be codified. The sort of code Story envisioned would be comprised of "general principles of law." It would not include "all the diversities, expansions, exceptions and qualifications of those principles" found in the numerous volumes of reports.[92]

Lest the commissioners be accused of attempting to revolutionize the operation of the legal system through codes, Story offered several "fundamental rules" that would govern the application of the sort of code he suggested as practicable. The code would be "interpreted and applied to all future cases, as a code of the common law of Massachusetts, and not as a code of mere positive or statute law." It would "furnish the rules for decisions in courts of justice, not only in cases directly...within its terms, but indirectly and by analogy." In cases unprovided for by the code or not governed by analogy, "the common law of Massachusetts, as now existing, is to furnish the rules of decision."[93] Story's point was clear: the common law, in matters of both content and technique, would continue much as before.

Of course, the form of the law would be revolutionized, and therein lay the benefits of codification for Story. In the first place, the law would be made more accessible. Instead of being "spread over many ponderous volumes...nowhere collected together in a concise and systematic form," it would be condensed and systematically arranged. While this would have the desirable effect of helping laymen to understand the laws that govern his "rights, duties, relations and business," it would not make every man his own lawyer. In this regard, a chief benefit of codification would be the elimination of unnecessary labor and research for the attorney. "[O]ften a single page of a code," Story remarked, "would contain, in a clear explicit statement, all that researches of a week, or even a month, would justify them in affirming them with unfailing confidence."[94]

Codification, however, would not result in the reduction of all the common law, exactly as it was, to a concise form. This was neither possible nor desirable. "[T]here are," Story observed, "in the common law many points, which...are not absolutely beyond the reach of forensic controversy, if learned counsel should choose to stir them." On some rules, there were "not only occasional diversities of judicial opinion, but many nice distinctions and differences, and many incidential dicta which serve greatly to perplex the inquiries of the ablest lawyers." This situation, not only added to the labor of the attorney, but also consumed the time of the courts unnecessarily. Codification would remedy this situation by establishing the "true rule" in cases of conflict. However, Story remarked that while this would "suppress useless and expensive litigation," it would not "dry up all the common sources of litigation." New cases would constantly arise, and "[t]hese must necessarily be left to be disposed of by the courts of justice." Similarly, Story suggested, codification afforded "a fit opportunity" to undertake a limited substantive reform of the common law by supplying "acknowledged defects," curing "admitted anomalies," and correcting "erroneous doctrines," which, "in a long succession of ages have gradually been ingrafted upon our common law." This, he added, "ought to be only done with a cautious and skillful hand," and no changes should be attempted "except such as have the sanction of experience and the support and approbation of enlightened judges and jurists."[95]

Story included in the report his suggestions of those portions of the common law that could be suitably and safely codified to the benefit of the state's legal system. He believed it would serve no useful purpose to apply the reform formula to that part of the common law that was largely obsolete but nonetheless still in force. Much of this ancient legal lore inherited from England, such as writs of pasture and of *ejectione firme* and the law of fines and recovery, was not only rarely appealed to but was full of intrinsic difficulties and technical principles that made its codification most difficult.Even if it could be easily accomplished, it would serve no useful purpose and, in fact, would be positively detrimental to the system of codified law by unnecessarily extending its length. However, he suggested, the law "which is of daily occurrence in the common business of life and furnishes the rules for the rights of persons and rights of property of the community—in civil cases" was a different matter. Indeed, he declared unreservedly, that "the labors of codification should be strenuously and sedulously" applied to that portion of the common law. It was there "that the benefits of a code will be most extensively felt, and in which the task may be performed with the greatest certainty of success." Additionally, Story asserted that commercial law, as well as the whole law of crime and punishment, should be codified. He believed the good results that would follow were so apparent that it was "wholly unnecessary" to develop them in the report. To carry out the work of codification, he recommended that a commission of five men "of high standing in the profession" be appointed.[96]

Story had written a careful, but enthusiastic, report favoring the implementations of codification. Intellectually, at least, he seemed to have removed the last obstacles to the reform by answering all the arguments of the anti-codifiers. Certainly the moderate codifiers could not have hoped for more. Not only did he present the best possible case, but not a word of his analysis could be labeled radical. Indeed, radical codifiers took little solace in Story's point of view. Some actually found it objectionable. One writer in the Boston *Statesman* took issue with the essential premise of Story's analysis—that there was a common law constitutionally in existence in Massachusetts. Expressing his disappointment in the report, he asserted that only statute law as approved by the people's representatives carried any real legal force. The common law was the source of judicial usurpation of legislative power, and as such, was a positive danger to the commonwealth.[97] However, radical antagonism to the results of the inquiry made by the special commission was not translated into opposition to the project in the legislature. It was from the other end of the ideological spectrum that the codifiers had most to fear.

The moderates greeted the report with enthusiasm, hopeful of its effect. The *American Jurist,* close to the situation in Massachusetts, reprinted the entire report and declared that it was "received with much favor" in the state.[98] Everett took great "satisfaction" in reading the report and declared to Story that he was "proud" to present it to the legislature. He continued, saying, "I feel that if my connection with the government of the Commonwealth is to be remembered for anything, it will be for my humble agency in getting this great subject into your hands and those of your associates."[99]

The enthusiasm with which the General Court took up codification was somewhat restrained. The senate refused to follow the recommendation that private law be codified. Instead, they resolved that the governor select a commission that would reduce only the criminal law to a code. Since it did not deal directly with property rights, its codification appeared a safe step.

The *American Jurist* greeted the action by the legislature with great pleasure, confident that it marked the beginning of a new era in American law.[100] Others, however, were not as sure that that bright prospect would be fulfilled. The future of codification, Charles Sumner observed shortly after the legislature had voted to codify the criminal law, "will depend, in great measure" on the success of that project.[101] Edward Everett was not even that optimistic. After the senate refused to go beyond the codification of the criminal law he knew that the reform he once believed would add so much to his historical image was doomed to failure. Everett correctly observed that the inherent opposition of the bar to reform stood in the way of the codification of the common law in Massachusetts. As he wrote in his diary, "[s]everal legal gentlemen in the house and senate are opposed" to anything more than the codification of the criminal law. He acidly added, "[w]as it ever found that the members of the legal profession were in favor of legal reform?"[102] He saw the sort of opposition he and the codifiers were up against in a conversation with Daniel Webster, who he found himself to be largely compatible with on other matters. He and Webster "had a long argument on the subject of codification, to which he [Webster] is bitterly opposed." Everett chided Webster that practitioners were usually antagonistic to the most elemental and beneficial improvements in the law. He cited the opposition of the English bar to an act of Parliament in 1730 that required that legal proceedings and instruments be in the native English language instead of the archaic law French, which had been the custom for centuries. Webster replied, manifesting the very trait that Everett condemned, that "they were right...the English Law Bill produced no benefit!"[103]

Given this sort of mentality among the leaders of the bar, it is not surprising that codification met with failure in Massachusetts despite the increased acceptability of the reform, the pressures of democratic reformers, bipartisan support, the approval of Story, and the moderate nature of his reform proposals. To such individuals, the legal status quo, even though defective, was preferable to unsettling reform, especially in matters of property law. They were generally men of property themselves. No ulterior motive derived from this fact. Rather, it was an element in their conservative point of view. They could, however, approve, if reluctantly, the codification of the criminal law. Not only did it not encompass property rights, but, by general consent, the genius of American government required that criminal law should be in writing as a guarantee of personal liberty. Furthermore, its improvement was compatible with a strong contemporary interest in penal reform.

Leading lights of the Massachusetts bar were appointed to codify the state's criminal law: Willard Phillips, John Grey Rogers, Luther S. Cushing, Samuel B. Wolcott, and Charles Jackson, who was later replaced by James Alvord. They were mandated by the legislature to "reduce so much of the Common Law of Massachusetts, as relates to crime and punishments, and the incidents thereof to a written and systematic code." They immediately set about the task, which, according to their own testimony, put their abilities sorely to the test. It was necessary, of course, for them to make sense out of the common law as it related to crimes and to systematize it. In doing so, they experienced first hand what the codifiers had been complaining about. The commissioners had to deal with the problems of reception and with ambiguities, lacunae, and contradictions that were replete throughout the amorphous mass of the unwritten law. So difficult did they find the task that after two years of labor, they informed the legislature that they could not fix a time when the project would be completed.[104]

By the time the commission completed its work in 1841, codification had become decreasingly important as a political issue within the state and as an issue within the legal profession. One indication of this can be seen in the request of Governor John Davies to the commissioners in 1840 to delay their report to the legislature until the following year, as he desired to keep its session short.[105]

The General Court held the draft code in abeyance for several sessions and at last refused in 1844 to implement it. The cause lay not so much in active opposition to codification as in a growing lack of interest, even among its proponents. Some of the problem that had given energy to the reform impulse in Massachusetts were being solved in other ways. Furthermore, other reforms, seemingly more direct and more easily accomplished, were suggested by the lay reformers. This pattern of diminished fascination with codification was generally visible in the United States in the 1840s. There was, however, one significant exception to this development: a highly visible codification movement continued to exist in New York. Considering its leading role in legal matters, success there held the potential for a regeneration of the reform effort throughout the country.

NOTES

1. Frederick Robinson, "A Program for Labor," in *Social Theories of Jacksonian Democracy,* Joseph Blau, ed. (Indianapolis: Bobbs-Merrill Co. 1954), p. 331.

2. Gilbert Vale, "Practical Reform, and Review of Home and Foreign Politics," *The Diamond* 1 (1841): 79.

3. Frederick Robinson, *A Letter to the Hon. Rufus Choate, Containing a Brief Exposure of Law Craft and Some of the Encroachments of the Bar upon the Rights of the People* (n.p.: 1832): pp. 5, 12, 16-17.

4. See David Brion Davis, "Some Themes of Counter-Subversion: An Analysis of Anti-Masonic, Anti-Catholic, and Anti-Mormon Literature," *Mississippi Valley Historical Review* 47 (1960): 205-24.

5. Robinson, *A Letter,* pp. 4, 11, 13, 14. 17.

6. Ibid., p. 10.

7. "Introduction," *United States Magazine, and Democratic Review* 1 (1838): 6.

8. "Duties of the State to Its Citizens," *United States Magazine, and Democratic Review* 22 (1848): 469.

9. "Legerdemain of Law Craft," *United States Magazine, and Democratic Review* 22 (1848): 529.

10. Robinson, "A Program for Labor," p. 328.

11. Boston *Statesman,* 18 July 1835.

12. Ibid., 27 August 1835.

13. Ibid., 25 July 1835.

14. "The Supreme Court of the United States," *United States Magazine, and Democratic Review* 1 (1838): 144.

15. See Boston *Statesman,* 27 August 1836.

16. Robert Rantoul, Jr., *Memoirs, Speeches and Writings of Robert Rantoul, Jr.,* Luther Hamilton, ed. (Boston: J.P. Jewett and Co., 1854), p. 280.

17. Boston *Statesman*, 26 Dec. 1835. See also "Elective Judiciary," *United States Magazine, and Democratic Review* 22 (1848): 199-206.

18. Rantoul, *Memoirs*, p. 278.

19. "Edward Livingston and His Code," *United States Magazine, and Democratic Review* 9 (1841): 12.

20. Boston *Statesman*, 26 Dec. 1835.

21. Robinson, "A Program for Labor," p. 331.

22. "Edward Livingston and His Code."

23. The notion that this was possible had apparently become quite widespread by the mid-1830s. See Boston *Courier*, 21 May 1836.

24. See Boston *Statesman*, 18 Feb. 1837.

25. "Trial by Jury," *United States Magazine, and Democratic Review* 6 (1839): 470-72.

26. "Introduction," pp. 6-7.

27. P. W. Grayson, *Vice Unmasked, an Essay: Being a Consideration of the Influence of Law upon the Moral Essence of Man, with Other Reflections* (New York: G. H. Evans, 1830), pp. 159, 163, passim.

28. John Pickering, "A Lecture on the Alleged Uncertainty of the Law; Delivered Before the Boston Society of the Diffusion of Useful Knowledge, March 5, 1830," *American Jurist and Law Magazine* 12 (1834): 278, 309.

29. "Usury Laws," *American Jurist and Law Magazine* 6 (1831): 282, 308.

30. "Subjecting Lands to the Debts of the Deceased," *American Jurist and Law Magazine* 10 (1833): 457.

31. "Rules of Evidence v," *American Jurist and Law Magazine* 10 (1833): 5, 6-7.

32. "On the Plan and Objects of the *American Jurist and Law Magazine*," *American Jurist and Law Magazine* 19 (1838): 9.

33. See *American Jurist and Law Magazine* 14 (1835): 280-302; 15 (1836): 16-43; 16 (1836): 59-87, 289-315; 17 (1837): 71-93; 20 (1839): 305-24; 21 (1839): 352-72; 22 (1840): 282-303; 24 (1841): 32-62.

34. "Hilliard's Abridgement," *American Jurist and Law Magazine* 19 (1838): 487.

35. David Hoffman, *A Course of Legal Study*, 2d ed. (Baltimore: Joseph Neal, 1836): p. 657.

36. Timothy Walker, *Introduction to American Law* (Philadelphia: P. H. Niklin & T. Johnson, 1837): p. v.

37. "Notices of New Books," *Law Reporter* 6 (1844): 425.

38. S. F. Dixon, "Codification and Reform of the Common Law," *American Jurist and Law Magazine* 14 (1835): 284.

39. Ibid., p. 283.

40. Simon Greenleaf, *A Collection of Cases, Overruled, Denied, Doubted or Limited in Application*, 2d ed. (New York: W. & A. Gould and Co., 1838), n.p.

41. See "Ohio Reports," *American Jurist and Law Magazine* 7 (1832): 261-85; "Revised Code of Pennsylvania," *American Quarterly Review* 19 (1836): 399-420.

42. "Revision of the Laws in Massachusetts," *American Jurist and Law Magazine* 13 (1834): 344-45.

43. For Metcalf's earlier opinion on codification and legal reform, see [Theron Metcalf], "Tyng's Reports, Vol. XIV," *North American Review* 7 (1818): 184-87.

44. Charles Fairman, "Theron Metcalf," *Dictionary of American Biography*, Dumas Malone, ed., 20 vols. (New York: Charles Scribner's Sons, 1934), XII: 582.

45. Joseph Story to Edward Everett, 4 April 1836, Edward Everett Papers, Massachusetts Historical Society, Boston, Massachusetts.

46. Luther Cushing, "The Greatest-Happiness-Principle," *American Jurist and Law Magazine* 20 (1839): 334.

47. "Written and Unwritten Systems of Law," *American Jurist and Law Magazine* 9 (1833): 33.

48. [Willard Phillips], "Bentham's *Theory of Legislation," North American Review* 51 (1840): 395. Phillips had also earlier opposed codification. See his "Pickering's Reports," *North American Review* 20 (1825): 181-83.

49. "Revision of the Laws in Massachusetts," pp. 345-56.

50. See "Written and Unwritten Systems of Law," *American Jurist and Law Magazine* 5 (1831): 23-52; 9 (1833): 5-36.

51. Ibid., 5: 36.

52. "Revision of the Laws in Massachusetts," p. 345.

53. On the contemporary perception of the differences between partial and general codification, see Hoffman, *Course of Legal Study,* 2d ed., pp. 612-13.

54. Boston *Courier,* 21 May 1835.

55. The condition of Mississippi law was particularly bad. One local attorney called it "a perfect chaos." "Legislation in Mississippi," *American Jurist and Law Magazine* 11 (1834): 364.

56. "Criminal Code of Maine," *American Jurist and Law Magazine* 27 (1842): 148.

57. Report of the Commissioners Appointed to Revise the General Statutes of the Commonwealth, 4 vols., I: vi. See also, "Revision of the Laws in Massachusetts," pp. 356-58, suggesting that there was little likelihood that such action would produce the desired result.

58. "Revised Code of Pennsylvania," *American Quarterly Review* 13 (1833): 55.

59. Ibid., p. 53.

60. "The Statute Law of Tennessee," *American Jurist and Law Magazine* 8 (1832): 305.

61. "Revised Code of Pennsylvania," vol. 13.

62. "Proposed Insolvent Law of Massachusetts," *American Jurist and Law Magazine* 6 (1831): 116.

63. "The Statute Law of Tennessee," p. 313. See also Mark DeWolfe Howe, "The Creative Period of Law in Massachusetts," *Proceedings of the Massachusetts Historical Society* 69 (1949): 234-35.

64. "Criminal Code of Maine," p.148.

65. "Limited Partnerships," *American Quarterly Review* 19 (1836): 48.

66. "Revised Code of Pennsylvania," 13: 59.

67. See "Revised Statutes of Massachusetts," *American Jurist and Law Magazine* 15 (1836): 306-307, for commentary on these changes.

68. "Revised Code of Pennsylvania," 13: 56.

69. Ibid., p. 58.

70. "Revised Statutes of Massachusetts," p. 310.

71. See ibid.; "The Creative Period of Law in Massachusetts," pp. 234-35.

72. "Report of the Commissioners," p. x.

73. On Kneeland, see, generally, Leonard Levy, *The Law of the Commonwealth and Chief Justice Shaw* (Cambridge: Harvard University Press, 1957): pp. 43-58; Henry Steele Commager, "The Blasphemy of Abner Kneeland," *New England Quarterly* 8

(1935): 29-41.

74. Arthur Darling, *Political Changes in Massachusetts, 1824-1848* (New Haven: Yale University Press, 1925), p. 198.

75. Boston *Courier,* 13 Dec. 1836. See also Boston *Statesman,* 18 July 1835, 5 and 12 March, 23 April 1836, 11 and 18 Feb., 7 Dec. 1837.

76. Boston *Statesman,* 10 Oct. 1835.

77. *Columbia Centinel* (Boston), 5 Oct. 1835.

78. "Tyson's Discourse," *North American Review* 51 (1840): 234.

79. Boston *Courier,* 21 May 1836.

80. Ibid.

81. Joseph Story to James John Wilkinson, 26 Dec. 1836, *Proceedings of the Massachusetts Historical Society,* 2d ser., XV (1889): 221.

82. Boston *Statesman,* 23 Jan. 1836.

83. Boston *Daily Advertiser,* 1 Feb. 1836. See also Luther S. Cushing, "Codification of the Common Law in Massachusetts," *American Jurist and Law Magazine* 15 (1836): 112.

84. Boston *Daily Advertiser,* 19 Feb. 1836.

85. Cushing, "Codification of the Common Law," pp. 111, 112, 116.

86. Edward Everett to George Grinnell, 5 March 1836, Everett Papers.

87. Joseph Story to Edward Everett, 17 March 1836, Everett Papers.

88. Josph Story to Edward Everett, 22 March 1836, Everett Papers.

89. Charles Sumner to Francis Lieber, 17 Nov. 1836, Charles Sumner, *Memoir and Letters of Charles Sumner,* Edward L. Pierce, ed. 2 vols. (Boston: Roberts Bros., 1893), I: 186.

90. Joseph Story, "Codification of the Common Law," in Joseph Story, *Miscellaneous Writings of Joseph Story,* William W. Story, ed. (Boston: Charles C. Little and James Brown, 1852), p. 706.

91. Ibid., pp. 708, 709-10, 712-13.

92. Ibid., pp. 714,715.

93. Ibid., p. 716.

94. Ibid., pp. 721, 723.

95. Ibid., pp. 724, 725, 726.

96. Ibid., pp. 726, 728, 730, 731.

97. Boston *Statesman,* 11 Feb. 1837.

98. "Intelligence and Miscellany," *American Jurist and Law Magazine* 17 (1837): 487.

99. Edward Everett to Joseph Story, 27 Dec. 1836. Everett Papers.

100. "Intelligence and Miscellany."

101. Charles Sumner to Prof. Mittermaier, 27 March 1837, Sumner, *Memoir,* I: 189.

102. Diary of Edward Everett, 8 Feb. 1837, Everett Papers.

103. Ibid., 13 April 1837.

104. Preliminary Report of the Commissioners to Reduce So Much of the Common Law as Relates to Crimes and Punishments, and the Incidents Thereof, to a Written and Systematic Code," n.d., pp. 5, 7-30.

105. William Lincoln to Willard Phillips, 27 Dec. 1840, quoted in Gerald W. Gawalt, "Massachusetts Lawyers: A Historical Analysis of the Process of Professionalization, 1760-1840," unpublished Ph.D. dissertation, Clark University, 1969, p. 187.

8

WORKING FOR CODIFIED LAW: NEW YORK, 1830-1860

If interest in codification was generally on the wane in the United States in the early 1840s, it continued to exist without diminution in New York. The codification movement was largely sustained there by the state's inability to correct persistent deficiencies in the workings of its legal system. Specifically, onerous delays in litigation, with attendant high costs, continued. The state's unique role on the cutting edge of American legal development meant that success there might be translated into renewed efforts to codify American law in the country as a whole.

One source of legal abuse was found in a faulty judicial system, capped by a hydra-headed set of appellate courts, that was inadequate to handle the increasing deluge of business brought before the bench. No court was free from criticism. The court of errors, one of the common law appellate courts, according to contemporary professional analysis, had a "cumbrous character." Because of the "uncertainty of its decisions," it was "very unpopular with the great body of the profession." The Court of Chancery was "still more disliked" because of "the intolerable delays to which suitors were subjected." In 1841, it was two years behind in its calendar of cases.[1] The Supreme Court was "disliked on account of the separation of its judges into judges of law and judges of fact, and the evils resulting from this sequestration of the higher judges from jurors and witnesses, and the active business of the profession." The Court of Common Pleas, the most active of the lower courts, was considered "petty" and "notorious for incompetency." The retention of the inherited dual court system—law and equity—in the state was the cause of much uncertainty as to the proper mode of redress and, consequently, a source of additional bitter complaint. Furthermore, with the exception of the improvements made in real property actions in the Revised Statutes and in certain other minor statutory reforms, New York remained saddled with the antiquated, complex, verbose, and, of necessity, dilatory system of English procedure.[2] It was a system of remedial law that was hardly fitted to the needs of a busy commercial area like New York.

The resulting widespread sense of legal abuse encouraged the governors of the state, beginning in 1834, to make urgent pleas annually to the legislature for reform.[3] William L. Marcy's message in 1836 was typical. He observed to the lawmakers that the "vast increase of business in our higher courts has demonstrated their inadequacy" and declared that "[s]omething must be done for public relief."[4]

Individual practitioners promoted the work of law reform with vigor. For example, in 1838, Theodore Sedgwick, Jr., published a pamphlet analyzing the nature and cause of delay in the legal system, with suggestions for change by which he hoped the legislature would take remedial action.[5] Gulian Verplanck, a lawyer of reformist bent as well as a minor American literary figure, led what was a largely futile fight for procedural reform as a member of the legislature.[6] Among the strongest and most persistent voices heard demanding the amelioration of the legal system was that of David Dudley Field, who was to emerge as the pre-eminent figure in American law reform during the second half of the nineteenth century. Beginning in 1839 and for nearly the next half century, Field indefatigably agitated the question of law reform in the state.[7]

For the most part, interest in reform was directed toward structural improvements in the court system, a matter on which a majority of the legal profession agreed that something had to be done. Codification was not a necessary component of this reform. Nonetheless, varying applications of the reform formula were viewed by many as an essential element in any comprehensive and satisfactory effort to improve the state's legal order. For some the experience with codification with the revised statutes encouraged interest in the reform. Gulian Verplanck, for example, citing the beneficial effect of the revision, suggested that judicious codification would improve the workings of the legal system. By that means, the state could, in his words, "fix by enactment what is floating and uncertain...expunge what is contradictory to the wiser rule...improve what is imperfect...amend what is defective...[and] repeal what is obsolete." The result, he suggested, would be a body of "brief declaratory rules" that would lessen the burden on the courts by preventing unnecessary litigation and speeding the resolution of many disputes by giving the judge in a given case a "ready and perspicuous rule of action and decision."[8] No doubt, Verplanck's statement reflected, not only New York's particularly onerous situation, but also his perception of those enduring problems of the common law that had fostered the codification movement in the United States and that were especially acute in New York. For example, in 1836, David Hoffman counted seventy-five volumes of New York reports.[9] The multiple appellate courts of the state boasted an annual output of opinions unrivaled in any other jurisdiction in the common law world. Their very numbers prompted one law writer to ponder, "[w]hat may be effected when some modern Tribonian shall appear with the capacity and powers of compiling from the now almost countless volumes of law, a rational and uniform system of jurisprudence?" He suggested that "it would be idle even to hazard a conjecture."[10]

While the general codification of the common law remained popular in New York, the concept of the partial codification of procedural law met with even greater approbation. Many were satisfied with the state of the substantive law, believing that its most important areas of law had already been successfully reformed, at least as much as they ought to be, but that practice should be improved. Indicative of this attitude was one contemporary's observation that "[o]ur real law has undergone a complete modification; our commercial law is based on reason; but we are practicing in the 19th century, with all the formulas and fuss of the 17th."[11] The legal profession was in near-universal agreement that something had to be done to improve and streamline practice.

Familiar complaints were heard concerning the inherited remedial law used in the state. It was slow, arbitrary, overly technical, archaic, artificial, and labyrinthine.[12] There was, however, little harmony within the legal profession as to what sort of specific reforms should be undertaken, although it was recognized that change had to come through legislation. There was a predilection toward the codification formula, regardless of any divergence in matters of content, and the state's encounter with codification in the Revised Statutes gave added weight to that tendency.

It was David Dudley Field who led the second phase of the codification effort in New York. For his work, Field has been accorded a paramount position among law reformers by legal historians. While this conclusion is essentially correct, his role in the American codification movement is in need of reassessment. It has generally been suggested that Field was the fountainhead of the codification effort in America, and that the brand of codification he promoted bore his particular stamp. Maurice Lang, in a brief study of codification in the common law world, declared that it was through Field that "[t]he movement for the codification of the law in the United States originated in New York."[13] Similarly, Alison Reppy has suggested that with the exception of Livingston's penal code, nothing tangible in the way of a reform effort could be found in England or America before Field appeared on the scene. "It remained, therefore," Reppy observed, "for Field to launch an Anglo-American movement for codification."[14] In a recent overview of America's legal past, Lawrence M. Friedman refers to Field as the "hero" of the "codification movement... one of the set pieces of American legal history."[15]

That Field deserves the highest commendation for his law reform efforts no one can doubt. However, the American codification movement hardly began with him. Codified law, as we have seen, had been a matter of serious debate within the legal fraternity and had actually been successfully attempted, if in a limited way, by the time he became a practitioner in 1830. Field's exposure and attachment to codification came in part from reading the works of Livingston, Sampson, and others, as well as from his professional association with Henry Dwight Sedgwick, who had established his credentials as a codifier by 1824.[16] In fact, Field came to participate in the movement rather late, just as the effort to codify American law had begun to ebb, at least in the older eastern states. While sporadic and localized interest in the reform would continue, and while some states adopted codes, no broad-based movement favoring general codification existed after the mid-1840s. By that time, the effectual perimeters of the codification formula had been well established: partial codification was widely and increasingly acceptable as a method to improve the legal system, but general codification was not. Similarly, Field's concept of codification differed not at all from the moderates' approach to the reform.[17] In his analysis of the need for the reform or the reform itself, he added nothing new. The same might be said of his chief opponent James C. Carter, who is frequently credited with being the agent of the defeat of the codification movement.[18]

None of these considerations detract from Field's contributions; rather, they place them in their proper perspective. Field's importance as a codifier derives in good measure from his relentless, but what became his almost solitary, promotion of codification throughout most of his professional career. For decades, he struggled to keep the idea of codification before the public and professional eye. His perseverance, coupled with his position among the leadership of the bar, insured recognition for his efforts, even though they were largely fruitless. Field's true greatness, however, lies in his codes. Unlike most codifiers, whose efforts did not include the drafting of codes, Field actually formulated a number of draft codes for his native New York. While, with one exception, they were spurned there, many other states adopted a number of them. This was especially true of his procedural code. This one code, promulgated in New York, was extensively borrowed throughout the United States. Not only did it cement what was widely acknowledged in theory—the desirability of partial codification—but it also went a long way toward revolutionizing civil procedure in the United States.

The first tangible action in the movement for codified law that Field led in New York did not come from the legislature. In spite of the annual pleas of the governors and the ferment for legal reform in the state, the legislature did little beyond discussing the matter and appointing a special commission of practitioners to examine the cause of delay in the courts and to suggest remedies. The commission submitted recommendations designed to "diminish litigation, facilitate the progress of suits, and prevent the unnecessary accumulation of expenses and costs" through largely structural changes. Codification was not among the proposals.[19] However, the lawmakers responded to this and other suggestions by doing nothing that remedied the situation. The cause of their inaction can be found in a combination of legislative inertia, the traditional reluctance of legislators to move in the area of law reform, and their inability to agree on specifically what should be done.

The indisposition of the lawmakers to reform the legal system led to a successful call for a constitutional convention, which met in 1846. While that body took up a host of matters, it was generally agreed that the "chief reason" for its existence was "to remedy the defects in the legal system to produce speedy inexpensive justice."[20]

Urged on by Field and others through newspaper articles, correspondence, and conversation, the convention took up the matter of judicial reform with enthusiasm.[21] The court structure was completely refashioned, with the most important change being the abolition of separate courts of equity and of law, the powers of both being unified in a single court. This had long been sought as a means of streamlining justice and bringing greater certainty to the legal system. "Few will fain to regret," one commentator suggested at the time, "the extinction of the ancient title of chancellor." He saw the concurrent existence of equity and law in one court as a step toward "the scientific administration of justice," which, if carried out to its logical conclusion through the unification of equity and common law procedures, would give New York "an opportunity...to place her jurisprudence on a basis of simplicity and order as never before enjoyed."[22]

Some sort of reform of procedure was necessitated by the reorganization of the courts. Merely to change the court structure without ameliorating defective procedures would have been a half measure toward the improvement of the administration of justice in the state. Furthermore, in combining the jurisdictions of law and equity into one court, the constitutional convention did not actually abandon the distinction between the two or modify in any way their distinctly different systems of pleading and practice. If left alone, this system of dual jurisdiction would have represented no improvement at all and would have created an impossible situation in terms of practice.

Accordingly, reform of practice was, in the words of Charles Z. Lincoln, the constitutional historian of New York, "[o]ne of the most important subjects which engaged the Convention."[23] Instead of undertaking the improvements themselves, which was not only impracticable but also hardly in keeping with their purpose of refashioning the organic law of the state, the convention delegates provided, in the new constitution, that the legislature should carry out the reform. Specifically, it mandated the legislature to appoint "three commissioners whose duty it shall be to revise, reform, simplify and abridge the rules of practice, pleadings, forms and procedures of the courts of record in this state."

Obviously, the vague nature of the constitutional requirement permitted all manner of speculation about what form procedural law should take. However, its intent as well as its wording implied that New York's procedural law would be codified. No doubt this was understood and accepted by at least some of the delegates to the convention.

If codification appeared to be assumed in this part of the constitution, it was explicit elsewhere. Influenced by the tireless efforts of Field, the convention also included a section in the organic law that charged the legislature to "appoint three commissioners whose duty it shall be to reduce into a written and systematic code the whole body of the law of this state, or so much and such parts thereof as to the said commissioners shall seem practicable and expedient." However, they adopted the section with something less than total enthusiasm. Forty-five of the 105 members voting opposed the action. Consequently, while the codification formula was given the strongest tangible impetus toward implementation thus far seen in America, the strong opposition that greeted it in the convention boded ill for its success.[24]

The constitutional directives on procedural reform, plus the strongly felt need for legal change in the state, overcame the previously strong reluctance on the part of the legislature to reform practice. Following the ratification of the constitution, the lawmakers were greeted with several suggestions concerning the sort of procedural reform they should attempt to effect. Field, for example, published a pamphlet entitled *What Should Be Done with the Practice of the Courts* that urged a total revamping of New York procedure.[25] In a further effort to influence legislative action, he also prepared a memorial, signed by sixty-one prominent members of the bar, which asserted

> that a radical reform of legal procedure in all its departments is demanded by the interests of justice and by the choice of the people; that a uniform course of proceedings in all cases, legal and equitable, is entirely practicable and no less expedient; and that a radical reform should aim at such uniformity and at the abolition of all useless forms and proceedings.[26]

The codification formula was quite naturally implicit in this declaration. However, the degree to which it would be implemented depended on the extent to which the prospective commissioners on the reform of practice were willing to go in reducing the existing law to codified form or in replacing it with new legislation.

Because of his views of law reform, which were considered too revolutionary for some, Field was not appointed to the commission for the reform of practice. The appointees were Arphaxed Loomis, a prominent law reformer who had led the fight for improvement of practice in the constitutional convention; David Graham, a leading authority on New York procedure; and Nicholas Hill, Jr., an eminent practitioner. They were instructed by the legislature to draft a bill that would provide

> for the abolition of present forms of action and pleading, in all cases at common law; for a uniform course of proceedings in all cases whether of legal or equitable cognizance, and for the abandonment of all Latin and foreign tongues so far as the same shall be deemed practicable and of any form of proceedings not necessary to ascertain or presume the rights of the parties.[27]

On the same day, 8 April 1847, the legislature also appointed Reuben H. Walworth, Alvah Worden, and John A. Collins, all well-known lawyers, as Commissioners of the Code, pursuant to the directive of the new constitution that the law of the state should be codified. For codifiers, it must have been a great day, indeed. Until then, except for the limited gains made in the form of partial codifications of statute law, the codification movement had largely been limited to discussion and debate. Now, tangible, positive action had been taken. While success was not assured, prospects must have seemed bright.

The first, and most successful, fruits of the dual reform effort came from the Commissioners on Practice and Pleading, but not before a change occurred in their membership. Field's ostensible radicalism had precluded his appointment to the commission. However, Nicholas Hill soon found that his two fellow commissioners were of a like mind with Field. Hill considered it the duty of the commission merely to reform existing practice, not to abandon it and build anew as Loomis and Graham seemed bent on doing. Consequently, he resigned, stating that he could not agree with their intent to recommend changes "so purely experimental, so sudden and general, and at the same time so perilous," as he believed them to be.[28] His resignation suggests that there were possibly strong opposition within the bar to the sort of reforms Field had been recommending. However, in the general enthusiasm for reform, Field was appointed to replace Hill.

The three commissioners, now thinking alike, proceeded apace and, in five months, submitted their first draft code of procedure to the legislature. While it would be called the Field Code, it was a product of the labors of all three commissioners.[29] The code, which covered a number of subjects in civil procedure, was considered the first installment of an entire code of remedial law. On matters where it was silent, the old law was expressly retained. Yet to come were additions to this first code, covering evidence and testimony in civil actions as well as an entire code of criminal procedure.

Entitled "An Act to Simplify and Abridge the Practice and Pleadings and Proceedings of the Courts of the State," this partial code was enacted by the legislature in April 1848, a month and a half after they had received the draft, and it went into effect 1 July 1848. Comprised of 391 sections, it was, stylistically speaking, the most perfect concrete expression of the codification formula yet seen in the United States, outside of Louisiana. As Lawrence Friedman has observed, it was

> tightly worded and skeletal; there was no trace of the elaborate redundancy, the voluptuous heaping on of synonyms so characteristic of Anglo-American statutes. It was, in short, a code in the French sense, not a statute. It was a lattice of reasoned principles, scientifically arranged, not a thick thumb stuck into the dikes of the common law.[30]

The content of the code departed no less from the past than did its form. The procedural distinction between law and equity was completely eliminated, and a single highly simplified procedural law was created to replace it. Among other things, the ancient forms of action at common law were eliminated, as was special pleading and the rules that determined the sufficiency of pleadings. Only one form of action was provided for in the code, with but one method of commencing it. Parties in a suit were called upon to plead the facts of the case, not to plead the issue as at common law. A litigant, in the words of the code, was to state his case "in ordinary and concise language, without repetition, and in such a manner as to enable a person of common understanding to know what is intended."[31] The code made a distinct break with the past. While it did not usher in an era of procedural reform, as much had been done before in New York as elsewhere, it nonetheless gave a new direction and increased energy to efforts to improve the procedural law in the United States.[32]

As one might expect, the implementation of the new codified form of practice provoked no uniform response. Typical of those who looked favorably on the change was John W. Edmonds, a judge of the state supreme court. While Edmonds considered the changes made in the law "radical," he also believed them "essential" and saw "nothing novel or startling" in the code. He believed it radical in the sense that it utterly did away with old forms and practices, but many of these were time-consuming, served no useful purpose, and had long been sources of much complaint. "Nothing," he asserted, "has been lopped off, which had not been condemned by some of the most enlightened members of the profession; and nothing introduced that is calculated to impair the rights of property or to interfere with the enjoyment of liberty or the pursuit of happiness."[33] Professional periodicals, reflecting the reformist inclination so characteristic of them in the antebellum years, generally applauded the code.[34] Typical of their analysis was that of the *Law Reporter,* which commended the code's "simple and compact form" and found its content a welcome remedy to the verbose and complicated proceedings it replaced.[35]

This enthusiasm was not shared by the more conservative members of the profession. These were men who were, according to one contemporary observer, "strongly opposed to experiments" and who looked upon reform as a "vandal spirit...invading the province of jurisprudence."[36] No doubt characteristic of their point of view was Thomas Dunscomb, James Fenimore Cooper's fictional lawyer in his last novel, *The Ways of the Hour,* which Cooper used as a vehicle to criticize the reforms that had resulted from the constitution of 1847. Dunscomb was " 'emphatically' a common lawyer," who was undoubtedly arche typical of many of Cooper's contemporaries within the bar. He was "not at all 'agreeable' to this great innovation [the procedural code] on 'the perfection of reason.' " It was, he said, "as extravagant and high flying an invention as ever came from the misguided ingenuity of man." Manifesting the conservative opposition to change, Dunscomb declared that he found "no pleasure in managing a cause since this Code of Procedure has innovated on all our comfortable and venerable modes of doing business."[37]

It was this sort of mentality that helped to defeat each code subsequently proposed by the Commissioners on Practice and Procedure. However, more was involved in their rejection than the conservative forces once again gaining the upper hand in the legislative struggle for legal reform. The code itself proved to be defective; which simultaneously strengthened the forces of opposition and weakened the position of its advocates. Shortly after the code went into effect, it was found necessary to amend it significantly to supply omisions and to cure defects. Originally, it contained 391 sections. In less than a year, it had grown to 473. By the time it was repealed in 1877, its size had swelled nearly tenfold.[38] It should be noted that the courts, generally manned by conservative common lawyers, were generally hostile to the code and used their courtrooms to subvert it.[39]

One could make a strong case for the suggestion that not all these additions were in fact necessary, and that the legislature destroyed the code's ability to function as intended by constantly tinkering with it and making it more complex. However, the fact remains that contemporaries believed the code deficient and thus attempted to ameliorate it. To the anti-codifiers, this felt necessity to improve the code annually proved their argument that it was impossible to deal legislatively with matters that required the flexibility of the common law. As one law writer of the day noted, "every subsequent amendment" to the code after it was put in effect "was regarded as a tacit admission that the projectors themselves viewed it in the light of an experiment. Generally it was classed in the category of impractical theories."[40]

No doubt dissatisfaction with the code and its new simplified system of procedures arose from its novel format and content and practical legal skills. Instead of relying on his "accustomed blanks or his precedents," one legal light observed, the practitioner was "sent back to the fountainhead of principle" as stated in the code in sparse unadorned language.[41] The common lawyers naturally felt out of their element in the business of code pleading. Instead of the massive tomes that required labor, but nonetheless familiar labor, the lawyer and judge had to rely on a systematically arranged spare set of legal principles. Naturally, they felt uncomfortable, and, naturally, they attempted to bring back that accustomed comfort through amendments to the code that made it more elaborate and more complex. As Field himself later said of these common lawyers, "as a general rule we might as soon expect a Mohammedan to take a Christian to his bosom as a case lawyer, no, I might say, a case-hardened lawyer, to take a code to his."[42]

Defects in the code, however, were quite real. From the very beginning of the codification process in New York, the legislature attempted to see that the work was completed as rapidly as possible. The three commissioners were given something over a year and a half to codify all the procedural law of the state. They had to request two separate extensions of their commissions before they completed their task. The legislature, Judge Edmonds complained, appeared "to expect a code of practice by return mail." This, he continued, "denied to the proposed reforms before enactment, that due examination, in or out of the legislature, so essential to the perfection of such a work."[43]

A second cause of the code's shortcomings was its lack of a strong empirical base, which was the result of the commissioners' approach to the codification of procedural law. Like their counterparts in Louisiana a generation earlier, these codifiers believed it possible to experiment in matters of practice since procedural issues did not directly involve property rights. Consequently, they drew upon "ideal of right reason," as one commentator has observed, "rather than from a careful study of what actually happened in American courts, and what function and interests courts and their law suits served."[44] The code, as a result, appeared to confirm the objections of anti-codifiers, that codification would result in a system of laws poorly related to real legal needs. Adding to this difficulty was the fact that the original Code of 1848 was never intended to be a complete system of remedial law; it was but one part of a greater whole. The rejection of the other proposed portions of a completed code of practice, because of dissatisfaction with the original installment, left what could best be called a hybrid system—part code, part common law. The Code of 1848, however, was written as one part of a completely codified system of procedure, not as a supplement to the common law. As such, it could never be a satisfactory system of law by itself without extensive changes.

Lacking the broad-based support that stood behind procedural reform, the codification of New York's substantive law was never implemented, although the state went further in that direction than any other up to that time. The inclusion of the directive in the constitution of 1847 that all the law of the state, or as much as was believed practicable, should be codified was the result of the generally reformist spirit of the convention generated by the defective legal system and the urging of Field. Enthusiasm for the project, however, rapidly waned, and opposition to the reform, always strong, asserted itself.

In keeping with constitutional authority, the legislature in 1847 appointed three Commissioners of the Code for a term of two years to codify the law of the state. After some initial difficulties in securing three individuals willing to serve, the legislature began to have second thoughts about the wisdom of the project. Demonstrating a characteristic reluctance to engage in matters of legal reform, the lawmakers requested that the commissioners report to them on the advisibility of limiting their labors to a new revision of the statute law. The commissioners replied that they had a constitutional mandate to codify all the law, and that it was not within their power to question it. However, as they pursued their labors, at least two of the commissioners began to doubt the expediency of the project. Expressing the view of common law orthodoxy in their report to the legislature at the end of their term of office, they asserted their belief that the statute law and common law "are distinct in their character and cannot really be assimilated in their general and leading features." Instead of a codification of the common law, they included in the report their revision of the first six chapters of the Revised Statutes, without a recommendation for legislative approval.[45] A new commission was then appointed for a term of two years, but, when one of its members, John C. Spencer, an author of the Revised Statutes, refused to serve, the law providing for the commission was repealed, and codification was dead in New York at least for the time being. One commentator observed that given the climate in the state following this blow to the codification movement, "[t]o resuscitate the Commission would be like raising the dead, and this was not an age of miracles."[46]

Field charged that this initial effort to codify the substantive law of New York failed because the commissioners "had no faith in a codification of the common law, and neither appeared to understand what was meant by it nor [were] competent to undertake it if they had. They thought only of a new revision of statutes. What we wanted was a codification of the Common Law."[47] Whether or not the commissioners had confidence in the project, the immensity of the task and the brief period of time alloted to them by the legislature to complete it discouraged them from approaching codification with vigor. The apparent rapidity with which the legislature awaited the completed work dissuaded some appointees from serving at all and was a frequent source of complaint.[48]

However, more was involved. The codification movement in New York was confronted with two formidable problems that made the outlook for future success pessimistic, indeed. On the one hand, there was the strong opposition of many influential members of the bar, orthodox common lawyers, who saw codification of the substantive law as a dangerous experiment. This was the same sort of resistance the American codification movement had faced from its inception, and it was fed by the unsatisfactory experience with the procedural code. Such an impediment could have been overcome only if there were exceptionally strong enthusiasm for the reform among laymen and other lawyers dissatisfied with the legal order. This, New York lacked. There was not perfect contentment with the legal system, of course. But the abuses that gave the effort its initial thrust, specifically the onerous delays in the courts, no longer existed as a result of the constitution of 1846 and of subsequent legislation passed to enact its provisions. More general problems, such as an overly large objective body of law and a need for substantive reform, had also been solved to the extent that they no longer gave powerful impetus to reform. In New York as elsewhere after 1850, interest in codification was on the decline, though as long as Field was alive, it would not die.

Despite the setback codification received in New York, Field continued his efforts in behalf of the reform, aggressively agitating to revive the code commission. In 1855, he managed to get a bill before the legislature to that end, but it was rejected.[49] Two years later, he met with success. Partly because of his persistent efforts and also because of the continued existence of the constitutional mandate directing codification, the legislature reestablished the Commission on the Code. The lawmakers were also motivated by the knowledge that they would make the ultimate determination whether subsequent codes should be implemented. Furthermore, the autonomy of the commission was specifically limited by the requirement that draft codes would, at several stages before their presentation to the legislature, be distributed among legal officers of the state for criticism and suggestions for improvement. This requirement helped quell any fears of Field's supposed radicalism. No doubt the absence of any provision to compensate the commissioners also encouraged legislative action.[50]

For the next eight years, three commissioners, Field and two others, worked to complete their task and presented the final draft of penal and civil codes to the legislature in February 1865. A separate political code had been submitted in 1860. Like the original code of procedure, these documents were short and uncomplicated. The whole of the substantive civil law of the state was encompassed in 2,034 sections. The criminal code was slightly more than half as long, and the political code contained 1,136 sections. They contained none of the verbosity, fictions, complexities, or redundancies of the common law. In other words, they reflected the impulses and desires that had energized the American codification movement.

The movement, however, did not have enough strength to effect the implementation of these codes. In fact, the codification effort in New York after 1850 was sustained largely through the strength of David Dudley Field's efforts alone, while opposition to the reform remained strong. In the words of Field's biographer, "lawyers were quite willing, as a matter of professional curiosity, that Mr. Field and his associates should amuse themselves with their beautiful codes," but they considered it to "be quite another thing to ask the whole bar of the state to put their necks under the yoke."[51]

A crazy quilt legislative history covering two decades followed the submission of the draft codes to the legislature. They were constantly brought before the lawmakers for their approval, and Field annually trekked to Albany to work for their passage. Ultimately, a version of the penal code was ratified in 1881, but only after many attempts at passage and after it had been rewritten. Of course, resistance to the codification of criminal law was never as strong as that directed toward attempts to improve substantive civil law. This aversion to the reform of private law was translated into an insurmountable barrier to the passage of the proposed civil code. Indeed, at one point, the New York Bar Association named a special committee to see that the code was defeated in the legislature.[52] In spite of Field's efforts for two decades, the civil and political codes were rejected.

Initially, the second phase of the codification movement in New York had great advantages. David Dudley Field was one. Another was the widespread dissatisfaction with the legal system that was translated into demands for legal change. However, once the court system was reformed and the procedural code was implemented, although with not altogether satisfactory results, the momentum behind codification lagged. Without Field, it is doubtful that it would have continued to exist at all. The persistent opposition of influential members of the bar, such as James Carter, sealed its fate.

Had Field's codes been successfully implemented, the codification movement, flagging elsewhere in the United States, would perhaps have been revived, although the compelling problems that had originally energized the widespread effort were being ameliorated. Lacking the impelling force of widespread dissatisfaction, especially among practitioners, as seen in earlier decades, it seems unlikely that sucess in New York would have been translated into any universal triumph for codified law. The efforts in New York, nonetheless, did encourage sporadic and localized interest in codification elsewhere.

Even though the codification movement was dying by mid-century, the reform occasionally received strong endorsements. Timothy Walker, a student of Story's at Harvard, through his *Western Law Journal,* for example, attempted to develop support for codified law, but with no real success in his adopted state of Ohio.[53] Nonetheless, the western United States proved to be fertile ground for a limited revival of interest in codes. Being relatively new political units, there was quite naturally no powerful emotional or practical attachment to an entrenched legal system. Unlike the situation in the older states, the maintenance of property rights was not yet associated with an established system of law. Consequently, legal change did not represent disruption of those rights. Indeed, because of their very newness, the absence of a developed system of law, and the frequently conflicting attempts of individuals to take advantage of the opportunities these states were supposed to offer, property rights were uncertain and a source of litigation. This prompted a desire to be able to settle disputes as expeditiously and with as much flexibility as possible. The law of the eastern states, frequently complex, filled with treacherous uncertainty, and often inapplicable to the unique conditions found closer to the frontier, was unappealing. Furthermore, the bars of the new states and territories were made up largely of youthful individuals from numerous jurisdictions. These were ambitious men generally not overburdened with legal talent. The adoption of a new codified legal system of law, with all its appealing simplicity, was quite easy for them.[54] The alternative to adopting codes was unappealing. These jurisdictions could either adopt the reception formula, accepting the law of one or more of the older states that was applicable to their circumstances as of a given date, or they could develop a legal system from the ground up for themselves. Both solutions would be accompanied by potential problems of legal inaccessibility and uncertainty. A code might not bring perfect certainty, but a self-contained legal system could be created by that method in a stroke, without having to adopt a system of laws presumed as with reception.

The existence of the Field codes was essential to the adoption of codified law in a number of western states since Field offered a code or codes that could be implemented with little effort. Some of the very factors that encouraged the acceptance of codes—a youthful bar and the absence of a developed corpus of native law to draw upon—discouraged local efforts at drafting a code. As with the adoption of the fruits of other codification efforts, such as the New York Revised Statutes, the Field codes could be ratified, with whatever minor changes were needed, without taxing local professional skills.

Of the jurisdictions that adopted the Field procedural code before the end of the Civil War, only one (Georgia) was among the original thirteen states, and most had recently entered the Union or were still territories.[55] Only western states—California, the Dakotas, Idaho, and Montana—adopted any of the Field codes relating to substantive law. One older eastern state, Georgia, on the very eve of the Civil War, codified her law. This effort grew out of the state's unsatisfactory system of common law, which had developed in a highly haphazard fashion. Furthermore, the state had a tradition of legal reform through legislation that eased the effort.

The implementations of partial codifications or complete systems of codified law after 1845 represented localized efforts. Field, for example, was not aware of the Georgia code until some years after its ratification.[56] Such codes did not represent a general renewal of interest in codification as a reform formula; rather, they were the offspring of the codification movement. The significant debate over whether American law should be codified had been decided some years before. By 1845, it was generally established that partial codification was an acceptable and useful tool of law reform but that any general codification of the law was rejected. The shelving of the Field codes in New York only confirmed this fact. Complete systems of codified law in a small number of western states appear as aberrations whose variations from the norm had little meaning in fact. Their codes hardly took them out of the family of common law jurisdictions. The role of the courts as lawmakers in each of these states was not changed by codification. Soon, each of these states had a set of reports that were considered evidence of the law as much as were its statutes or codes. In effect, then, the codes had become partial codifications.

NOTES

1. Charles Z. Lincoln, ed., *Messages from the Governors, Comprising Executive Communications to the Legislature*.... 11 vols. (Albany: J. B. Lyon, 1909), III:871.

2. "The New Constitution of New York," *Law Reporter* 9 (1847): 485.

3. See Lincoln, *Messages from the Governors*, III:433, 489, 536, 608, 647, 716, 1009; IV:30, 53.

4. Ibid., III:536.

5. Theodore Sedgwick, *A Statement of Facts in Relation to the Delays and Arrears of Business in the Court of Chancery of the State of New York* (New York: A. S. Gould, 1838).

6. Robert W. July, *The Essential New Yorker: Gulian Crommelian Verplanck*

(Durham, N.C.: Duke University Press, 1951), pp. 226-30. See also Gulian Verplanck, "Administration of Justice in New York," *Law Reporter* 2 (1839): 33-42.

7. David Dudley Field, *Letter to G. C. Verplanck on the Reform of the Judicial System of the State* (New York: 1840); Henry M. Field, *The Life of David Dudley Field* (New York: Charles Scribner's Sons, 1898), pp. vi-xi, 42-56, 68-96. On the role of Field as a legal reformer in New York, and for a more complete discussion of the problems found in its legal system and the efforts made for their amelioration, see Michael Joseph Hobor, "The Forms of the Law: David Dudley Field and the Codification Movement in New York, 1839-1888," unpublished Ph.D. dissertation, University of Chicago, 1975; Daun Roell Van Ee, "David Dudley Field and the Reconstruction of the Law," unpublished Ph.D. dissertation, Johns Hopkins University, 1974.

8. Verplanck, "Administration of Justice, pp. 38-40.

9. David Hoffman, *A Course of Legal Study, 2d ed.* (Baltimore: Joseph Neal, 1836), pp. 659-60.

10. Elijah Spence, *The Equitable Jurisdiction of the Court of Chancery,* 2 vols. (Philadelphia: Lea & Blanchard, 1846-50), I: 715.

11. Theodore Sedgwick, "Law Reform," *Western Law Journal* 3 (1846): 151. See also Charles Hepburn, *The Historical Development of Code Pleading in America and England* (Cincinnati: W. A. Anderson and Co., 1897), p. 18.

12. On the sort of complaints leveled against English practice, see Hepburn, *Historical Development,* pp. 18-35.

13. Maurice Lang, *Codification in the British Empire and America* (Amsterdam: H. J. Paris, 1924), p. 117.

14. Alison Reppy, "The Field Codification Concept," in *David Dudley Field: Centenary Essays Celebrating One Hundred Years of Legal Reform,* Alison Reppy, ed. (New York: New York University School of Law, 1949), p. 21.

15. Lawrence Friedman, *A History of American Law* (New York: Simon and Schuster, 1973), p. 351.

16. Field, *Life of Field,* p. 43.

17. Compare David Dudley Field, *A Short Response to a Long Discourse* (New York: 1884) to Joseph Story, "Codification of the Common Law," in Joseph Story, *Miscellaneous Writings of Joseph Story,* William W. Story, ed. (Boston: Charles C. Little and James Brown, 1852), pp. 698-734.

18. Friedman, *History of American Law,* pp. 351-52. Compare James C. Carter, *The Proposed Codification of Our Common Law* (New York: Evening Post, 1884) and *The Provinces of the Written and Unwritten Law* (New York: Banks and Bros., 1889) with [John Porter], "The Necessity of the Common Law," *North American Review* 27 (1828): 167-91 and "Ohio Reports," *American Jurist and Law Magazine* 7 (1832): 261-85.

19. Lincoln, *Messages from the Governors,* IV: 648-49. See also Hepburn, *Historical Development,* pp. 80-81.

20. Charles Z. Lincoln, *The Constitutional History of the State of New York from the Beginning of the Colonial Period to the Year 1905,* 5 vols. (Rochester, N.Y.: Lawyers Co-Operative Publishing Co., 1906), II: 140.

21. Reppy, "The Field Codification Concept," pp. 31-32; David Dudley Field, *Reorganization of the Judiciary* (New York, 1846).

22. "The New Constitution of New York," p. 490.

23. Lincoln, *Constitutional History,* II: 164.

24. Ibid.; N.Y. Const., art. I, sec. 17 (1847).

25. David Dudley Field, *What Should Be Done with the Practice of the Courts* (New York: J. S. Voorhies, 1847).

26. Quoted in Field, *Life of Field,* p. 48.

27. New York Laws, chap. 59, sec. 8 (1847).

28. New York Assembly Journal, p. 1482 (1847).

29. John T. Fitzpatrick, "Procedural Codes of the State of New York," *Law Library Journal* 17 (1924): 15.

30. Friedman, *History of American Law,* pp. 340-41.

31. New York Laws, chap. 397, sec. 120 (1848).

32. On the amelioration of procedural law in the United States before the advent of the Field Code, see William E. Nelson, "Reform of Common Law Pleading in Massachusetts, 1760-1830: Adjudication as a Prelude to Legislation," *University of Pennsylvania Law Review* 122 (1973): 97-136.

33. John Worth Edmonds, "An Address on the Constitution and Code of Practice, and Modification of the Law Effected Thereby..." *Monthly Law Reporter* 11 (1848): 233-35.

34. See "New York Code of Procedure," *Monthly Law Reporter* 11 (1848): 97-112; "Law Reform in Missouri," *Western Law Journal* 6 (1849): 447.

35. "The New York Code," *Monthly Law Reporter* 13 (1850): 110.

36. Ibid.

37. James Fenimore Cooper, *The Ways of the Hour* (New York: G. P. Putnam, 1850), pp. 13, 43, 69.

38. Reppy, "The Field Codification Concept," p. 34; J. Willard Hurst, *The Growth of American Law* (Boston: Little, Brown and Co., 1950), p. 90.

39. See Van Ee, "David Dudley Field and the Reconstruction of the Law," pp. 102-10.

40. "Practice and Pleading," *New York Legal Observer* 10 (1852): 320.

41. "Notice of New Books," *Monthly Law Reporter* 11 (1849): 234.

42. Field, *A Short Response,* p. 10.

43. "Notice of New Books," *Monthly Law Reporter.*

44. Friedman, *History of American Law,* p. 343.

45. New York Senate Documents, vol. 2, number 69 (1848).

46. Field, *Life of Field,* p. 69.

47. David Dudley Field, *Speeches, Arguments, and Miscellaneous Papers of David Dudley Field,* A. P. Sprague, ed., 3 vols. (New York: Appleton and Co., 1884-90), I: 307.

48. Lincoln, *Messages,* IV: 489; Lang, *Codification,* p. 133.

49. Field, *Life of Field,* p. 74.

50. New York Laws, vol. 1, chap. 266 (1857).

51. Field, *Life of Field,* p. 86.

52. Lang, *Codification,* p. 147.

53. Timothy Walker, "Codification," *Western Law Journal* 1 (1844): 433-44.

54. Friedman, *History of American Law,* pp. 341-42.

55. The states were Missouri, California, Kentucky, Iowa, Minnesota, Washington, Nebraska, Wisconsin, Kansas, Georgia, Nevada, Dakota Territory, Idaho, Arizona, and Montana.

56. David Dudley Field, "Codification in the United States," *Juridical Review* 1 (1889): 19.

9

TRADITION IN TRIUMPH—ALMOST

An astute observer should have seen in the 1840s that the codification movement, as a viable agent of legal change, had reached its limits. To be sure, had Field's efforts met with greater success in New York, any announcement of its death at that time would probably have been premature. However, the major factors that precluded the achievement of its ultimate goal—the codification of the common law—existed long before Field had even drafted his first code. In New York as elsewhere, the codification movement faced a persistently strong opposition, while the ranks of its advocates thinned after an initial powerful expression of enthusiasm.

From the very inception of the codification movement, a large and potently influential group of practitioners stood impacably against the reform. There is no need to reiterate all their arguments. Suffice it to say that they were motivated to oppose codification by an attachment to what they considered a tried and true legal system, and a fear that change would produce legal uncertainty destructive of established rights. Codifiers frequently stated that their fellow practitioners were responsible for the defeat of necessary improvements in the law, and they were largely correct. Field, for example, toward the end of his life, observed that "[w]henever any considerable amelioration had been obtained, either in the form or in the substance of the law, in procedure, or in doctrine, it has come from a minority of lawyers supported by the voices of laymen." Field claimed that because of the "nature of the profession, the lawyer becomes wedded to old things by the course of his daily avocations. He reposes upon the past. He is concerned with what is, not with what should be, in the ages that have gone before him." While Field, at least at this point in his life, did not think this characteristic was "altogether to be regretted," others viewed it less charitably.[1] A law writer for the *American Jurist* in an article entitled "Legal Reform," declared of the legal profession that "if anyone was interested in the continuance of the present state of things, it is they." Practitioners, he said, "are the high priests" of the "mysteries" of the law. "With dismal perseverance they have delved amid black letter through the heyday of life, to master these abstrusenesses; and what would become of these years of toil, if the fate of legislation would proscribe the hidden lore?" As to their "motive to resist a reformation in the law," this same writer suggested it was a concern for their own personal gain. "Technicalities," he observed, "are to them a sort of franchise, a vested right, a monopoly. To legislate them away would be to legislate bread out of their mouths."[2] Laymen, as we have seen, frequently made the same criticism.

Whether these practitioners were motivated more by a desire for private profit or by a positive concern for the security of the legal order cannot be determined. No doubt, both elements were there. Regardless of the source of this negative impulse, it operated powerfully to limit the success of the reform effort. As such, it was in keeping with the Anglo-American legal tradition. A conservative faction of the bar, often a majority, had consistently fought demands for legal reform whenever they had appeared.[3]

The lack of complete success experienced by the codification movement, however, cannot be laid entirely at the feet of conservative professionals. A more complex dynamic was involved. Just as the codification movement originally flowed from no single source, so, too, its life was arrested by no single element. Rather, a number of factors, frequently interrelated, diminished interest in the reform.

It will be recalled that the codification movement was a response to the practical dissatisfaction of practitioners with the legal system. The law, it was claimed, was inccessible and uncertain. The size of the objective body of the law and the diversity of its contents, as well as the character of decision making in the common law system, were seen as causes of these problems. In addition, it was also asserted that the law received from England was unsuited to the circumstances of republican America and was consequently in need of substantive reform. Central to any understanding of the felt sense of abuse were the exigencies of legal development experienced in America during the antebellum period. A developing society was placing unprecedented demands on the legal structure, and those demands produced unparalleled growth and change in the law. However, as these demands were met, a legal system emerged in which the grievances of professionals were being satisfied. While a limited application of the codification formula helped to still demands for reform by assisting in the reduction of the problems of the antebellum legal order, for the most part, amelioration came through more traditional means in keeping with existing legal institutions and practices. As a result, the driving impulse behind the effort to codify American law—dissatisfaction—languished. Ultimately, apathy as much as resistance defeated the movement to codify American law.

The reliance on English law, so heavily disparaged by many codifiers, was made necessary by an absence of suitable and accessible native legal materials. The only alternative was to adopt a formula as the reformers suggested, or repeal all English law and build anew on a piecemeal basis. The latter would have created legal chaos and, consequently, would have appealed to no responsible spokesmen. As we know, the remedy of codes was opposed for many of the same reasons. However, the inherited system of law was not adopted uncritically. Rather, English legal science was being adapted to American circumstances and was given an American stamp by the court and the legislatures. Much of English jurisprudence was overthrown, and new doctrines were created. In addition, new areas of law, largely ignored in the received law, were developed. Of course, this process had been going on since the founding of the colonies, but, after 1815, it was accelerated by the rapid growth and development of the American society that had placed heavy demands on the legal system.[4] Although, the process of Americanization of the law did not occur fast enough for some.

By the 1840s, a distinct system of American law, made up of settled doctrines adopted to local needs, was beginning to emerge, at least in the older states. By that time, the basic legal problems facing the young republic—the necessity of creating an indigenous system of law compatible with American circumstances and capable of solving the legal problems created by a rapidly changing society—was well on its way to a satisfactory resolution. As one law writer commented in 1848: "[W]e are now in the transitory state, between the common law of England, and that which is to be the common law of federated America. The former is everywhere giving way, and the latter everywhere assuming its proper shape and consistency."[5] The only area of law where codification was widely adopted as a method of Americanization was procedure, and, then, only in those states that found their substantive law reformed and their procedural law lagging behind their needs. While the system of American law that emerged in the antebellum period was far from perfect, and while it continued to have a strong English flavor, the original cause of complaint—a direct reliance on English law—was largely removed. Furthermore, as ruling doctrines were established, one finds less and less talk about the legal uncertainty resulting from the common law method, though it was not completely eliminated. Legal growth and change continued at a rapid pace, but it occurred within a stabilized framework.

The development of a reasonably fixed indigenous system of law did not, in and of itself, scotch the codification movement. It was not enough to create a system of law for the new republic; the law had to be made accessible to practitioners and jurists if its existence were to be meaningful. In fact, the very growth of an American law, as evidenced by an ever increasing number of reports and statutes, had been a source of complaint that had generated support for the reform effort. Codifiers sought to make sense out of what they considered a chaotic mass of native law, frequently ambiguous and inconsistent, by reducing it to a set of concise statements. The solution to this problem, like the response to the need for an indigenous legal product, was less specific and direct than the codifiers' formula. The law was made accessible and was accorded a degree of stability and certainty through the growth and development of a body of American legal literature, chiefly treatises and digests.

Roscoe Pound, in his seminal book *The Formative Era of American Law,* declared that "more than anything else the books of our great nineteenth century text writers defeated the urge of a code."[6] While this observation is largely correct, Pound's notions about the nature of the role of early American legal literature in frustrating the codification movement require modification.

Text writers, Pound observed, "gave the courts at a critical period what they could take to be authoritative statements of received common law and so gave judges and legislators something from which to make required new starts in building a legal system."[7] As a result, they were able to develop a body of law that was able to resist codification, a reform that had been made appealing by the absence of an established legal system. The codification movement grew out of more than simply the desire for an indigenous legal product. It was, more importantly, a response to what was considered the unmanageable outpouring of American law. Texts were frequently consulted by lawmakers to find out what the law should be or, in Pound's words, to make "new starts." However, the bench and the bar also needed texts to discover what the law in its full detail was once it had been formulated, and they added to the ever growing mountain of reports and statute books. Treatises fulfilled this function, serving as a research tool, as Pound suggests. But alone, they were not enough. The use of treatises had serious limitations. They provided a perspective, or set of principles, on what the law was or, as often as not, what it should be. Certainly, they could be cited in support of a position, or they could be used as a reference work to discuss case law. But since they were written to develop a coherent and logical exposition of the law, they hardly presented a comprehensive picture of all the law that might be relevant to a given controversy. Alone, they did not provide attorneys access to all the potential weapons and shields available to do battle in the adversarial process as the champion of some litigant. It was an ever increasing number of digests that filled this need not met by the text writers. Together, digests and treatises made the law accessible to a satisfactory extent in the antebellum period. When one considers that by 1842 there were over 650 volumes of American reports alone, it seems likely that some type of codification would have been more nearly a reality without the development of these two research tools.[8]

While some important examples of American texts and digests were published before 1830—notably, Reeve's *Baron and Femme* (1816),[9] Phillip's *Insur-*

ance (1823),[10], Dane's *Abridgement* (1823-29),[11] and Kent's *Commentaries* (1826-30),[12]—native legal works do not appear in significant numbers until after 1830. By that time, there were enough indigenous legal materials to permit their composition and a concomitant demand for these research tools to synthesize and abridge the growing body of American law. Until then, practitioners had to depend either on their own inquiries into primary sources of the law or on English works, either in American editions or in their original forms. This was an impossible situation that provided an impulse toward codification. English texts prepared for American use were generally found wanting, though some—notably Chitty's *Pleading*—were popular enough to go through several American editions.[13] It was claimed by one law writer that such works were "made *to sell*" rather "than to be used by an intelligent profession." Most, he continued, were simply dressed up with "a few familiar cases in the shape of notes...and the publication is announced as an edition with *improvements,* or *additions,* or *references to the latest cases;* terms...applied with but little conscience."[14] Another claimed that "there are no books more clumsy in the use and more troublesome in the digestion, than the English treatises heaped with notes of American cases."[15] Because they were frequently makeshift affairs, and essentially expositions of English and not American law, practitioners could never be sure how closely they reflected the reality of American law. Unabridged English texts were, of course, even less productive of legal certainty, given the problems inherent in reception. Nonetheless, the strong sales of these works, despite their shortcomings, manifested a powerful felt need for some sort of implement by which to grasp the law.

Such books were abandoned as soon as native texts became available. As "the proportion of indigenous law begins to preponderate," one commentator observed in 1833, "elementary treatises and abridgements are...appearing in the form of original American works, the great mass of which is composed of results of our own legislation and judicial decisions."[16] American law writers were so productive that not many years later, another suggested that the United States was vying "with the mother country in the number and value of works on legal subjects."[17] These were looked upon as an indispensable means of coping with the ever growing mountain of native legal materials. Borrowing the words of an advertisement in a recent issue of the *American Bar Association Journal,* practitioners in the antebellum period discovered that there was "a difference between having law books and having a legal research system."[18]

Viewing the approximately 650 American reports in existence in 1842, a writer in the *American Jurist* suggested that without the numerous digests that had appeared to make this mass manageable, "the most inveterate book lawyer must have abandoned the use of reports as utterly hopeless."[19] Similarly, Charles Sumner observed that "[b]y the assistance of digests, we are enabled to reduce to some order and discipline this immense army [of reports] and to use it for our purpose when occasion requires....At the present...they cannot fail to be appreciated."[20] Another writer stressed the advantages of digests in cold economic terms. Stressing the necessity of digesting "in this country more than any other," he asserted that at least 800 new volumes of reports would be published in the next fifty years, at a cost of $3,200 to their purchaser. These, he suggested, could be distilled into fifty or sixty volumes and be available for a fraction of their original cost.[21]

Treatises also received the approbation of the legal profession for the same reasons.[22] As one writer claimed, an ably written text enabled the practitioner "to attain a certain point with more facility and less time, than he could before."[23] Another stressed the indebtedness of the profession to "printers and abridgers" because the "law is now oppressed by the multitude of precedents," and without "their mechanical assistance...we must reject the light of the experience of even our contemporaries."[24]

By their numbers and usefulness in making the law accessible, digests and treatises obviated the pressing felt need for codified law. Interest in codified law waned as the numbers of legal texts increased. Their relationship to the codification movement was sensed by contemporaries. One codifier declared in the *American Jurist* that "[w]hatever regret we may experience for want of a code of our law, certain it is that" commentaries and digests "afford powerful topics of consolation to them whose business it is to be particularly conversant with jurisprudence."[25] An orthodox common lawyer stressed the point differently. Suggesting that secondary legal works gave access to the vastness of American law, he declared that "by the opposite experiment of codification, we shall have all its benefits with few if any of its evils."[26] Thus it appeared that the legal fraternity could have access to the law without the disturbing and possibly disruptive effects they feared from authoritatively digesting and reformulating the law in a code.

Because they were seen as serving largely the same function, practitioners stressed as prerequisites for useful texts and abridgements the same elements found in codes—conciseness of statement and systematic arrangement. A good law book, one lawyer declared, gives a

> clear and concise statement to the point, a crystal purity of style, and a careful exclusion of all discussion, suggestions and insinuations which have no immediate reference to the matter at hand, and which serve to cover up the law, so that it is about as difficult to get at the true doctrine of the cause as it would be to catch a particular fish on the banks of New Foundland.[27]

Another wrote that a law writer should present rules of law "simply and distinctly," stripped of "inapt phraseology, and considerations not directly pertinent."[28] Pointedly, Charles Sumner recommended a treatise to the profession (Greenleaf on Evidence) because it stated the law so concisely that it reached "even to the brevity of a code."[29] Stressing arrangement, one commentator asserted that a treatise "should show that the law is a science, not a bundle of arbitrary precedents, tied up like a bundle of sticks."[30] Because the lawyer was faced with such an enormous mass of law in his practice, another writer declared that digests and treatises should reduce "the divided points to systematic arrangement."[31]

Digests exceeded treatises in number and in variety. In addition to digests of federal reports,[32] the decisions of nearly every state's appellate courts were abridged as soon as they comprised several volumes. Supplements and new digests followed as additional cases were reported.[33] More specialized abridgements were also printed. For example, O. L. Barbour and E. B. Harrington published a digest of American equity cases in 1837,[34] and Ellis Lewis and Pelig Chandler edited books of American criminal cases and statute law in 1841.[35] Some abridgements took on a surprisingly modern flavor. Early examples of regional reporters were seen in digests of southern and western case law compiled by Thomas J. Wharton.[36] James Conover prepared an index to all the reported law and equity cases of Ohio, Indiana, and Illinois.[37] Theron Metcalf, Jonathan C. Perkins, and George T. Curtis edited a three-volume abridgement that covered all the courts of common law and admiralty in the United States, or some 649 volumes of reports[38]. One contemporary called it "a kind of universal index."[39] However, no attempt was made to bring it up to date regularly, although at least one supplement was published.[40] There were also digests of statutes: some abridged all the statutes of a given jurisdiction,[41] while others were topical.[42] There were even abridgments of texts.[43] It would be difficult to say how many digests were published in the antebellum period without a list of American legal imprints. However, some idea of the number involved can be gained by a list of fifty-one different digests of American reports that were in progress or that had been published by 1842.[44]

While there were attempts to analyze the whole of American law in texts, Kent's *Commentaries* being an outstanding example, most treatises were more specialized. Generally, they were devoted to a single subject. Most did, however, attempt to survey all American law relevant to their topic, though the scope of some did not go past the boundaries of a single jurisdiction.[45]

The treatises of Joseph Story place him foremost among American law writers. Over a period of twelve years, he wrote nine texts (*Bailments, Constitutional Law, Conflict of Laws, Equity Jurisprudence, Equity Pleadings, Agency, Partnerships, Bills of Exchange,* and *Promissory Notes*). Other writers were less prolific, but their works were no less important. Nearly fifty major legal texts were written in the antebellum period. In addition to those by Story, among the most significant were: Greenleaf's *Evidence,*[46] Wharton's *Criminal Law,*[47] Parson's *Contracts,*[48] Gould's *Pleading,*[49] Hilliard's *Real and Personal Property,*[50] Angell and Ames' *Corporations,*[51] Sedgwick's *Damages,*[52] and Ray's *Insanity.*[53] By their excellence, variety, and number, they not only gave the legal fraternity access to the law, but they also gave elaborations on it to aid their understanding. Indexes of cases and statutes and John Bouvier's ever-popular law dictionary[54] also aided the legal profession in its quest for knowledge of the law, but it was digests and treatises that best filled that function. So great were their numbers that one law writer, in commenting that these secondary law books had the effect of systematizing the common law, declared that "the only embarrassment comes from the number and variety of means and facilities."[55]

The existence of numerous digests and treatises not only helped the attorney by giving him access to the law of the jurisdiction in which he practiced, but they also helped solve the legal problems caused by federalism. With these new tools, the legal fraternity could, with relative ease, consult the law of other states. Furthermore, treatises, covering as they did all relevant law, brought a degree of unity to the American legal system. Perfect consistency would never be achieved, but these books cemented, in many particulars, the general sort of harmony brought by the near universal adoption of the common law in the United States.[56]

Like lawyers, laymen also lost interest in codes. While the sources of their discontent were not eliminated, their diminished zeal for the reform, as with the legal fraternity, resulted from changes in the legal system short of codification. From their point of view, reforms in the law, especially in matters of practice, had the effect of removing the more obvious defects. While these changes did not result in a situation in which every man could become his own lawyer, at least the nonprofessional could understand more or less what was going on in the court that was trying his case, and judgements were apparently made on the relevant facts. Furthermore, in many states, legal matters that laymen were most frequently involved with, such as conveyancing, were also simplified. The limited codifications of the statute law also possibly had the effect of creating the impression that the legal system was being improved along lines they desired. One of their champions within the profession, Robert Rantoul, suggested to a lay audience that this was the result of the codification of Massachusetts' statute law. He told a Fourth of July audience that the revision had taken an important step to the "great end" that the law be made "intelligible to all." Calling the revision "the most important act of our legislation since the revolution," he declared that it left the law "systematized, simplified, modernized, and...consistent with itself."[57]

Many laymen nonetheless continued to feel the necessity for reform. However, the focus of their interest was no longer codification but rather institutional changes that reflected their emphasis on democracy. Specifically, they called for the de-professionalization of the bar and for the popular election of the judiciary. By midcentury, many states had responded to these efforts by changing or abolishing admission requirements for the bar and by making judicial tenure dependent on success at the ballot box. The hoped-for results, however, did not occur. Legal training still remained a prerequisite for success at the bar, and despite the fact that they were now elected, judges did not prove as responsive to the popular will as did the other two branches of government. However, the effort largely absorbed the lay reformers' energies, and codification slipped on their list of priorities. Furthermore, the bar itself had had some success in improving its popular image, which diminished interest in the reform.[58]

The codification movement thus failed to achieve its ultimate goal of reducing the common law to a written text. The great mass of our law, especially that relating to private rights, is still found in the opinions of jurists rather than in the statute books. However, the codification movement was not a failure. As a result of the reform effort, partial codification is a prominent and important feature of our legal system. In the words of one legal historian, partial codification is "epidemic" in the United States.[59] Possibly, given the nature and growth of legal development and change in the United States since the beginning of the nineteenth century, the limited use of codification or some means by which the law could be made accessible was inevitable.

Volumes of reports have remained the chief repository of our law. Nonetheless, the American legal system has also witnessed a proliferation of statutes. American jurisdictions have relied on statute law both as a means of meeting the legal needs of a constantly changing society and as a means of reform. In every state, the statute book has grown proportionately larger with every passing decade.[60] As a result, some tool was necessary to keep this growth comprehensible. As we have seen, the codification formula was widely adopted as a means of procedural reform. After the Civil War, and especially in the twentieth century, partial codification was widely used both as a way of making the statute law accessible and as a tool of legal reform.[61]

Codification has also been used to reform other areas of law as well. Since the beginning of the twentieth century, the American Law Institute has attempted to bring greater uniformity to American law through the development of model codes such as the Uniform Sales Act, which are offered to all the states to adopt. Success in this area has been achieved to a limited extent. All the states, for example, have adopted the Uniform Commercial Code.

For some, the codification formula has not been utilized enough. Periodically, the legal community has heard renewed demands for the codification of American law.[62] However, the limited use of the reform and the existence of secondary law books as research tools have precluded the possibility of renewal of a codification effort on the scale that existed in the antebellum period.

Most of the early codifiers would probably be pleased with the use of codification in the United States today. However, the radicals would hardly consider it a victory. Our codes have not bridled the discretionary powers of our common law judges; they function in much the same fashion whether they are interpreting a code or the common law. The meaning of the codes is frequently affected by their decisions, so much so that annotated codes have become far more important in understanding the law than have the bare codes themselves.

If we can learn anything from the American codification movement, it is the limitations of legal reform in the American legal environment or in any established legal environment. Law reform efforts are a response to dissatisfaction with some elements of the legal structure. While lay complaints about the legal order may have some influence about the extent and character of any remedies adopted to cure defects, the most effective voices for legal change are those of practitioners. Furthermore, when demands for legal change are translated into action, the nature and process of reform are controlled by the legal profession. There can be, of course, a difference of opinion on the matter within the profession, which can be divisive. Nonetheless, a consensus of the legal fraternity, in which the leading members of the bench and the bar have an influential voice, must give its assent to any improvement in the law. This consensus can only be achieved when it is agreed that a grievous situation exists or when the object of reform is an inconsequential anachronism. Important prerequisites for the establishment of this consensus are a tradition of reform and established experience with the proposed change. Consequently, American law reform has been a limited, if not conservative, affair.

If some improvements appear to be revolutionary, such as the adoption of the Field Code of Civil Procedure, it should be remembered that the profession was largely united in the belief that something should be done to improve practice, and that significant reforms relating to practice, such as those found in the Revised Statutes, had previously been enacted. Furthermore, even if the Field Code did exceed the limits of acceptable legal change, an opinion soon recognized generally among New York practitioners, it was limited to only a portion of procedural law and was soon emasculated by constant legislative and judicial interference. Nonetheless, meaningful reform did occur. Often, it is the result of piecemeal changes and improvements in the law, which, if undertaken cumulatively at once, would spell legal revolution. Yet, a comprehensive reform movement may also result in significant legal change, especially when it reflects strongly felt legal needs. The American codification movement was such an effort. While its most sweeping goals were not achieved, largely because the major grievances that energized the reform were satisfactorily remedied by other means, the American legal environment had a different appearance as a result of the reform effort. Some codifiers were disappointed, but their work was far from fruitless.

NOTES

1. David Dudley Field, "Codification in the United States," *Juridical Review* 1 (1889): 19-20.

2. "Legal Reform," *American Jurist and Law Magazine* 9 (1833): 302.

3. See Donald Veall, *The Popular Movement for Law Reform, 1640-1660* (Oxford: Clarendon Press, 1970), pp. 328-35; Charles Hepburn, *Historical Development of Code Pleading in America and England* (Cincinnati: W. A. Anderson and Co., 1897), p. 69; Lawrence Friedman, "Law Reform in Historical Perspective," *St. Louis University Law Journal* 13 (1969): 351-74.

4. See, generally, William E. Nelson, *Americanization of the Common Law: The Impact of Legal Change on Massachusetts Society, 1760-1830* (Cambridge: Harvard University Press, 1975); Morton J. Horwitz, *The Transformation of American Law, 1780-1860* (Cambridge: Harvard University Press, 1977).

5. "On the Plan and Objects of the *American Jurist and Law Magazine," American Jurist and Law Magazine* 19 (1838): 11.

6. Roscoe Pound, *The Formative Era of American Law* (Boston: Little, Brown and Company, 1938), p. 154.

7. Ibid., p. 151.

8. "A List of the Various Reporters Arranged in Order of Time, with Remarks, etc.," *American Law Magazine* 2 (1884): 271-345.

9. Tapping Reeve, *The Law of Baron and Femme...* (New Haven: Oliver Steele, 1816).

10. Willard Phillips, *A Treatise on the Law of Insurance*, 2 vols. (Boston: Wells and Lilly, 1823-34).

11. Nathan Dane, *A General Abridgement and Digest of American Law*, 9 vols. (Boston: Cummings, Hilliard & Co., 1823-29).

12. James Kent, *Commentaries on American Law*, 4 vols. (New York: O. Halsted, 1826-30).

13. Joseph Chitty, *A Treatise on the Parties to Actions, and on Pleadings...with Additions and Notes by John A. Dunlap*, 8th American ed. (Springfield, Mass.: Gordon C. Merriam, 1840).

14. Charles Sumner, "Chitty's Pleadings," *American Jurist and Law Magazine* 11 (1834): 337.

15. "Greenleaf's Evidence," *Law Reporter* 5 (1842): 54.

16. "Mistakes in the Westminster Review on the Subject of American Jurisprudence," *American Jurist and Law Magazine* 8 (1832): 276-77.

17. [George S. Hilliard], "Hoffman's Course of Legal Study," *North American Review* 46 (1838): 72.

18. *Journal of the American Bar Association* 60 (1974): 885.

19. "Digests of American Law Reports and American Law Periodicals," *American Jurist and Law Magazine* 23 (1840): 129.

20. Charles Sumner, "Barbour's Equity Digest," *American Jurist and Law Magazine* 17 (1837): 367.

21. "Digests of Reported Cases in Equity," *United States Law Intelligencer and Review* 1 (1829): 102.

22. "Conflict of Laws," *American Jurist and Law Magazine* 11 (1834): 369.

23. "Life and Writings of Sir William Blackstone," *American Jurist and Law Magazine* 1 (1829): 130.

24. "Wharton's Digest," *American Law Journal* 1 (1843): 231.

25. "Life and Writings of Sir William Blackstone," p. 129.

26. "Wharton's Digest," p. 232.

27. "Notices of New Books," *Law Reporter* 9 (1846): 90.

28. "Notices of New Books," *American Jurist and Law Magazine* 12 (1834): 569.

29. Charles Sumner, "Greenleaf on Evidence," *American Jurist and Law Magazine* 27 (1842): 393.

30. "Greenleaf's Evidence," p. 52.

31. "Cowen's Digest," *American Jurist and Law Magazine* 5 (1831): 294.

32. Richard Peters, *A Full and Arranged Digest of the Decisions in Common Law, Equity, and Admiralty, of the Courts of the United States,* 24 vols. (Philadelphia: Thomas Cowperthewait, 1838-39).

33. For example, Lewis Bigelow published a digest of the first twelve volumes of Massachusetts Reports in 1818. The work was brought up to date in 1825. Five years later, a supplement was published. In 1827, Francis Hilliard published an abridgement of reported Massachusetts cases covering the intervening years.

34. O. L. Barbour, *An Analytical Digest of Equity Cases, Decided in the Courts of the Several States, and of the United States* (Springfield, Mass.: G. & C. Merriam, 1843).

35. Pelig Chandler, *American Criminal Trials*, 2 vols. (Boston: Charles C. Little and James Brown, 1841-44); Ellis Lewis, *An Abridgement of the Criminal Law of the United States* (Philadelphia: Thomas Cowperthewait & Co., 1848).

36. Thomas J. Wharton, *A Digest of Southern and Western Cases*, cited in "Digests of American Reports," p. 134.

37. James F. Conover, *A Digested Index of All the Reported Decisions in Law and Equity of the Supreme Courts of the States of Ohio, Indiana, and Illinois* (Philadelphia: Key & Biddle, 1834).

38. Theron Metcalf, Jonathan C. Perkins, and George T. Curtis, *Digest of the Decisions of the Courts of Common Law and Admiralty in the United States*, 3 vols; vol. 1 (Boston: Hilliard, Gray and Co., 1840); vols. 2-3 (Boston: C. C. Little and J. Brown, 1845-46).

39. George T. Curtis to the editors of the *Law Reporter*, 20 Aug. 1846, *Law Reporter* 9 (1846): 234.

40. John Phillips Putnam, *A Supplement to the United States Digest*, 2 vols. (Boston: Charles C. Little and James Brown, 1847).

41. Thomas Gordon, *A Digest of the Laws of the United States* (Philadelphia: I. Ashmead and Co., 1844).

42. W. P. Gregg and Benjamin Pond, *The Railroad Laws and Charters of the United States* (Boston: C. C. Little and J. Brown, 1851).

43. J. Eastman Johnson, *An Analytical Abridgement of Kent's Commentaries on American Law* (New York: Halsted and Voorhies, 1839).

44. "Digests of American Reports," pp. 128-37.

45. Elijah Paine, *The Practice in Civil Actions and Proceedings at Law in the State of New York* (New York: G. & C. Crowell, 1830).

46. Simon Greenleaf, *A Treatise on the Law of Evidence*, 3 vols. (Boston: C. C. Little and J. Brown, 1842-53).

47. Francis Wharton, *A Treatise on the Criminal Law of the United States* (Philadelphia: J. Keys, 1846).

48. Theophilus Parsons, *The Law of Contracts*, 2 vols. (Boston: Little, Brown and Co., 1853-55).

49. James Gould, *A Treatise on the Principles of Pleading, in Civil Actions* (New York: B. & S. Collier, 1832).

50. Francis Hilliard, *An Abridgement of the Law of Real Property* (Boston: C. C. Little and J. Brown, 1838); Francis Hilliard, *A Treatise on the Law of Personal Property* (New York: Halsted and Voorhies, 1841).

51. Joseph K. Angell and Samuel Ames, *A Treatise on the Law of Private Corporations, Aggregate* (Boston: Hilliard, Gray, Little, Wilkins, 1832).

52. Theodore Sedgwick, *A Treatise on the Measure of Damages* (New York: J. S. Voorhies, 1847).

53. Isaac Ray, *A Treatise on Medical Jurisprudence and Insanity* (Boston: C. C. Little and J. Brown, 1838).

54. John Bouvier, *A Law Dictionary, Adapted to the Constitution and Laws of the United States and of the Several States of the American Union*, 2 vols. (Philadelphia: T. and J. W. Johnson, 1839).

55. "Kent's *Commentaries on American Law," North American Review* 74 (1851): 108.

56. Pound, *The Formative Era,* pp. 153-54.

57. Robert Rantoul, Jr., *Memoirs, Speeches and Writings of Robert Rantoul, Jr.,* Luther Hamilton, ed. (Boston: J. P. Jewett and Co., 1854), pp. 277-78.

58. See Maxwell Bloomfield, "Law v. Politics: Self-Image of the American Bar (1830-1860)," *American Journal of Legal History* 12 (1968): 306-23; "Lawyers and Public Criticism: Challenge and Response in Nineteenth Century America," *American Journal of Legal History* 15 (1971): 264-77.

59. Lawrence Friedman, "Law Reform in Historical Perspective," *St. Louis University Law Journal* 13 (1969): 351.

60. For example, Maryland, a state hardly on the forefront of nineteenth-century legal development, during the 1820s increased the size of its statute book by an average of twenty pages with each session of its legislature. In the 1840s, the average output of each session had increased to 452 pages. Grace E. MacDonald, comp., *Check-list of Session Laws* (New York: W. H. Wilson Co., 1936), p. 83.

61. See I. Dee Mallonee, "Revised Statutes and Codes," *American Law Review* 48 (1914): 37-49.

62. See Hessel E. Yntema, "The Jurisprudence of Codification," and Carl McFarland, "Administrative Law and the Codification of Statutes," in *David Dudley Field: Centenary Essays Celebrating One Hundred Years of Legal Reform*, Alison Reppy, ed. (New York: New York University School of Law, 1949), pp.204-14, 251-64.

SELECTED BIBLIOGRAPHY

PRIMARY SOURCES

Case Law

Bodgardus v. Trinity Church. 4 Paige (N.Y.) 178 (1833).
Canal Appraisers v. People. 17 Wendell (N.Y.) 571 (1824).
Commonwealth v. Hutchinson. 1 Mass. 7 (1804).
Marks v. Morris. 4 Hening and Munford (Va.) 463 (1809).
Morris' Lessee v. Vanderen. 1 Dallas 64 (Sup. Ct. of Pa. 1782).
Rensselaer Glass Factory v. Reid. 5 Cowen (N.Y.) 586 (1825).
State v. Mairs. 1 N.J. 335 (1795).
Trial of the Journeymen Cordwainers of the City of New York...New York: I. Riley, 1810.

Law Reports

Chipman's Reports (Vt. 1793).
1 Cranch (U.S. 1804).
1 Johnson (N.Y. 1804).
Kirby's Reports (Conn. 1789).
1 Root (Conn. 1799).

Statute Law and Legislative Materials

Maryland

State of Maryland. *Index to the Laws and Resolutions of the State of Maryland from 1800 to 1813, Inclusive*...Annapolis: F. Green, 1815.

Kilty, William, ed. *The Laws of Maryland...*Annapolis: F. Green, 1799.

Massachusetts

Acts and Laws Passed by the General Court of Massachusetts (1803).

*The Perpetual Laws of the Commonwealth of Massachusetts...*Boston: Adams and Nourse, 1789.

Thomas, Isaiah, ed. *The Perpetual Laws of the Commonwealth of Massachusetts...* Worcester, Mass.: Isaiah Thomas, 1788.

———. *The Perpetual Laws of the Commonwealth of Massachusetts...*2 vols. Boston: I. Thomas, 1799.

Stearns, Asahel; Shaw, Lemel; and Metcalf, Theron, eds. *General Law of Massachusetts...*2 vols. Boston: Wells & Lily and Cummings & Hillard, 1823.

Report of the Commissioners Appointed to Revise the General Statutes of the Commonwealth. 4 vols. Boston: 1834.

Preliminary Report of the Commissioners to Reduce So Much of the Common Law as Relates to Crimes and Punishments, and the Incidents Thereof, to a Written and Systematic Code. Boston: 1839.

New Jersey

Acts of the Sixteenth General Assembly of the State of New Jersey (1792).

Acts of the Nineteenth General Assembly of New Jersey (1795).

Acts of the Twenty-fifth General Assembly of New Jersey (1800).

Acts of the Twenty-sixth General Assembly of New Jersey (1801).

Acts of the Forty-third General Assembly of New Jersey (1819).

Allinson, Samuel, ed. *Acts of the General Assembly of the Province of New Jersey...* Burlington, N.J.: Isaac Collins, 1776.

Patterson, William, ed. *Laws of the State of New Jersey...*Newark: Matthias Day, 1800.

New York

New York Laws (1847), (1848), (1857).

Jones, Samuel, and Varick, Richard, eds. *Laws of the State of New York...*New York: Hugh Gaine, 1789.

The Revised Statutes of the State of New York, Passed in the Years 1827-1828 (1830).

New York Assembly Journal (1847).

New York Senate Documents. Vol. 2, number 69 (1848).

Report from the Commissioners Appointed to Revise the Laws of the State of New York...Communicated March 15, 1826. Albany: 1826.

Chapter 1 of the Second Part of the Proposed Revision of the Statute Laws of the State of New York. Albany: 1827.

Pennsylvania

Acts of the General Assembly of the Commonwealth of Pennsylvania (1792).

South Carolina

Grimke, John Faucheroud, ed. *The Public Laws of the State of South Carolina.* Philadelphia: R. Aitken and Son, 1790.

Brevard, Joseph. *An Alphabetical Digest of the Public Statute Law of South Carolina.* 3 vols. Charleston: John Huff, 1814.

James, Benjamin. *A Digest of the Laws of South Carolina*...Columbia, S.C. Telescope Press, 1822.

The Committee Appointed 20th December Last, to Report on the Practicability of a Code of Statute and Common Law of the State...Beg Leave to Report as Follows. Columbia, S.C. 1827.

Vermont

Williams, John A., ed. *Laws of Vermont.* Vol. 14 of *State Papers of Vermont.* Montpelier, Vt.: State of Vermont, 1966.

Virginia

Collection of Acts of the General Assembly of Virginia (1803).

Hening, Richard, ed. *The Statutes at Large* . . . 13 vols. New York: R. & W. & G. Bartlow 1819.

United States

2 United States Statutes at Large (1799-1813).

U.S. Congress. *American State Papers.* Class X, vol. 1 Miscellaneous (1789-1809).

Foreign Law

Justinian I. *The Institutes of Justinian.* Thomas Cooper, trans. Philadelphia: P. Byrne, 1812.

The Commercial Code of France with the Motives or Discourses of the Councellors of State, Delivered Before the Legislative Body, Illustrative of the Principles and Provision of the Code . . . [John Rodman, trans.] New York: C. Wiley, 1814.

Constitutions

Thorpe, Francis Newman, comp. *The Federal and State Constitutions* . . . 7 vols. Washington, D.C.: Government Printing Office, 1909.

Law Journals

American Jurist and Law Magazine, 1828-1843.

American Law Journal (Hall's), 1808-1817.

American Law Journal (n.s.), 1848-1852.

American Law Magazine, 1843-1846.

Carolina Law Repository, 1814-1816.

Law Reporter, 1838-1866.

New York Legal Observer, 1842-1854.

United States Law Intelligencer and Review, 1829-1831.

United States Law Journal, 1822-1826.

Western Law Journal, 1843-1853.

Articles

"American Law—Kent's Commentaries." *United States Law Intelligencer and Review* 2 (1830): 231-40.

"Bentham on Codification" *Edinburgh Review* 29 (1817): 217-37.

"The Civil Law" *American Jurist and Law Magazine* 2 (1829): 39-65.

"The Civil Law" *American Law Journal* 1 (1807): 491-96.

"Codification" *American Quarterly Review* 6 (1829): 104-16.

"Codification" *United States Law Intelligencer and Review* 2 (1830): 268.

"Codification" *United States Law Intelligencer and Review* 3 (1831): 101-102.

"Common Law" *Atlantic Magazine* 1 (1824): 23-30.

"Conflict of Laws" *American Jurist and Law Magazine* 11 (1834): 365-408.

"Constitution and Penal Code of France" *United States Law Journal* (1823): 405-45.

Cooper, Thomas. "Bentham's Rationale" *Southern Review* 5 (1830): 381-426.

"Cowen's Digest" *American Jurist and Law Magazine* 5 (1831): 294-97.

"Criminal Code of Maine" *American Jurist and Law Magazine* 27 (1842): 147-69.

[Cushing, Caleb]. "Law Reports" *North American Review* 18 (1824): 371-82.

———. "The Greatest-Happiness-Principle" *American Jurist and Law Magazine* 20 (1839): 332-62.

Cushing, Luther S. "Codification of the Common Law in Massachusetts" *American Jurist and Law Magazine* 15 (1836): 111-28.

"Dane's Abridgement" *American Jurist and Law Magazine* 4 (1830): 62-86.

"Difficulties Under the Revised Statutes of New York" *United States Law Intelligencer and Review* 2 (1830) 147-48.

"Digests of American Law Reports and American Law Periodicals" *American Jurist and Law Magazine* 23 (1840): 128-37.

"A Digest of the Law of Maritime Captures and Prizes" *North American Review* 2 (1816): 218-20.

"Digests of Reported Cases in Equity" *United States Law Intelligencer and Review* 1 (1829): 101-105.

Dixon, S. F. "Codification and Reform of the Common Law" *American Jurist and Law Magazine* 14 (1835): 280-302; 15 (1836): 16-43; 16 (1836): 59-87, 289-315; 17 (1837): 71-93; 20 (1839): 305-24; 21 (1839): 352-72; 22 (1840): 282-303; 24 (1841): 32-62.

"Doctrine of Contracts" *American Quarterly Review* 1 (1827): 106-29.

Du Ponceau, Peter S. "*Tesimon. Erudit. Viror.*" *Journal of Jurisprudence* 1 (1821): 3-8.

"Duties of the State to Its Citizens" *United States Magazine, and Democratic Review* 22 (1848): 493-99.

Edmonds, John Worth. "An Address on the Constitution and Code of Practice, and Modification of the Law Effected Thereby . . . *Monthly Law Reporter* 11 (1848): 232-35.

"Edward Livingston and His Code" *United States Magazine, and Democratic Review* 9 (1841): 1-20, 209-23.

"Elective Judiciary" *United States Magazine, and Democratic Review* 22 (1848): 199-206.

[Everett, Edward]. "Code Napoleon" *North American Review* 20 (1825): 399-417.

Field, David Dudley. "Codification in the United States" *Juridical Review* 1 (1889): 18-25.

[Gardiner, William H.]. "Pickering's Reports." *North American Review* 23 (1826): 217-19.

— . "Revision of the Laws of New York" *North American Review* 24 (1827): 193-209.

"Greenleaf's Evidence" *Law Reporter* 5 (1842): 49-55.

[Haven, Nathaniel]. "English Common Law Reports" *North American Review* 21 (1825): 377-88.

———. "Greenleaf's Reports" *North American Review* 22 (1826): 27-34.

[Hilliard, George S.]. "Hoffman's Course of Legal Study" *North American Review* 46 (1836): 72-82.

"Hilliard's Abridgement" *American Jurist and Law Magazine* 19 (1838): 476-87.

"Il Consolato Del Mare" *American Law Journal* 3 (1810): 21-56.

"An Industrious Man" "On Redress of Grievances" American Museum 1 (1787): 114-16.

"Intelligence and Miscellany" *American Jurist and Law Magazine* 17 (1837): 486-88.

"Introduction" *United States Magazine, and Democratic Review* 1 (1838): 1-15.

"Johnson's Reports, Vol. XIX" *United States Law Journal* 1 (1822): 174-213.

"Judiciary in New York" *United States Law Journal* 2 (1826): 120-41.

"Jurisprudence of Louisiana" *American Quarterly Review* 4 (1828): 53-85.

"Kent on American Law" *American Quarterly Review* 1 (1827): 162-88.

"Law Drafting" *American Jurist and Law Magazine* 3 (1830): 182.

"Law Reform in Missouri" *Western Law Journal* 6 (1849): 445-53.

"Legal Reform" *American Jurist and Law Magazine* 9 (1833): 239-304.

Legare, Hugh S. "Codification" *Southern Review* 7 (1831): 391-412.

"Legerdemain of Law Craft" *United States Magazine, and Democratic Review* 22 (1848): 529-40.

"Legislation in Mississippi" *American Jurist and Law Magazine* 11 (1834): 363-65.

"Life and Writings of Sir William Blackstone" *American Jurist and Law Magazine* 1 (1829): 116-31.

"Limited Partnerships" *American Quarterly Review* 19 (1836): 48-67.

"A List of the Various Reporters Arranged in Order of Time, with Remarks, etc." *American Law Magazine* 2 (1844): 271-345.

"Manufacturing Corporations" *American Jurist and Law Magazine* 2 (1829): 92-118.

[Metcalf, Theron]. "Wheaton's Reports" *North American Review* 17 (1823): 118-30.

———. "Tyng's Reports, Vol. XIV" *North American Review* 7 (1818): 184-97.

"Mistakes in the Westminster Review on the Subject of American Jurisprudence" *American Jurist and Law Magazine* 8 (1832): 275-83.

"The New Constitution of New York" *Law Reporter* 9 (1847): 481-93.

"The New York Code" *Monthly Law Reporter* 13 (1850): 109-18.

"New York Code of Procedure" *Monthly Law Reporter* 11 (1848): 97-112.

"Notices of New Brook" *American Jurist and Law Magazine* 12 (1834): 569-71.

"Notices of New Books" *Law Reporter* 6 (1844): 425; 9 (1846): 90-91.

"Notices of New Books" *Monthly Law Reporter* 11 (1849): 234-35.

"Ohio Reports" *American Jurist and Law Magazine* 7 (1832): 261-85.

"On the Plan and Objects of the *American Jurist and Law Magazine" American Jurist and Law Magazine* 19 (1838): 1-12.

"On the Substitution of a Written Code in Place of the Common Law" *Atlantic Magazine* 1 (1825): 281-92.

Parker, Isaac. "Inaugural Address Delivered in the Chapel of Harvard University, by the

Hon. Isaac Parker, Chief Justice of Massachusetts, and Royall Professor of Law" *North American Review* 3 (1816): 11-27.

"Penal Code of the French Empire" *American Review of History and Politics* 2 (1811): appendix, 1-69.

[Phillips, Willard]. "Bentham's Theory of Legislation" *North American Review* 51 (1840): 384-96.

———. "Pickering's Report" *North American Review* 20 (1825): 180-91.

Pickering, John. "A Lecture on the Alleged Uncertainty of the Law; Delivered Before the Boston Society of the Diffusion of Useful Knowledge, March 5, 1830." *American Jurist and Law Magazine* 12 (1834): 285-311.

[Porter, John]. "The Necessity of the Common Law" *North American Review* 27 (1828): 167-91.

"Practice and Pleading" *New York Legal Observer* 10 (1852): 320.

"Proposed Insolvent Law of Massachusetts" *American Jurist and Law* 6 (1831): 116-28.

"Provincial and Colonial Laws" *American Jurist and Law Magazine* 3 (1830): 115-21.

"Recent Reports" *American Jurist and Law Magazine* 3 (1830): 314-51.

"Revised Code of Pennsylvania' *American Quarterly Review* 13 (1833): 30-60; 19 (1836): 399-420.

"Revised Statutes of Massachusetts" *American Jurist and Law Magazine* 15 (1836): 294-321.

"The Revision of 1830—The Innovations of 1847 and 1848" *New York Legal Observer* 6 (1848): 49-53.

"Revision of the Laws" *Atlantic Magazine* 2 (1825): 458-66.

"Revision of the Laws in Massachusetts" *American Jurist and Law Magazine* 13 (1834): 344-78.

"Rules of Evidence" *American Jurist and Law Magazine* 10 (1833): 5-40.

[Rush, Richard]. *"American Jurisprudence" Carolina Law Repository* 2 (1816): 347-63, 543-56.

Sampson, William. "The Common Law" *Atlantic Magazine* 2 (1825): 281-92.

"Scott's Life of Napoleon" *Southern Review* 1 (1828): 159-92.

[Sedgwick, Henry Dwight]. "The Common Law" *North American Review* 19 (1824): 411-39.

Sedgwick, Theodore. "Law Reform" *Western Law Journal* 3 (1846): 145-51.

"The Statute Law of Tennessee" *American Jurist and Law Magazine* 8 (1832): 298-315.

[Story, Joseph]. "Hoffman's Course of Legal Study" *North American Review* 6 (1817): 45-77.

"Subjecting Lands to the Debts of the Deceased" *American Jurist and Law Magazine* 10 (1833): 457-60.

Sumner, Charles. "Barbour's Equity Digest" *American Jurist and Law Magazine* 17 (1837): 366-72.

———. "Chitty's Pleadings" *American Jurist and Law Magazine* 11 (1834): 320-38.

———. "Greenleaf on Evidence" *American Jurist and Law Magazine* 27 (1842): 379-408.

"The Supreme Court of the United States" *United States Magazine, and Democratic Review* 1 (1838): 143-72.

"To the Public" *American Jurist and Law Magazine* 1 (1829): i-vi.

"Trial by Jury" *United States Magazine, and Democratic Review* 6 (1839): 463-72.

"Tyson's Discourse" *North American Review* 51 (1840): 234-36.

"Uniacke's Letter to the Lord Chancellor of England" *New York Review and Antheneum Magazine* 2 (1826): 126-30.

"Usury Laws" *American Jurist and Law Magazine* 6 (1831): 282-309.

Vale, Gilbert. "Practical Reform, and Review of Home and Foreign Politics" *The Diamond* 1 (1841): 78-79.

Verplanck, Gulian. "Administration of Justice in New York" *Law Reporter* 2 (1839): 33-42.

"Verplanck on Contracts" *United States Law Journal* 2 (1826): 72-120.

Walker, Timothy. "Codification" *Western Law Journal* 1 (1844): 433-44.

[Webster, Daniel]. "Wheaton's Reports, Vol. III" *North American Review* 8 (1818): 63-71.

"Wharton's Digest" *American Law Journal* 1 (1843): 231-32.

"Written and Unwritten Systems of Law" *American Jurist and Law Magazine* 5 (1831): 23-52; 9 (1833): 5-36.

Books and Pamphlets

Angell, Joseph K., and Ames, Samuel. *A Treatise on the Law of Private Corporations, Aggregate.* Boston: Hilliard, Gray, Little, Wilkins, 1832.

[Austin, Benjamin]. *Observations on the Pernicious Practice of the Law.* Boston: Adams and Nourse, 1786.

Barbour, O.L. *An Analytical Digest of Equity Cases, Decided in the Courts of the Several States, and of the United States.* Springfield, Mass.: G. & C. Merriam, 1843.

Bentham, Jeremy. *The Works of Jeremy Bentham.* John Bowring, comp. New York: Russell and Russell, 1962 edition.

Blackstone, Sir William. *Blackstone's Commentaries: With Notes of References to the Constitution and Laws, of the Federal Government of the United States, and of the Commonwealth of Virginia* St. George Tucker, ed. 5 vols. Philadelphia: William Young and Abraham Small, 1803.

———. *Commentaries on the Laws of England* 4 vols. Philadelphia: Robert Bell, 1771.

Bouvier, John. *A Law Dictionary, Adapted to the Constitution and Laws of the United States and of the Several States and of the American Union* 2 vols. Philadelphia: T. and J. W. Johnson, 1839.

[Brackenridge, Hugh Henry]. *Considerations on the Jurisprudence of the State of Pennsylvania, No. 1.* Philadelphia: [W. Duane?], 1808.

———. *Law Miscellanies.* Philadelphia: P. L. Byrne, 1814.

Carter, James C. *The Proposed Codification of Our Common Law.* New York: Evening Post, 1884.

———. *The Provinces of the Written and Unwritten Law.* New York: Banks and Bros., 1889.

Chandler, Pelig. *American Criminal Trials.* 2 vols. Boston: Charles C. Little and James Brown, 1841-44.

Chipman, Nathaniel. *Sketches of the Principles of Government.* Rutland, Vt.: J. Lyon, 1793.

Chitty, Joseph. ***A Treatise on the Parties to Actions, and on Pleadings...with Additions and Notes by John A. Dunlap*** **8th American ed. Springfield, Mass.: Gordon C. Merriam, 1840.**

Conover, James F. *A Digested Index of All the Reported Decisions in Law and Equity of the Supreme Courts of the States of Ohio, Indiana, and Illinois.* Philadelphia: Key & Biddle, 1834.

Cooper, James Fenimore. *The Prairie.* New York: Airmont Publishing Co. 1964 edition.

———. *The Ways of the Hour.* New York: G. P. Putnam, 1850.

Crevecoeur, J. Hector St. John. *Letters From an American Farmer.* Gloucester, Mass.: Peter Smith, 1965.

Dane, Nathan. *A General Abridgement and Digest of American Law* 9 vols. Boston: Cummings, Hilliard & Co., 1823-29.

Du Ponceau, Peter S. *A Dissertation on the Nature and Extent of the Jurisdiction of the Courts of the United States.* Philadelphia: Abraham Small, 1824.

Field, David Dudley. *Letter to G. O. Verplanck on the Reform of the Judicial System of the State.* New York, 1840.

———. *Re-organization of the Judiciary.* New York, 1846.

———. *A Short Response to a Long Discourse.* New York, 1884.

———. *Speeches, Arguments and Miscellaneous Papers of David Dudley Field* A. P. Sprague, ed, 3 vols. New York: Appleton and Co., 1884-90.

———. *What Should Be Done with the Practice of the Courts.* New York: J. S. Voorhies, 1847.

[Goodenow, John Milton]. *Historical Sketches of the Principles and Maxims of American Jurisprudence in Contrast with the Doctrines of the English Common Law on the Subject of Crimes and Punishments.* Steubenville, Ohio: James Wilson, 1819.

Gordon, Thomas. *A Digest of the Laws of the United States.* Philadelphia: I. Ashmead and Co., 1844.

Gould, James. *A Treatise on the Principles of Pleading, in Civil Actions.* New York: B. & S. Collier, 1832.

Grayson, P. W. *Vice Unmasked, an Essay: Being a Consideration of the Influence of the*

Law upon the Moral Essence of Man, with other Reflection. New York: G. H. Evans, 1830.

Greenleaf, Simon. *A Collection of Cases Overruled, Doubted, or Limited in Application.* Portland, Maine: Arthur Shirley, 1821.

———. *A Collection of Cases, Overruled, Denied, Doubted or Limited in Applications* 2d ed. New York: W. & A. Gould and Co., 1838.

———. *A Treatise on the Law of Evidence* 3 vols. Boston: C. C. Little and J. Brown, 1842-53.

Gregg, W. P., and Pond, Benjamin. *The Railroad Laws and Charters of the United States.* Boston: C. C. Little and J. Brown, 1851.

Griffith, William. *Annual Law Register of the United States,* vols. 3-4. Burlington, N.J.: D. Allinson, 1822.

Grimke, Thomas. *An Oration on the Practicability and Expediency of Reducing the Whole Body of the Law to the Simplicity and Order of a Code.* Charleston, S.C., 1827.

Hammond, Jabez D. *The History of the Political Parties in the State of New York from the Ratification of the Federal Constitution to December 1840.* Albany: C. Van Benthuysen, 1842.

Higgins, Jesse. *Sampson Against the Philistines. . . .* Philadelphia: William Todd, 1807.

Hilliard, Francis. *An Abridgement of the Law of Real Property.* Boston: C. C. Little and J. Brown, 1838.

Hoffman, David. *A Course of Legal Study.* Baltimore: Coale & Maxwell, 1817.

———. *A Course of Legal Study* 2d ed. Baltimore: Joseph Neal, 1836.

———. *Legal Outlines.* Baltimore: E. J. Coale, 1829.

[Hopkinson, Joseph]. *Considerations on the Abolition of the Common Law in the United States.* Philadelphia: W. P. Farrand and Co., 1809.

Humphreys, Charles. *A Compendium of the Common Law in Force in Kentucky.* Lexington, Ky.: William Gibbs Hunt, 1822.

Jefferson, Thomas. *The Works of Thomas Jefferson* Federal Ed. Paul Leicester Ford, ed. New York: G. P. Putnam's Sons, 1905.

———. *The Writings of Thomas Jefferson* H.A. Washington, ed. 12 vols. Philadelphia: J. B. Lippincott and Co., 1864.

Johnson, J. Eastman. *An Analytical Abridgement of Kent's Commentaries on American Law.* New York: Halsted and Voorhies, 1839.

Kent, James. *Commentaries on American Law.* 4 vols. New York: O. Halsted, 1826-30.

Kerr, Lewis. *Exposition of the Criminal Laws of the Territory of Orleans.* New Orleans: Bradford & Adison, 1806.

Kilty, William. *A Report of All Such English Statutes. . . .* Annapolis: William Chandler, 1811.

Lewis, Ellis. *An Abridgement of the Criminal Law of the United States.* Philadelphia: Thomas Cowperthewait & Co., 1848.

Livingston, Edward. *The Complete Works of Edward Livingston on Criminal Jurisprudence,* 2 vols. Montclair, N.J.: Patterson Smith, 1968 reprint edition.

Madison, James. *The Writings of James Madison,* Gaillard Hunt, ed. 9 vols. New York: G. P. Putnam's Sons, 1901.

Martin, Francois Xavier. *The Office and Authority of a Justice of the Peace . . .* New Bern: Francois Xavier Martin, 1791.

Metcalf, Theron; Perkins, Jonathan C.; and Curtis, George T. *A Digest of the Decisions of the Courts of Common Law and Admiralty in the United States,* 3 vols. Vol. 1. Boston: Hilliard, Gray and Co., 1840; Vols. 2-3. Boston: C. C. Little and J. Brown, 1845-46.

Paine, Elijah. *The Practice in Civil Actions and Proceedings at Law in the State of New York.* New York: G. & C. Crowell, 1830.

Parsons, Theophilus. *The Law of Contracts.* 2 vols. Boston: Little, Brown and Co., 1853-55.

Parsons, Theophilus, Jr. *Memoir of Theophilus Parsons.* Boston: Ticknor and Fields, 1859.

Paulding, James Kirk. *The Merry Tales of Three Wise Men of Gotham.* New York: Harper & Brothers, 1826.

Peters, Richard. *A Full and Arranged Digest of the Decisions in Common Law, Equity, and Admiralty, of the Courts of the United States,* 24 vols. Philadelphia: Thomas

Cowperthewait, 1838-39.

Phillips, Willard. *A Treatise of the Law of Insurance,* 2 vols. Boston: Wells and Lilly, 1823-34.

Putnam, John Phillips. *A Supplement to the United States Digest,* 2 vols. Boston: Charles C. Little and James Brown, 1847.

Rantoul, Robert, Jr. *Memoirs, Speeches and Writings of Robert Rantoul, Jr.* Luther Hamilton, ed. Boston: J. P. Jewett and Co., 1854.

Ray, Isaac. *A Treatise on Medical Jurisprudence and Insanity.* Boston: C. C. Little and J. Brown, 1838.

Reeve, Tapping. *The Law of Baron and Femme.* . . . New Haven: Oliver Steele, 1816.

Robinson, Frederick. *A Letter to the Hon. Rufus Choate, Containing a Brief Exposure of Law Craft and Some of the Encroachments of the Bar upon the Rights of the People.* n.p.: 1832.

Sampson, William. *Sampson's Discourse, and Correspondence with Various Learned Jurists Upon the History of the Law,* Pishey Thompson, comp. Washington, D.C.: Gales & Seaton, 1826.

[Sedgwick, Henry Dwight]. *The English Practice.* New York: J. Seymour, 1822.

Sedgwick, Theodore. *A Statement of Facts in Relation to the Delays and Arrears of Business in the Court of Chancery of the State of New York.* New York: A. S. Gould, 1838.

———. *A Treatise on the Measure of Damages.* New York: J. S. Voorhies, 1847.

Spence, Elijah. *The Equitable Jurisdiction of the Court of Chancery,* 2 vols. Philadelphia: Lea & Blanchard, 1846-50.

Story, Joseph. *Miscellaneous Writings of Joseph Story,* William W. Story, ed. Boston: Charles C. Little and James Brown, 1852.

———. *A Selection of Pleadings in Civil Actions, Subsequent to the Declaration.* Salem, Mass.: Barnard B. MacNulty, 1805.

Sullivan, James. *History of Land Titles in Massachusetts.* Boston: I. Thomas and E. T. Andrews, 1801.

Sumner, Charles. *Memoir and Letters of Charles Sumner.* Edward L. Pierce, ed. 2 vols. Boston: Roberts Bros., 1893.

Swift, Zephaniah. *A System of Laws of the State of Connecticut,* 2 vols. Windham, Conn.: John Byrne, 1795-96.

Walker, Timothy. *Introduction to American Law.* Philadelphia: P. H. Niklin & T. Johnson, 1837.

Wharton, Francis. *A Treatise on the Criminal Law of the United States.* Philadelphia: J. Keys, 1846.

Wilson, James. *The Works of James Wilson,* Robert Green McCloskey, ed, 2 vols. Cambridge: The Belknap Press of Harvard University Press, 1967.

Wilson, John L. *Codification.* New York: Gray and Bunce, 1827.

Wyche, William. *A Treatise on the Practice of the Supreme Court of Judicature of the State of New York in Civil Actions.* New York: T. and J. Swords, 1794.

Newspapers

Aurora (Philadelphia), 1803-05.

Boston *Courier,* 1834-37.

Boston *Daily Advertiser,* 1818, 1832-36.
Boston *Statesman,* 1834-37.
Charleston *Courier,* 1821-30.
Columbia Centinal (Boston), 1834-37.
National Advocate (New York), 1823-30.
New Hampshire *Gazette,* 1818.
New Hampshire *Patriot,* 1818.
New York *American,* 1823-30.
New York *Evening Post,* 1823-27.
New York *Statesman,* 1823-30.

SECONDARY SOURCES

Articles

Bechman, Gail McKnight. "Three Penal Codes Compared" *American Journal of Legal History* 10 (1966): 148-73.

Bloomfield, Maxwell. "Lawyers and Public Criticism: Challenge and Response in Nineteenth Century America," *The American Journal of Legal History* 15 (1971): 269-77.

———. "Law v. Politics: Self-Image of the American Bar (1830-1860)," *American Journal of Legal History* 12 (1968): 306-23.

Briceland, Alan V. "Ephraim Kirby: Pioneer of American Law Reporting," *The American Journal of Legal History* 16 (1972): 297-319.

Commager, Henry Steele. "The Blasphemy of Abner Kneeland," *New England Quarterly 8 (1935): 29-41.*

Davis, David Brion. "Some Themes of Counter-Subversion: An Analysis of Anti-Masonic, Anti-Catholic, and Anti-Mormon Literature", *Mississippi Valley Historical Review* 47 (1960): 205-24.

Eggleston, Sir Frederic William "Legal Development in a Modern Community" In *Interpretations of Modern Legal Philosophies,* Paul Sayre, ed. New York: Oxford University Press, 1947.

Fitzpatrick, John T. "Procedural Codes of the State of New York" *Law Library Journal* 17 (1924): 12-21.

Friedman, Lawrence M. "Law Reform in Historical Perspective" *St. Louis University Law Journal* 13 (1969): 351-74.

Gawalt, Gerard W. "Sources of Anti-Lawyer Sentiment in Massachusetts, 1740-1840" *The American Journal of Legal History* 14 (1970): 283-307.

Henderson, Elizabeth K. "The Attack on the Judiciary in Pennsylvania, 1800-1810" *The Pennsylvania Magazine of History and Biography* 61 (1937): 113-36.

Horwitz, Morton J. "The Emergence of an Instrumental Conception of American Law, 1780-1820" *Perspectives in American History* 5 (1971).

———. "The Transformation in the Conception of Property in American Law, 1780-1860" *University of Chicago Law Review* 40 (1974): 248-90.

Howe, Mark DeWolfe. "The Creative Period of Law in Massachusetts". *Proceedings of the Massachusetts Historical Society* 69 (1949): 234-51.

Mallonee, I. Dee. "Revised Statutes and Codes" *American Law Review* 48 (1914): 37-49.

Nelson, William E. "Emerging Notions of Modern Criminal Law in the Revolutionary Era: An Historical Perspective". *New York University Law Review* 42 (1967): 450-82.

———. "Reform of Common Law Pleading in Massachusetts, 1760-1830: Adjudication as a Prelude to Legislation" *University of Pennsylvania Law Review* 122 (1973): 97-136.

Pound, Roscoe. "The Development of American Law" *Law Quarterly Review* 67 (1955): 49-66.

Senese, Donald. "Building the Pyramid: The Growth and Development of the State Court System of Antebellum South Carolina, 1800-1860." *South Carolina Law Review* 24 (1972): 357-89.

Smith, Jonathan. "The Depression of 1785 and the Daniel Shays' Rebellion." *William and Mary Quarterly*. 3d ser. 5 (1948): 77-94.

Surrency, Erwin C. "Revision of Colonial Laws" *The American Journal of Legal History* 9 (1965): 189-202.

Utter, William T. "Ohio and the English Common Law." *Mississippi Valley Historical Review* 16 (1929): 321-33.

Wallach, Kate. "The Publication of Legal Treatises in America from 1800 to 1830." *Law Library Journal* 45 (1942): 136-48.

Waterman, Julius. "Thomas Jefferson and Blackstone's Commentaries." *Illinois Law Review* 27 (1933): 629-49.

Books

Association of American Law Schools, ed. *Select Essays in Anglo-American Legal History*, 3 vols. Boston: Little, Brown and Co., 1907.

Baker, J. H. *An Introduction to English Legal History*. London: Butterworths, 1971.

Bailyn, Bernard. *The Ideological Origins of the American Revolution*. Cambridge: The Belknap Press of Harvard University Press, 1967.

Blau, Joseph, ed. *American Philosophic Addresses, 1700-1900*. New York: Columbia University Press, 1946.

———, *Social Theories of Jacksonian Democracy*. Indianapolis: Bobbs-Merrill Co., 1954.

Brown, Elizabeth Gaspar. *British Statutes in American Law, 1776-1836*. Ann Arbor: University of Michigan Law School, 1964.

Butler, William A. *The Revision of the Statutes of New York and the Revisors*. New York: Banks and Bros., 1889.

Cardozo, Benjamin N. *The Nature of the Judicial Process*. New Haven: Yale University Press, 1921.

Chroust, Anton-Herman. *The Rise of the Legal Profession in America*, 2 vols. Norman: University of Oklahoma Press, 1965.

Commager, Henry Steele, ed. *Documents in American History*. 2 vols. 7th ed. New York: Appleton-Century-Crofts, 1963.

Darling, Arthur. *Political Changes in Massachusetts, 1824-1848*. New Haven: Yale University Press, 1925.

Ellis, David M., et al. *A History of New York State*. Ithaca, N.Y.: Cornell University Press, 1957.

Ellis, Richard E. *The Jeffersonian Crisis: Courts and Politics in the Young Republic*. New York: Oxford University Press, 1971.

Field, Henry M. *The Life of David Dudley Field*. New York: Charles Scribner's Sons, 1898.

Freehling, William W. *Prelude to Civil War*. New York: Harper and Row, 1966.

Friedman, Lawrence M. *A History of American Law*. New York: Simon and Schuster, 1973.

Furnas, J. C. *The Americans: A Social History of the United States, 1587-1914*. New York: G. P. Putnam's Sons, 1969.

Goebel, Julius. *Antecedents and Beginnings to 1801*, vol. 1 of *The Oliver Wendell Holmes Devise History of the Supreme Court of the United States*. Paul Freund, ed. New York: Macmillan Co., 1971.

Hatcher, William B. *Edward Livingston*. Baton Rouge: Louisiana State University Press, 1940.

Hepburn, Charles. *The Historical Development of Code Pleading in America and England*. Cincinnati: W. A. Anderson and Co., 1897.

Hicks, Frederick C. *Materials and Methods of Legal Research*, 2d ed. Rochester, N.Y.: Lawyers Co-Operative Publishing Co., 1933.

Hobbes, Thomas. *Leviathan*. Cambridge: Cambridge University Press, 1904.

Horwitz, Morton J. *The Transformation of American Law, 1780-1860*. Cambridge: Harvard University Press, 1977.

Hurst, J. Willard. *The Growth of American Law*. Boston: Little, Brown and Co., 1950.

———. *Law and the Conditions of Freedom in Nineteenth Century America*. Madison: University of Wisconsin Press, 1956.

July, Robert W. *The Essential New Yorker: Gulian Crommelian Verplanck*. Durham, N.C.: Duke University Press, 1951.

Lang, Maurice. *Codification in the British Empire and America*. Amsterdam: H. J. Paris, 1924.

Lerner, Gerda. *The Grimke Sisters*. New York: Schocken Books, 1967.

Levy, Leonard. *The Law of the Commonwealth and Chief Justice Shaw*. Cambridge: Harvard University Press, 1957.

Lincoln, Charles. Z. *The Constitutional History of the State of New York from the Beginning of the Colonial Period to the Year 1905*. 5 vols. Rochester, N.Y.: Lawyers Co-Operative Publishing Co., 1906.

———. ed. *Messages from the Governors, Comprising Executive Communications to the Legislature*. . . . 11 vols. Albany: J. B. Lyon, 1909.

McClellan, James. *Joseph Story and the American Constitution*. Norman: University of Oklahoma Press, 1971.

MacDonald, Grace E., comp. *Check-List of Session Laws*. New York: W. H. Wilson Co, 1936.

Malone, Dumas, ed. *Dictionary of American Biography*, 20 vols. New York: Charles

Scribner's Sons, 1934.

———. *The Public Life of Thomas Cooper.* New Haven: Yale University Press 1926.

Mellinkoff, David. *The Language of the Law.* Boston: Little, Brown and Co., 1963.

Miller, Perry. *The Life of the Mind in America from the Revolution to the Civil War.* New York: Harcourt, Brace and World, 1965.

Nelson, William E. *Americanization of the Common Law: The Impact of Legal Change on Massachusetts Society, 1760-1830.* Cambridge: Harvard University Press, 1975.

Pimsleur, Meira G., ed. *Checklist of Basic American Legal Publications.* S. Hackensack, N.J.: Fred B. Rothman and Co., 1962.

Pound, Roscoe. *The Formative Era of American Law.* Boston: Little, Brown and Co., 1938.

Reppy, Alison, ed. *David Dudley Field: Centenary Essays Celebrating One Hundred Years of Legal Reform.* New York: New York University School of Law, 1949.

Sabine, Lorenzo. *Biographical Sketches of Loyalists of the American Revolution with an Historical Essay.* 2 vols. Boston: Little, Brown and Co., 1864.

Smith, Charles Page. *James Wilson: Founding Father, 1742-1798.* Chapel Hill: University of North Carolina Press, 1956.

Veall, Donald. *The Popular Movement for Law Reform, 1640-1660.* Oxford: Clarendon Press, 1970.

Walters, Raymond, Jr. *Alexander James Dallas.* Philadelphia: University of Pennsylvania Press, 1943.

Warren, Charles. *A History of the American Bar.* Boston: Little, Brown and Co., 1911.

Wood, Gordon. *The Creation of the American Republic, 1776-1789.* Chapel Hill: University of North Carolina Press, 1969.

Unpublished Works

Gawalt, Gerald W. "Massachusetts Lawyers: A Historical Analysis of the Process of Professionalization, 1760-1840." Ph.D. dissertation, Clark University, 1969.

Hobor, Michael Joseph. "The Forms of the Law: David Dudley Field and the Codification Movement in New York, 1839-1888." Ph.D. dissertation, University of Chicago, 1975.

Roper, Donald. "An Atmosphere of Flux—An Objective of Certainty: The New York Supreme Court in the Early Nineteenth Century." Unpublished paper delivered to the American Society for Legal History, 10 Nov. 1973.

Senese, Donald. "Legal Thought in South Carolina, 1800-1860." Ph.D. dissertation, University of South Carolina, 1970.

Van Ee, Daun Roell. "David Dudley Field and the Reconstruction of the Law." Ph.D. dissertation, Johns Hopkins University, 1974.

INDEX

About the Author

CHARLES M. COOK is Assistant Director of the Commission on Institutions of Higher Education of the North Central Association of Colleges and Schools in Evanston, Illinois, and a visiting faculty member of the School for New Learning of DePaul University.